Renaissance Festivals

D1553016

WITHDRAWN

Renaissance Festivals

Merrying the Past and Present

KIMBERLY TONY KOROL-EVANS

Lincoln Public Library   DUPL
3 7496 00326559 9

McFarland & Company, Inc., Publishers

Jefferson, North Carolina, and London

LIBRARY OF CONGRESS CATALOGUING-IN-PUBLICATION DATA

Korol-Evans, Kimberly Tony, 1966–
    Renaissance festivals : merrying the past and present /
Kimberly Tony Korol-Evans.
        p.   cm.
    Includes bibliographical references and index.

    ISBN: 978-0-7864-4014-6
    softcover : 50# alkaline paper ∞

    1. Maryland Renaissance Festival — History.   2. Carnivals —
United States.   3. Festivals — United States.   I. Title.
GV1835.5.K67   2009
394'.60973 — dc22   2009022107

British Library cataloguing data are available

©2009 Kimberly Tony Korol-Evans. All rights reserved

*No part of this book may be reproduced or transmitted in any form
or by any means, electronic or mechanical, including photocopying
or recording, or by any information storage and retrieval system,
without permission in writing from the publisher.*

Cover image: jousting at the Maryland Renaissance Festival, 2007
(photograph by Jeff Kubina); background ©2009 Shutterstock

Manufactured in the United States of America

McFarland & Company, Inc., Publishers
  Box 611, Jefferson, North Carolina 28640
    www.mcfarlandpub.com

The Past
In Memoriam of the two Henrys in my life
Henry Peter Korol
10 March 1922 to 7 May 2001
My father, who taught me always to "keep my eye on the
donut and not on the hole." This book is the donut I offer you.
You are in my heart always. I love you, and I miss you.
and
William Huttel
11 January 1953 to 12 November 2001
His thirteen years portraying King Henry VIII at the
Maryland Renaissance Festival will never be forgotten.
You are legendary, "Big Mr. Bill King Henry."
I miss you, my colleague and my friend.

and

The Present
To my son, Wallace Casimir "Walkir" Korol,
as he embarks on his performance career at the
contemporary American Renaissance festival.
Thank you for all your love and for all the time
with me you gave up so I could write this book.

Table of Contents

Acknowledgments

The creation of this book required the proverbial "cast of thousands," but there are those who I need to specially acknowledge for their contributions. I want to give special acknowledgment to my mentor, Dr. Tracy C. Davis, who read these pages from their inception while I was still a doctoral candidate at Northwestern University. Two other NU faculty members, Dr. Bernard Beck and Dr. Linda Austern, each spent numerous hours working with me on the foundation of this book. Other members of the academy to whom I owe special acknowledgment include Dr. Carol Burbank; Dr. Margaret Drewal; Dr. Shulamith "Shuly" Lev-Aladgem; Dr. Ed Muir; and Dr. Jennifer Gunnels, my colleague, mentor, and friend. I offer my gratitude to commentators from the 2005 International Federation for Theatre Research (IFTR), 2005 American Society for Theatre Research (ASTR), 2005 Mid America Theatre Conference (MATC); and 2003 and 2004 Group for Early Modern Cultural Studies (GEMCS) conferences. Finally, I must recognize the late Dr. Dwight Conquergood, who introduced me to the co-performer/witness methodology and urged me to explore, engage, theorize, and define it.

I also offer my appreciation to everyone at the Maryland Renaissance Festival. Thank you to the Smith family — Mr. Smith (Jules Sr.), Jules Jr., Justin, Adam, and Mark — who allowed me access to the festival, and to Jaki Shives, with whom I worked closely during my time in the Maryland Renaissance Festival (MDRF) office. To Carolyn Spedden, MDRF's artistic director, thank you for your trust, and for being my director and friend. Thank you to all of the performers at the MDRF with whom I worked. Though I am certain to miss someone, I nonetheless must single out for recognition a few performers with whom I engaged extensively: Kate Cox and Roy Cox, who taught me more about embodied knowledge than I thought I could ever learn; Mary Ann Jung, who was a constant source of comfort during the long rehearsal and performance process, especially when I was missing my son; Melissa McGinley, who, in her first year at the MDRF, became an integral part of my performance day and a wonderful sounding board; Diane Wilshere, who loves history as much as I do; Lisa Ricciardi-Thompson, who offered unparalleled insights into the festival and its *raison d'être*; Laura Kilbane, a performer as well as a fellow scholar, who listened patiently to my attempts to theorize my work; Timothy McCormick, who on Sunday nights would share a bottle of Zin with me and discuss anything theatrical but the book, hereby reminding me that all of this work is about a love of theatre; Michael Winchester and Jeff Bryant, my daily robbers; and to Larry and Paula Peterka, the most academic non-"official" scholars I have ever met, who, along with Mr. and Mrs. Smith and Kenneth, took me into their home, fed me, clothed me (Paula made my costume), and housed me during inclement weather. I offer my most sincere appreciation to Paula, with whom I had endless conversations about festival, Tudor history, and most important, our sons; your pragmatic yet humorous voice of reason grounded me when I was lonely, lost, and confused during my research.

Many patrons at the MDRF whose names I never even knew contributed heavily to this work. However, I am compelled to mention by name the following: Judy Streeb, whose words and introductions were invaluable; Craig Rhymer, whose videotapes were an invaluable asset; and performers Liz Herman and Joe Shelby, whose references opened doors for me with patrons that my Northwestern credentials did not. I also wish to thank the vendors who participated in this study for their unique views. I also owe a debt of gratitude to my new-found friends from the Midwest festivals — especially Di Johnson-Taylor, Becky Grotts, and Susi Matthews Cannon for their insights. Also, I thank the hundreds of thousands of patrons who enter the gates of Revel Grove and other festival sites every year; it is your continued patronage of this venue and the others like it that made this book not only possible, but necessary.

To the fabulous Carrie Jane Cole, your support during the research and writing of this book was instrumental in keeping me relatively sane, and your photographs in this work are integral to a better understanding of the intrastice. I could never have completed my ethnography without the help of a very special friend, Gwynn Valentine Fulcher, who nannied my son while I was away compiling my initial research. To my Northwestern University compatriots: Christina McMahon, for "unpacking" the co-performer/witness concept with me; Stefka Mihaylova, for always believing in me and being my biggest supporter and fan; Jesse Njus, my early modern colleague; Dan Smith, for calming my angst on more occasions than I can count. I wish also to thank Marie DeBenedictis, for her work as a reader, and Greg DeBenedictis for his support during the time I was researching this book. To P. Anthony Mast and

Brenda Carstensen, friends new and old, who supported me through the process, and to Alicia James, whose work in the classroom made it possible for me to have the time to finish the final edits.

Finally, and most of all, I wish to thank my family. To my brothers — John, Ken, and Dave Korol — for talking to me about anything BUT my book. I do not think you all know how much those conversations — usually about sports — meant to me. To Patricia Korol, my maman, thank you for loving me for me. To my sisters, Jude and Jean Korol: your support, your love, your commitment to family, and your belief in me would all have been more than anyone could hope for, but you also gave unselfishly to your nephew, Walkir. Your constant love for my son and your continuous care for him are beyond compare. Thank you so much. My sister-in-law, Laura McDowell (lmdstudio), was a godsend as she took all of the pictures taken by Dr. Cole and changed their format to make them printable in this work. To Mark A. Korol-Evans — my husband, my partner, my friend, my research assistant — I am eternally grateful for your continual support, your gentle guidance, your calm control, your persistent encouragement, and your infinite love. Last, and yet first and foremost, my thanks to Walkir — Wallace Casimir Korol — my son, my light, my reason for being. Your hugs and kisses and cuddles and schnuggles at the end of a long day of reading, researching, or writing made it all worthwhile. Nothing in this world is as important as your love for me or my love for you. Thank you, Walkir, for helping me become a better person and a better mommy. I love you.

Preface

This book focuses on the Maryland Renaissance Festival (MDRF) and examines how performers and patrons in a carnivalesque setting experience intrasticiancy — the state created by the overlapping of the actuality of twenty-first-century America and the historical record of sixteenth-century England. Anthropologist Victor Turner's studies of liminality explore temporal-spatial confluence, and my study of the intrastice builds upon his work and provides for differing levels of immersion within the performances at the MDRF. The theatrical convention that spectators are able to "willingly suspend disbelief" is the foundation of study of the intrastice, and it is also what allows for the audience to "play at belief" and "actively create belief." I explore the manner in which spectators frame the contiguous performances at the festival and thus influence the level of intrasticiant immersion.

A history of the festival movement in the United States contextualizes the carnivalesque and its contributions to intrasticiancy, and an exploration of the sensescape at the MDRF and how it contributes to the temporal-spatial intrastice expands current landscape and soundscape scholarship. This work augments previous research on living history by considering both the tactile nature of these performances and the importance of embodied knowledge to their representation, while analyzing the difference between living history and historical elaboration and the resulting effects on intrasticiancy. I examine how actor-patron improvisational interaction imparts a deeper understanding of non-scripted performances within the milieu the MDRF offers and consider how the interface as a system of communication contributes to the understanding of the negotiation that exists between performer and spectator at theatrical events. My analysis of immediate post 11 September 2001 performance illustrates how actors complete cultural work in a carnivalesque setting during a time of crisis. Finally, I consider the ways different patrons frame the MDRF to illuminate roles spectators play and how those choices influence immersion within the intrastice.

My exploration of the Maryland Renaissance Festival and other contemporary American Renaissance faires contributes to opening new areas of academic study. By examining such concepts as the sensescape, intrasticial immersion, historical elaboration, and the co-performer/witness, I establish that contemporary American Renaissance festivals are worthy of serious scholarship, and I hope that in doing so I combat some of the prejudice against these faires which exists within the academy. I contribute to the literature on Renaissance festivals a brief history of the contemporary faires and provide a solid foundation upon which members of the academy can build further scholarship. In addition, my study of the performance at the MDRF the weekend following 11 September 2001 exemplifies how festival performers do cultural work in the carnival setting during a time of crisis.

This study augments previous research on living history by considering both the tactile nature of these performances and the importance of embodied knowledge to their representation. Building upon scholarship about "site-specific" performances such as Colonial Williamsburg, Gettysburg, and Plimoth Plantation, this study establishes that living historians can stage meaningful shows in created spaces. Furthermore, by demonstrating the differences between living history and historical elaboration, I provide a new way for scholars to analyze historically-based performances. Prior scholarship has focused on questions of "accuracy" and "authenticity" within living history venues, while this study concentrates on the levels of intrasticial immersion that occur when patrons experience the very different performances of living history and historical elaboration.

My examination of the sensescape of Revel Grove supplies an alternative way to read a research site. While the privileged senses of sight and sound remain important aspects of the overall scene, by analyzing how smell, taste, and touch effect spectators' reactions to an environment, I offer a more detailed method of analyzing social environments, both within and outside the theatrical discipline. While Erving Goffman's frame analysis provides a nexus to examine individual choices, it does not recognize that the overall sensescape in which those decisions are made influences the participants' level of intrasticial immersion. For example, the prospect of dining at a restaurant with a 1920s theme may encourage some patrons to dress in clothing similar to the pre–Depression-era style, while planning to eat at a local burger joint fosters no desire to don clothing particular to a period or style. Thus, the theory of the sensescape makes available a relevant method for sociological and anthropological examination of spaces in which work and leisure coincide: theme restaurants, sporting arenas, local pubs.

This work impacts the fields of theatre and performance studies both theoretically and methodologically. I demonstrate the festival as a modern carnivalesque form, and, in doing so, I expand the field of application for Mikhail Bakhtin's work. By examining the intrasticiant state as one of "both/and," I propose an alternative to Turner's "neither/nor" liminality, launching an innovative approach to theatre, performance, and ritual. The theory of the intrastice provides a method for examining a wide range of performance situations, my theatrical lexicon equating immersion to dimensions of belief enhances the understanding of the well-known theatrical convention of the "willing suspension of disbelief." Richard Schechner writes that festivals are a form of environmental theatre, and my examination of the actor-patron improvisational interaction imparts a deeper understanding of non-scripted performances within that milieu. Analyzing the ways in which actors and patrons interact both during scripted and improvisational performances, often taking place within minutes of each other, demonstrates the fluid nature of the stage/audience boundary the MDRF milieu allows and highlights a new way to examine other theatrical events — both current and historical — in which performers and spectators mingle. Furthermore, my consideration of the interface as a system of communication contributes to the understanding of the negotiation that exists between performer and spectator at theatrical events.

Finally, I know that personally I would not have received much of the data integral to this work had I not employed the co-performer/witness methodology. This research methodology, based upon Dwight Conquergood's ethnographic model, tests its boundaries and limits while illustrating its benefits and efficacy. On many occasions, people only agreed to speak with me after verifying my credentials, not as a scholar, but as an insider, a co-performer. "Northwestern University" and "Ph.D. candidate" as points of reference opened far fewer doors for me than a single e-mail from a fellow performer or a patron attesting to my integrity. Through my work as a co-performer/witness, I demonstrate the manner in which to conduct this type of study and, hopefully, illuminate the methodology Dwight Conquergood proposed.

Introduction: How Merriment Abounds

On a sweltering summer afternoon fifteen minutes before three o'clock, I walked proudly into the Market Inn, grateful for the respite from the sun offered by the roofed pub. I meandered between two sets of wooden tables, three on each side, filled with patrons eating, drinking, and chatting. My dark green Tudor dress with gold club pattern and a gold lace trim covered my salmon undergown. The French hood of matching salmon stood proudly atop my head, adorned with light green aventurine, dark green jade, and burnt red carnelian beads, and I wore a matching necklace and girdle. In a loud voice, I began to address those assembled: "Good morrow, my Lords and Ladies. I be Elizabeth Seymour, Lady Ughtread, and thou art all most graciously invited to attend the betrothal ceremony betwixt my sister, Jane Seymour, and His Most Royal Majesty, King Henry VIII. It shalt take place just thither upon the Lyric Stage [pointing in the direction of the stage] at four and thirty of the clock."[1] Most people applauded lightly, gasped at the invitation to such an important event, or asked more specific questions. Finally, I concluded: "And tell them thou art on the Seymour side. Thou shalt gain a better seat." Following the patrons' laughter, I prepared to leave, only to run into a tall, dark-haired and bearded, sheepskin vest-clad man with a quarterstaff.

"Well, well, well. What do we have here?" he asked with a peasant accent. "Looks like a court lady. And court ladies have lots of money." Brandishing his quarterstaff at me about chest high, this uncouth behemoth demanded money. Swatting away the staff with my hand, I declared in righteous indignation, "Knowest thou not who I be? I be Elizabeth Seymour, elder sister to Jane Seymour, thy future QUEEN, and future sister-in-law to His Most Royal Majesty, King Henry VIII. Art thou MAD to threaten me so?" While he was

5

blabbering an attempt at an apology, another man approached me from the other side. "Little John," the handsome newcomer called out. Dressed in black hat, dark red velvet tights, and high black boots, he appeared as charismatic and civilized as the other man — Little John — seemed unappealing and ill-mannered. "What art thou doing?" he added.

"Just what Robin Hood said to do, Will," Little John replied. "Robbing from the rich to give to the poor." Looking disgusted, Will pressed on: "And how wert thou planning on doing that?" Menacingly wielding his quarterstaff, Little John replied: "The only way I know how: BRUTE FORCE." With a look of disgust thrown at his compatriot, Will addressed me. "My dear lady, allow me to introduce myself. I be Will Scarlet. And that there, that be Little John. Little John, there are better ways to get a donation. Watch and learn." With that he turned his attention completely toward me. He took my hand, gently raised it to his lips, and fixed his eyes upon my own. "Please excuse my friend. He knows not any better. We are indeed in the employ of Robin Hood, and if you could spare something, anything. A small donation for charity. To help the poor of the village. We wouldst be most grateful."

Abandoning my decorum in his chivalry, I began to stammer, for the first time losing some of my composure. "But I have nothing to give. I hath spent all mine money on a gift for my goodly sister and the king. All I have are the clothes upon my back." He would continue to stare into my eyes until I finally said, "Oh, well, aye, take my DRESS. Aye, it shall fetch quite a sum." Unbeknownst to me, Little John had already been unlacing the back of my dress during the plea Will Scarlet gave. Usually by the time I said to take the dress, all Little John had to do was lift it over my head. As Will Scarlet thanked me for my "donation," I walked somewhat dazed out of the pub. Clad now only in my salmon underskirt and underbodice ensemble, I announced to the spectators that "I simply cannot understand why removing my overdress doth make me all that much more hotter." As I left the pub, Little John mockingly donned the gown and asked his companion in crime, "Why is it every time you are with a woman, she winds up *out* of her dress?" To which the sweet-talking Will Scarlet replied, "Why is it every time thou art near a woman, thou winds up *wearing* her dress?" At the laughter that usually ensued from those gathered in the pub, Little John and Will Scarlet would slip away.

On most days, this improvised piece of street theatre in Revel Grove, Oxfordshire — the village depicted at the 2004 Maryland Renaissance Festival (MDRF) — followed this pattern quite closely. However, on one particular September afternoon, as soon as Little John (played by veteran festival performer Michael Winchester) began to unlace my dress, four or five girls — roughly between the ages of four and eleven — began to shout, "Lady. Hey, Lady. Hey, queen's sister! He's stealing your dress." Even though I had spoken to the girls earlier and had issued them a personal invitation to the royal betrothal, which they keenly accepted with starry eyes, I acted as if I were completely oblivious to their warnings and focused my attention upon Will Scarlet (played by Jeff Bryant). I gazed into his eyes, not totally conscious of what was happening behind me. Winchester was fully aware of what was happening, as the little girls, unable to garner my attention, took matters into their own hands and began to jump on the man unlacing my dress. They were pulling and tugging at him, trying to get him to stop while they continued to vie for my attention. Eventually, despite their best attempts, Winchester did manage to remove my dress, and the girls sat down.

Children, such as these young girls, have no difficulty in entering into the world of make-believe. They willingly suspend disbelief with ease, can play at believing at a moment's notice, and actively create belief at will. Whether it is entering the tree house of a large purple dinosaur, a land filled with multi-colored dragons, or a village that includes a tall, sheepskin-vested, quarterstaff-wielding "sixteenth-century" peasant, children easily maneuver from one world to the next. The young girls who attacked Winchester appeared to truly think in that moment that he was trying to steal my dress. They almost as eagerly clamored at the opportunity to attend the royal betrothal, at the queen-to-be's sister's behest. These children actively created a belief that they were in a world where a band of do-gooders would rob from the rich to give to the poor, and they acted accordingly by trying to stop him. Adults look upon children's ability to actively create belief as naïve, winsome, cute, or charming. These same adults do not expect to enter the world of make-believe with such alacrity. Nonetheless, during my research, most of the adults with whom I worked were at least willing to suspend their disbelief; many wanted to play at belief; and some even actively created belief.

Theoretical and Methodological Concerns

Anthropologist and theatre and ritual commentator Victor Turner's work on liminality strongly influences this work, as does cultural theorist Mikhail Bakhtin's writing on carnival. Turner defined liminality as "a temporal interface whose properties partially invert those of the already consolidated order which constitutes any specific cultural 'cosmos.'"[2] I argue that the culture of the contemporary American Renaissance festival provides the opportunity for such an interface, an ability to invert social order and create from it something new. Turner's liminality within a particular cultural cosmos appears to speak directly to Bakhtin's concept of carnival: "Carnival celebrates the destruction of the old and birth of the new world—the new year, the new spring, the new kingdom."[3] The destruction of the old and birth of the new are conceptually akin to the inversion of a particular cultural cosmos. By examining the nature of performance in a carnival setting and applying to it a theatrical theory derived from Turner's anthropological model, I question how participants experience the intrastice between the historical knowledge of sixteenth-century England and the reality of twenty-first-century America as they occur within a pretext of Tudor Oxfordshire at the Maryland Renaissance Festival.

Turner divided liminality into two distinct categories, the liminoid and the liminal. The liminoid was marked by the option a person had to engage in a particular experience. "Optation pervades the liminoid phenomenon, obligation the liminal. One is all play and choice, an entertainment, the other is a matter of deep seriousness, even dread, it is demanding, compulsory."[4] Turner argued that the liminal was achieved in "simpler" societies as a ritual occurrence, while the liminoid transpired in more "complex" societies as a form of diversion. Liminoid events include many types of cultural performances, including theatre.[5] Only in the liminal state could true transformation exist, according to Turner. Despite the similarities between Turner's definition of liminality and the rites of carnival, he specifically excluded carnival from being able to achieve the liminal status. He writes, "The carnival is unlike a tribal ritual in that it can be attended *or* avoided, performed or merely watched, at *will*. It is a genre of leisure enjoyment, not an obligatory ritual, it is play-separated-from-work."[6] By defining liminoid and liminal in this manner, Turner created a binary and placed the emphasis on the event in which a person participated and the place in which that involvement occurred, thus limiting who could experience the interface he described and who could achieve liminal or liminoid states.

In this project, I seek to expand upon Turner's writing on liminality, but I diverge from his work in three significant ways. First, Turner's definition of liminality is a state betwixt and between, a time in which a person has crossed a threshold and is neither here nor there, neither now nor then. Rethinking Turner's position and interpretation of the betwixt and between, I see the contemporary American Renaissance festival not as an empty *inter*stice, but as a filled *intra*stice, not as being of a neither/nor function, but rather as a both/and function in which the person enters a state that is both here and there, both now and then. I have coined the term intrastice as a way of delineating the difference between Turner's "state between" and my "state within." The prefix "intra-" means "occurring or situated within." Rather than the space between here and there/now and then, the void of Turner's liminality, the intrastice is a place within. In this particular study, the here and now of twenty-first-century America and the there and then of historical sixteenth-century England meld to create the pretext of Tudor Oxfordshire. Furthermore, Turner posits that it is the nature of the event that determines the state of liminality a person experiences, as I illustrate above. I deviate from Turner's assessment that a society's label as industrial or non-industrial is the key to the differing ways of experiencing the space between or, as I have defined it, the "occurrence within." Rather, I argue, the degree to which someone becomes immersed in the intrastice is a function of the manner in which the individual frames the event, not the actual nature of the event. Finally, I posit that there are (at least) three different ways to experience the occurrence within, so I expand Turner's binary states of liminality to three levels and add a specific theatrical meaning to each in order to explore how the intrastice is experienced at contemporary American Renaissance festivals.

Within this study, I have defined partaking in the intrastice at any level as "intrasticiancy," having chosen the "-ancy" suffix because it expresses a "quality or state."[7] I relate the first level of experiencing intrasticiancy to the theatrical convention in which spectators participate when they *willingly suspend disbelief.* This state of intrasticiancy is the intrasticial, which I create by taking the root "intrastice" and adding the "-al" suffix, which means "relating to." The intrasticial state is thus the least immersive level of intrasticiancy.

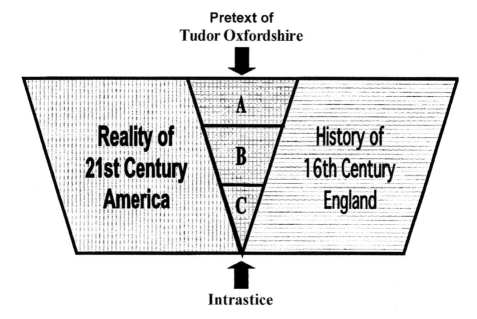

The triangular overlapping sections of the trapezoids representing twenty-first-century America and sixteenth-century England illustrate the Intrastice, which consists of three levels of immersion: A, the Intrasticial; B, the Intrasticive; and C, the Intrasticious.

INTRASTICIANT LEVELS OF IMMERSION

State of Intrasticiancy	Depth Immersed in Intrastice	Lexicon of Corresponding Theatrical Convention
Intrastical	Least immersive state; surface engagement; most common level	*Willingly suspending disbelief*
Intrasticive	Intermediate immersive state; playful engagement	*Playing at belief*
Intrasticious	Most immersive state; ritualistic engagement; least common level	*Actively creating belief*

The "intrasticial" state corresponds to "A" in figure 1; "intrasticive" corresponds to "B" in figure 1; and intrasticious to "C" in figure 1.

Those who experience the intrasticial phenomenon participate in the basic mode of theatregoing, one in which they temporarily put aside their knowledge of the real world to better enjoy the world of the theatrical event they are witnessing. In the second state of intrasticiancy, the intrasticive — created by adding the "-ive" suffix denoting "doing or tending toward an action" — the audience member actually *plays at belief.* This is a key distinction, as it requires the patron to make both a mental and physical move — an action — first from "suspension of disbelief" to a form of belief, and also from a mere receiver of performance to an active participant in its creation. The intrasticious is the third and final state which I propose. This level of immersion requires the participant to *actively create belief.* The "-ous" suffix means "full of;" thus it describes the state of becoming completely immersed within the intrastice. More than the intrasticive, which is playing at belief, this state indicates that those partaking of it experience a tangible transformation, a ritualistic move in which they enter the temporal-spatial intrastice in so deep a manner that the lines between "the here and there" and "the now and then" become completely blurred.

Erving Goffman's frame analysis provides a methodology for analyzing how different people participate in these various states of intrasticiancy. He writes that a frame is a "definition of a situation ... built up in accordance with principles of organization which govern events — at least social ones — and our subjective involvement in them."[8] In my case study, the frame is the Maryland Renaissance Festival's created realm of Revel Grove — the pretext of the Tudor Oxfordshire village that occurs within the overlap of the reality of twenty-first century America and the historical knowledge of sixteenth-century England. Furthermore, Goffman defines a primary framework as something which renders "what would otherwise be a meaningless aspect of the scene into something that is meaningful."[9] This framework is a manner of examining what is happening within the frame at a particular place and time in order to explicate its significance, value, or consequence.

Framing is of particular importance to the levels of immersion within the intrastice. How patrons frame the MDRF influences the states of intrasticiancy they experience. If spectators frame the MDRF as they would a play, then they will only enter the least immersive level of intrasticiancy, which corresponds to the theatrical convention of the willing suspension of disbelief. If, however, visitors enter into the intrastice and decide to play at belief, framing the MDRF as a performance in which they are co-creators, they may then experience the intrasticive level of immersion. Finally, when patrons actively create belief within the intrastice, they are participating at the deepest level of immersion, the intrasticious, and they experience the potential for tangible transformation. Spectators may rekey the frame of the MDRF, perhaps several times throughout the event, and though neither the location of the festival nor the primary performers change, this rekeying may substantially alter the visitors' experience of the theatrical event that is the MDRF. For the purposes of this study, I employ a definition proposed by theatre and performance scholar and theorist Temple Hauptfleisch, who writes of the theatrical event as the "*entire complex of processes occurring in and around a playing space at a particular time.*"[10] The "playing space" is the physical site of Revel Grove; the "particular time" consists of the nineteen days of the festival's run; and the processes I treat within this study concern the interaction between patrons, performers, and the multi-sensory environment of the village.

Those who participate in the primary framework view the faire (I use festival and faire interchangeably within this work) as a theatregoing experience, with expectations similar to those they would have attending a conventional theatre performance, and thus they participate as theatregoers in the willing suspension of disbelief, the intrasticial level of immersion. However, when spectators change the primary framework by becoming involved intrasticively or intrasticiously, they re-key the frame. Goffman writes of keying "a systematic transformation is involved across materials already meaningful in accordance with a scheme of interpretation, and without which the keying would be meaningless. Participants in the activity are meant to know and to openly acknowledge that a systematic alteration is involved, one that will radically reconstitute what it is for them that is going on."[11] Simultaneous framing occurs as different members of the audience re-key the frame to fit their own desires or needs with regard to levels of participation and belief. Turner writes of Goffman's work, "to frame is to discriminate a sector of sociocultural action from the general on-going process of a community's life."[12] Considering the different frames indicates a change from the commonplace routines of everyday life. Festival provides contiguous frames for the same event as people key their own frames based upon their personal schema causing varying levels of intrasticiancy. Thus, the framed event is out of the ordinary, sometimes even exotic or mysterious. Because it has no common referent in the mundane world, it requires a separate explanation, definition, and analysis. This is the world of the MDRF.

In order to gather data for this study, I employed an ethnographic approach. Since I attended the MDRF as a patron from 1992 to 1997 and worked an actor, improvisational instructor, and director over the course of the next five seasons (1998–2002), I also drew upon personal knowledge that spanned a decade before commencing this project. I also worked in the MDRF office during the 2004 season and had the opportunity to interact with performers, vendors, and patrons in that capacity and, most significantly, participated as a member of the cast at the festival during that season. Following the principles of performance studies scholar and ethnographer Dwight Conquergood, I sought as a co-performer/witness not merely to observe during the 2004 season in which I collected the bulk of my data, but to become in a true visceral way a part of the milieu within which I was working.[13] Conquergood called the co-performer/witness methodology "multisensory," refusing to just privilege sight. For Conquergood, being a co-performer meant understanding that "fieldwork is performance" and that we had to "question and critique" that performance while living the experience. Witnessing requires taking an active role, not only in recording information but also in disseminating it. Like Conquergood, Turner sought a more personal connection with the people with whom he worked. He wrote of his desire to become more intimately involved in his ethnographic technique: "I've long thought that teaching and learning anthropology should be more fun than they often are. Perhaps we should not merely read and comment on ethnographies, but actually perform them."[14] I had the opportunity to engage with patrons and performers first hand, and to observe the behaviors of visitors to the village without the patrons' knowledge of my research interests. The need for this in-depth type of research is based upon Conquergood's observation that

> the dominant way of knowing in the academy is that of empirical observation and critical analysis from a distanced perspective: "knowing that," and "knowing about." This is a view from above the object of inquiry: knowledge that is anchored in paradigm and secured in print. This propositional knowledge is shadowed by another way of knowing that is grounded in active, intimate, hands-on participation and personal connection: "knowing how," and "knowing who."[15]

I have since had hundreds of conversations with patrons and performers in order to gain further knowledge into the way that each frames his or her own experience at the MDRF. It is only after reaching this level of co-performer/ witnessing that I feel able to attend to my critical analysis of the festival.

Because my primary question concerns the manner in which performers and patrons participate in various intrasticiant levels at the MDRF, I am not interested in rehashing arguments over authenticity and accuracy with regard to the portrayal of historical sites, people, and pieces. How can we be authentic when we cannot even agree on what authentic means? How can we be accurate when we do not have the points of reference by which to judge our accuracy? The words themselves are highly contested. One performer at the festival explained her definitions of accurate and authentic to me: "Authentic would be if we had an actual sixteenth-century goblet on site. No one is authentic. Accurate means we try to replicate the items from the period as closely as possible based upon our most current research" (field notes). This is almost the exact opposite of the way many scholars would at least begin to define the words. Often the definitions are no clearer than the words themselves. For example, Jenny Adams writes, "the quest for the authentic, which here is defined by an object's claim to historical authenticity, and its continual frustration will resurface in the novel's main narrative."[16] Note the tautological nature of Adams's definition. She defines "authentic" with the word "authenticity." The problem of authentic is revealed as one in which tautological definitions abound while scholarly concepts and ideals of those actually performing the object of study at the MDRF are at odds. Therefore, I am not interested in explaining the authenticity or accuracy of the stories portrayed at the MDRF. Rather, I analyze how these storylines illustrate the levels of intrasticiancy which I set forth.[17]

Contemporary American Renaissance festivals are a commercial success; at the beginning of the twenty-first century, they collectively draw over ten million patrons each year. The faires fail to demonstrate any new form of cutting-edge theatre, relying instead upon the tried and true methods that have made them commercial successes. As more and more research into the Renaissance era accumulates, contemporary American Renaissance festivals can present more detailed historical information, but the sword swallowers, stilt walkers, mimes, musicians, and interactive improvisational street characters are still at the heart of successful festivals. One such performer explained both why he thinks little scholarly attention is paid to festivals despite their pedagogical aspects and commercial success and why it is a legitimate theatrical venue worthy of study:

> Some people think the Renn fest is not theatre. I studied and worked with such people. They spend their time in some converted warehouse, on a street better known for legitimate prostitution, working to provoke minimal audiences into seeing horrible plays. They attempt to [resuscitate] a model of theatre that has

been dead for years with arrogance and grant money. On a good day, twenty
thousand people go to the faire. If I put something exciting on stage, I get a
decent share of them. Over twelve years I have directed classical plays, performed improv and sketch comedy, done magic and hypnosis. The check always
clears [field notes].

As this veteran of more than a decade of festival performance notes, the faire
offers a wide variety of opportunities to participate in diverse theatrical
endeavors, from directing Shakespeare to street magic. The festivals are outside of both conventional and avant-garde theatre, and, using the terminology of cultural scholar Lawrence W. Levine, academics consider it a "lowbrow"
entertainment.[18] Perhaps because of this prejudice, contemporary American
Renaissance festivals have remained mainly within the purview of graduate
students, and there is no extended, published academic study focusing
specifically upon such festivals.

Leading theatrical researchers — including Richard Schechner — mention
Renaissance faires as part of larger studies but do not concentrate upon them
in any breadth or depth. A 1976 article by Sam Blazer in *TDR: The Drama
Review* treats the Northern California Renaissance Pleasure Faire, but pictures
fill more than half of the less than seven-page article. Jennifer Gunnels, a
recent graduate in Theatre at the University of Texas-Austin, wrote her M.A.
thesis on the Michigan Renaissance Festival and her Ph.D. dissertation on
three of the modern faires.[19] However, her work concentrates on concepts of
tourism, heritage, and consumerism, which are clearly separable from the
focus of my research on intrasticiancy. Gunnels's study does provide a depar-
ture point for my own work, primarily with regard to terminology specific
to faires. These "keywords," as sociologist Raymond Williams would call
them, are nearly universal among faire performers but are not necessarily a
part of the lexicon of the general acting community.[20] Three M.A. theses —
by Kimberly O'Brien, Brenda Reneé Pontiff, and Delanna Kay Reed — all
treat some aspect of the modern American Renaissance festival, but none
examine performer and patron intrasticiancy.[21]

I draw from a variety of other academic disciplines to complement this
study. Scholarship on living history heavily informs this project. Research on
Colonial Williamsburg, Virginia, includes studies by Richard Handler and
Anders Greenspan, who both examine historical interpretations at the Virginia village.[22] While Colonial Williamsburg, which is open every day, draws
nearly a million visitors each year, the MDRF brings more than 250,000
patrons through its gates in just nineteen days. Rory Turner's work on Civil
War re-enactors provides a guideline for examining performer immersion.[23]
Stephen Eddy Snow played a pilgrim at Plimoth Plantation for two seasons
and chronicled the experiences of first-person interpreters and patrons there

in his seminal work, *Performing the Pilgrims: A Study of Ethnohistorical Role-playing at Plimoth Plantation.*[24] I extend his ethnographic strategy to incorporate the deeper co-performer/witness tradition. This type of "research from within" is an important new anthropological method, and I seek to illuminate role of co-performer/witness to an extent heretofore unexplored.

While Snow and I explore the performance of living history, incorporate years of accumulated knowledge into our writings, focus upon individual re-enactments, and analyze both performers and patrons, we differ in several key ways. My analysis investigates living history as only one aspect of the festival performance. Second, while Snow focuses upon both heritage and tourism as substantial factors in Plimoth's continued existence, I have avoided this area of investigation largely because of Gunnels's prior work on the Michigan, Scarborough, and Texas festivals. Finally, and most significantly, while Snow treats performers and patrons, he neither examines in depth their relationship to each other nor their contributions to creating and participating within the states of intrasticiancy I have proposed. I also draw heavily from another scholar who has examined Plimoth Plantation, Barbara Kirshenblatt-Gimblett. Though Kirshenblatt-Gimblett focuses on museum studies, tourism, and heritage, much as Jennifer Gunnels's dissertation does, her explication of the environment at Plimoth Plantation is essential to my study of the sensescape of the MDRF. Furthermore, Kirshenblatt-Gimblett, like Snow, addresses the benefits of first-person interpretation, which impacts not only on the living history portion of the present study, but on interactive improvisation as a whole.

Questions of the role of the audience in the creation of the performance are also paramount to this study. In his book *Warlocks and Warpdrive: Contemporary Fantasy Entertainments with Interactive and Virtual Environments*, Kurt Lancaster examines a wide variety of events, ranging from live-action fantasy role-playing to cyberspace performances.[25] Lancaster does not examine any of the modern American festivals, which rely heavily upon the concept of focused play as practiced by writers, actors, re-enactors, musicians, dancers, variety performers, and visitors to the village, so I expand upon his work with performances that are not dependent upon an audience. In the present study, I seek to examine the role the audience plays for participants: both paid performer and paying patron.

Using the extensive studies by scholars such as Bakhtin, Conquergood, Snow, and Victor Turner as a starting point for my research, I focus upon several questions in this book. How are various levels of intrasticiancy illustrated in the carnivalesque setting of the MDRF? How does the co-performer/witness methodology impact the ability to research sites like the MDRF? How do performers and patrons engage in a milieu which employs interactive improvisation as a primary theatrical form? How do different performances facilitate varying degrees of immersion into the intrastice for both actor and audience?

Chapters

The first three chapters of this book illustrate the historical, theoretical/cultural, and physical context against which the rest of the work should be read. In the final three chapters, I examine the different participants — performer and patron alike — who contribute to creating the realm of the Maryland Renaissance Festival. The first chapter, "Seeking the New in the Old: A Brief History of the Contemporary American Renaissance Festival," explores Bakhtin's concept of the carnivalesque and relates it to the festival structure and provides a short history of the contemporary American Renaissance festival, tracing its lineage back to the first faire in 1963. I examine that festival in southern California, opened by Phyllis Patterson, and then trace the festival movement through the 1970s. I provide a detailed history of the Maryland faire and add an examination of the small festival circuit, focusing upon the White Hart Renaissance Faire in Hartville, Missouri. Finally, I conclude the chapter by explaining a new concept in Renaissance festivals, the plug-and-play faire as illustrated by the company Faire a la Carte.

In the second chapter, "Carnival Setting, Cultural Work," I detail what happens when the world outside the festival gates is turned upside down, and patrons and performers re-key the frame so that festival as intrastice becomes the norm that people seek. I accomplish this by analyzing the reactions of performers and patrons during the weekend following 11 September 2001. While my primary focus is upon the Maryland festival, performers from faires in Pennsylvania and New York, where the terrorist attacks occurred, as well as from the Kansas City faire, located in the heartland of America and far removed geographically from the epicenter of the events of 11 September 2001, also contribute their memories. Furthermore, this chapter begins the illustration of the intrastice and the levels of immersion that patrons and performers experience when they participate in this modern carnival.

In the third chapter, "A Stroll Through the Sensescape of the MDRF," I explore how the privileged senses of sight and sound as well as the lesser-studied taste, touch, and smell combine to create the overall theatrical environment at the festival. I argue that it is this sensescape that enables greater participation in the states of intrasticiancy. I explore the various elements of the sensescape that is Revel Grove by providing a tour of the village and illustrating how the various senses combine.

The fourth chapter, "Living History at MDRF: Performing Embodied Knowledge," focuses upon an analysis of the components of the festival in which either historical pedagogy is a primary goal or in which sixteenth-century tasks are actually engaged. Because these living history performers are actually completing the duties they would have conducted nearly 500 years ago, they also face the attendant risks those undertakings require. The members of the Household of Hengrave Hall provide the primary living history component at the faire, portraying residents of a grand manor home of the Tudor era. These Company of St. George members perform tasks such as cooking, wool carding and spinning, wood carving, and weapons training. A second troupe falling under the living history category is *Das TeufelsAlpdrücken Fähnlien* (the Devil's Nightmare Regiment). The Landsknechts, as they are commonly called at the festival, were King Henry's personal bodyguards as well as the primary standing army for the Holy Roman Emperor during the Tudor era. A third group I place within this category is The Free Lancers, the jousting troupe that performs four times each day in combat tilts. These unchoreographed lance passes present very real consequences for the participating jousters.

The fifth chapter, "Historical Elaboration: A Royal Day in Revel Grove," focuses upon what I term "historical elaboration," a rehearsal and performance process writers and actors at the MDRF employ. I examine the daily routine of the Royal Court in Revel Grove to illustrate how patrons interact with performers to facilitate participation in varying states of intrasticiancy. A patron in the intrasticial state will sit in the audience and watch one of the stage shows, willingly suspending disbelief, but enter no further into the intrastice. A patron in the intrasticive state will play along with a courtier who approaches him or her on the street and engages the patron in a meaningful conversation, thus playing at belief. A patron in the intrasticious state will dress in Tudor-style clothing, speak in an approximation of a sixteenth-century accent, bow to the royalty and nobility, and spend time performing various personal rituals throughout the day, thereby actively creating belief.

The sixth chapter, "Performers, Patrons, and Playtrons: Interactions and Interfaces in the Intrastice," focuses upon the relationship between the paid participants at the festival and the paying visitors in Revel Grove. While patrons at the MDRF certainly participate in ways other than those afforded by the states of intrasticiancy, the vast majority appear to fit into the intrasticial, intrasticive, or intrasticious states, and I examine how various patrons exemplify each of these three states of intrasticiancy. Furthermore, I analyze the manner in which performer-patron interaction influences and in turn is thus influenced by the state of intrasticiancy in which a patron participates.

Through examining the history of faires and the carnivalesque setting, the sensescape the festival provides, living history, historical elaboration, and audience participation, I provide a deeper understanding of the states of intrasticiancy. By choosing a carnivalesque setting, which Victor Turner limits to industrialized societies and thereby restricts to liminoid status, I demonstrate that multiple states of immersion can occur within an industrialized culture, which in turn opens up the theory of the intrastice for use in non-theatrical settings. I further illustrate that within the context of performance these states have specific theatrical attributes that can be applied at other venues, providing an addition not only to the theatre lexicon, but for anthropological and sociological work as well.

One final note before beginning this journey: I have changed the names of all of the patrons who participated in the research for this book, unless they were previously published in another source. Though many of them did not request anonymity, a significant portion did, and it seemed most reasonable to provide pseudonyms for the visitors to the village. I have changed performer names only when anonymity was requested by the performer, and in that specific case, it is noted that the name is a pseudonym. Most performers are well-known in the festival circuit, and at most faires there are playbills of some sort that list the actors and the characters they portray, and, indeed, most actors acknowledge the publicity is part of the job.

1

Seeking the New in the Old: A Brief History of the Contemporary American Renaissance Festival

Mikhail Bakhtin extols the virtues and vices of the carnivalesque through his landmark work *Rabelais and His World*, and he brings to the foreground the importance these festive activities had in the lives of the people of the time. He describes carnival as having

> a universal spirit; it is a special condition of the entire world, of the world's revival and renewal, in which all take part. Such is the essence of carnival, vividly felt by all its participants. It was most clearly expressed and experienced in the Roman Saturnalias, perceived as a true and full, though temporary, return of Saturn's golden age upon earth.[1]

Just as Bakhtin depicted the medieval and early modern carnival as descendants of the Roman Saturnalia, in this chapter I use Bakhtin's words as a guiding principle to explicate how the modern American Renaissance festival is a progeny (of sorts) of those long since past carnivals that so intrigued him. The essence of carnival, as Bakhtin describes above, is a condition of revival and renewal that all participants experience. At the modern American Renaissance festival, there is a range of experience of that essence, and those who participate in any level of immersion feel it to some degree. First, I will briefly explore the genesis of festivals in the United States in order to provide a background against which I can illustrate the carnivalesque elements common to most of these faires. Then I chronicle the history of the Maryland Renaissance Festival, the primary setting for the majority of this work. Finally, I will explore the circuit of smaller faires, explaining their importance to the continuing success of the renaissance festival culture, focusing on a single festival in Hartville, Missouri.

There are inherent problems with chronicling the history of the contemporary American Renaissance festival. No complete written narrative of the forty-plus years of contemporary American Renaissance festivals exists. Newspaper articles, often the only written primary sources about faires, rarely treat issues germane to the understanding of festival history and are often available only from the mid–1980s. Several magazine articles offer documentation unavailable elsewhere, but that information often requires further confirmation. A myriad of websites provide narratives about festivals, but Internet sources are often suspect since there is no indication of the genesis of the information or peer review to ensure accuracy. Nonetheless, I have used the Internet extensively to check sources against each other as I attempted to verify dates, places, and names. One Internet site, the SCRIBE network, describes itself as "The Renaissance Faire Information Clearinghouse" and is an invaluable source which provides links and histories otherwise unavailable.[2] Beyond these few written sources, much of the information about faire history has been passed down orally from one generation of performers to another; it is often this oral history against which I have verified written sources. This unusual form of documentation is part of the co-performer/witness methodology in which personal relationships hold equal — and sometimes greater weight — than written sources. I have often found during my research that four people will tell an almost identical story far more often than four written sources will agree with the same level of detail. It is within this paradigm that I present the following history of the contemporary American Renaissance festival.

The First Contemporary American Renaissance Festival

Tracing the genealogy of a particular theatrical movement can be difficult. Playwrights create new forms. Designers tinker with scenography. Directors find different ways to evoke emotions. Actors evolve a new natural style. However, with Renaissance festivals there is a clear path back to a single moment and a single person who began this theatrical form. Phyllis Patterson was the daughter of a former Memphis school superintendent. According to *Renaissance Magazine* reporter Ben Simons, Patterson has said that her father taught her that "'the classroom should be a circus for the five senses.'"[3] (See Chapter 3, which treats the five senses in detail.) In 1962, Patterson became the Director of Drama for the Wonderland Youth Center in Hollywood Hills, California. Her first year, she produced a history of theatre which included performances reminiscent of eras from antiquity to the Renaissance. The following year, Patterson had an idea for a fund raiser for a local station that produced BBC radio plays: a Renaissance festival. In planning that first faire, Patterson drew from her knowledge of theatre history. As performance theorist Kurt Lancaster writes, "New forms of performances are not created from a vacuum. Previous historical events, ceremonies, rituals, sporting events, and other kinds of performances have shaped and do influence the many new forms of performances occurring today."[4] Patterson — who had taught literature and was already well-versed in English history, Elizabethan drama, folk traditions, and philosophy — became enamored with the *commedia dell'arte* after a friend recommended that she read Pierre-Louis Ducharte's *Italian Comedy*. Weaving together her knowledge of English history and Elizabethan drama, her interest in folklife, and the spirit of the *commedia* within the medieval traveling tradition, Patterson created the first Renaissance festival.

A desire for the medieval marketplace in which bodies jostled amidst a cacophony of sound led Patterson to avoid the theatrical conventions of the proscenium stage. Simons writes that she wanted actors who would bring a "mix of improv and *Commedia* styles. Patterson's goal was to break down the wall between the stage and the audience so that the experience of immersion could combine with audience participation and patrons could play as large a part in the spectacle as they wanted."[5] From the beginning, the faire was designed so patrons could frame the festival in order to participate in their chosen level of intrasticiancy. According to Patterson,

> the faire I invented was truly an allegory concocted to appeal and invite participation on many varied levels. I believed there should be a great party atmosphere of Eat, Drink and Be Merry! for those who came to party. Additionally, there should be history, theater, art, music, dance and pageantry aplenty for those who want to plunge more deeply into the experience.[6]

Even today, spectators often attend festivals to experience a sense of belonging that perhaps they do not have in their lives outside of the faire. Patrons can become a part of the life of the festival; they participate in their own ways to their own degrees of comfort. While everyone may experience an essence of carnival, whether an individual acts upon it is a personal choice.

Initially, Patterson had difficulty finding participants to staff the festival, both performers and vendors. Eventually she found artists skilled in archaic music, including lute, recorder, sackbut, and crumhorn players, as well as madrigal singers. It was equally arduous for Patterson to find crafters for the faire, as Simons chronicles.

> At first it was difficult to find craftspeople who had any knowledge or expertise in traditional arts and crafts. The burgeoning of the 1960s handcrafts culture had not yet occurred, and there was yet no buying audience for handmade things. At first all she could find was one sandalmaker, but eventually she turned up a number of potters, some weavers and a handful of other hobbyists.[7]

These initial troubles in finding musicians and artisans are indicative of the early–1960s society that was still celebrating a renewed interest in mechanization supposedly designed to streamline work and provide more time for leisure.[8]

Despite having more time for leisure activities, the American family of the 1950s and early 1960s followed a tradition that rejected carnival and replaced it with more personal and less outwardly grotesque activities. Bakhtin explains the historical trajectory of carnival's fall:

> (Starting in the seventeenth century) we observe a process of gradual narrowing down of the ritual, spectacle, and carnival forms of folk culture, which became small and trivial. On the one hand the state encroached upon festive life and turned it into a parade; on the other hand these festivities were brought into the home and became part of the family's private life. The privileges which were formerly allowed the marketplace were more and more restricted. The carnival spirit with its freedom, its utopian character oriented toward the future, was gradually transformed into a mere holiday mood.[9]

For years the festival spirit had been celebrated privately, within the home. Christmas and Thanksgiving allowed for some level of celebration akin to the feast, but on a much smaller scale and held within private space and boundaries. It was more easily controlled within the home, where any potentially transgressive events were kept private. The perfect home of the 1950s as depicted in *Leave It to Beaver* or *The Donna Reed Show* ignores the possibility of transgression and especially the grotesque, which is expressed through the carnivalesque body. Moments of flatulence and the like are ignored in representations of the perfect home. Drunkenness is not part of the middle-class ideal. Mention of bodily functions such as urination would be met with disdain, and emphasizing not only the location but the size of the penis is beyond comprehension within a non-transgressive 1950s household. However, all of these parts of the grotesque come to the forefront in the 1960s rebellion against its supposedly perfect antecedent.[10]

The 1960s brought a huge upheaval in the *status quo* as Americans challenged racial, gendered, and classed lines. Against this backdrop, the early festivals became successful renditions of a new essence of carnival. For many years, any transgressive act relating to the lower body was discouraged in public. According to Bakhtin, "The carnival spirit and grotesque imagery continued to live and was transmitted as a now purely literary tradition, especially as a tradition of the Renaissance."[11] However, in the 1960s this tradition was reborn through folk culture and performance, not just literature: from Broadway musicals such as *Hair* to Happenings and Environmental Theatre, both of which utilized "found spaces" which were non-traditional theatrical spaces to produce performances. Turning again to Bakhtin, there is an explanation for why this occurred at this particular juncture in history. He writes:

> Through all the stages of historic development feasts were linked to moments of crisis, of breaking points in the cycle of nature or in the life of society and man. Moments of death and revival, of change and renewal always led to a festive perception of the world. These moments, expressed in concrete form, created the peculiar character of the feasts.[12]

The early and mid–1960s were a time of crisis in the United States. The Civil Rights Movement had begun, and Americans faced the Cuban Missile Crisis. A beloved President was assassinated, and a horrific war in Vietnam was ongoing. It was within this context, Bakhtin's "breaking points ... in the life of a society," that the festivals emerged. Whatever Patterson's pedagogical intents, the festival became much more, providing a place for carnival within a society at its breaking point.

Women's breasts are also part of Bakhtin's grotesque. The frequent, open, and sometimes even wanton display of women's bosoms at the festivals became a significant aspect of the modern carnival, in juxtaposition to the world of Rabelais. In the sixteenth century it was completely inappropriate for a woman to display ankles, shoulders, or elbows, i.e. any body part without a function requiring it to be exposed. However, artwork from the period clearly illustrates that women's breasts were prominent, with rounding of the bosom evident despite the underbodice, chemise, kirtle, and dress.[13] This discrepancy is easily explained: the breasts had a purpose. They gave mother's milk, and thus they gave life. However, in the twentieth century, especially in the 1950s when baby bottles were all the rage and breastfeeding seemed passé, the bosom came to be more and more covered. Therefore, the prominent display of breasts in the late twentieth and early twenty-first centuries marks them as part of the grotesque, the carnivalesque lower body, even if anatomically they would not initially fit into the definition. Exposure of the female body from ankles to thighs and shoulders to wrists is perfectly acceptable in the modern world. Women may wear miniskirts to the office and sleeveless camisoles in board meetings. However, if a woman displayed her breasts in corporate America as they are flaunted at the contemporary American Renaissance festival, at the very least she would be labeled as a slut, and she could possibly be fired for not wearing appropriate attire.

Thus, amidst this societal landscape of the early 1960s, the physical landscape of the early faires emerged. Simons writes specifically of the site for Patterson's first festival: "A five-acre country location was found for the event, with a small house that Patterson covered with a period-looking façade."[14] The next year the faire moved to a larger site, the Paramount Ranch, whose 500-year-old oak trees provided the ideal ambiance for the growing festival.

Patterson truly engaged with the environment as she worked to grow the size of the faire. Sam Blazer wrote in a 1976 edition of *TDR*, "the events merge into a texture where richness is conveyed through sheer density and sensory overload rather than through direct experience; through the knowledge that so much is happening everywhere rather than through the effect of any particular occurrence."[15] The interactive and immersive qualities Patterson stressed became part and parcel of the Renaissance festival experience, even as other faires began in different parts of the country and outside of her purview.

Familiar Faces, Different Places

Following Patterson's model, George Coulam, a former worker at the California faire, opened the first contemporary American Renaissance festival outside of California 1971. According to Patterson, "We were originators. The first of the many imitative versions of our RPF took place in Minnesota."[16] Following several years running the Minnesota faire, Coulam left to begin another festival, this time in Texas. In 1975, the Texas Renaissance Festival debuted, and the faire there, which is now incorporated as its own town, has thrived over the past thirty plus years. In 1977, the number of major faires doubled as the Colorado, Kansas City, Maryland, and Sterling Renaissance festivals opened their gates. No other single year has spawned so many major new faires or so many that continue to thrive decades later. In 1981, three new major festivals began: Camlann Medieval in Washington, the Pennsylvania Renaissance Festival, and Scarborough in Texas. By 1981, twelve major festivals flourished and hundreds more small educational or heavily craft-oriented faires also took place on single weekends. By 2008, at least twenty major faires — those running four or more weekends and drawing 80,000 or more patrons — were in operation around the country.

EARLY MAJOR FAIRES

1963	1964	1971	1975	1977	1980	1981
California (Southern)	California (Northern)	Minnesota	Texas	Colorado	Bay Area (FL)	Camlann (WA)
				Kansas City (MO)		Pennsylvania
				Maryland Sterling (NY)		Scarborough (TX)

The Maryland Renaissance Festival opened in 1977, fourteen years after Patterson's original faire in California. This chart illustrates the major festivals between 1963 and 1981.

HENRY'S VIII'S WIVES AT THE **MDRF**

Actual Year	Queen Portrayed	Historical Year
1989	Katherine of Aragon	152?
1990	Anne Boleyn	1534
1991	AnneBoleyn	1535
1992	Jane Seymour	1537
1993	Anna of Cleves	1540
1995	Catherine Howard	1542
1996*	Katherine Parr	1547
1997	Katherine of Aragon	1520
1998	Katherine of Aragon	1522
1999	Katherine of Aragon	1526
2000	Katherine of Aragon	1527
2001	Katherine of Aragon	1529
2002	Anne Boleyn	1533
2003	Anne Boleyn	1534
2004	Jane Seymour**	1536
2005	Jane Seymout	1537
2006	No Queen	1539
2007	Anna of Cleves	1540
2008	Catherine Howard	1541

**A list of the various queens portrayed since the Maryland Renaissance Festival
switched to a Henrician faire in 1989. At the time of this writing, the MDRF is
on its second time through the cycle of Henry VIII's wives. *Henry "died" off-
stage before the end of the festival day during the 1996 season. **See Chapter 4
for complete details on the 2004 storyline, which featured Katherine of Aragon,
Anne Boleyn, and Jane Seymour.**

The Maryland Renaissance Festival

As major festival sites go, Maryland was one of the earlier progeny of
Patterson's California faires. In the early 1970s, Jules Smith, Sr., the President
of the MDRF, initially invested $6,000 in Coulam's Minneapolis festival.
When Coulam left Minnesota to begin the Texas Renaissance Festival, Smith
"sold his shares for a nice gain."[17] Nonetheless, Smith, a successful Minnesota
lawyer, could not stay away from the festival business and eventually created
a faire of his own and literally, "with the help of his three oldest sons, started
building a Renaissance village in his driveway in Minneapolis and in a borrowed barn nearby."[18] The pieces were then erected on a site in Columbia,
Maryland, where the MDRF began its run in the summer of 1977. The festival originally ran for only four weekends, but it drew 17,000 people in its
first year. Acts that later become famous — including Penn and Teller and
members of the Flying Karamazov Brothers — performed at that first faire
alongside local amateur singers and dancers. When the development of the

planned community of Columbia encroached on the growing festival, Smith needed to find a new location. In 1985, he settled upon a location in Crownsville, Maryland, the current site of the faire.

In 1989, the MDRF made a major artistic change, moving from an Elizabethan faire featuring the virgin queen to a Henrician festival that celebrated her father and all six of his wives. Each year, Artistic Director Carolyn Spedden creates a new storyline for the festival based upon the historical record of sixteenth-century England. The basic premise of the storyline and times and locations for the In-House Stage Shows are listed in the program patrons receive as they enter the village gates. By 2004, the year of my ethnography, the festival was on its second cycle through the queens; the first cycle began in 1989 with Henry and Katherine of Aragon and ended in 1996 with Henry's death and the crowning of Edward. In 1997, the festival began the wife cycle over again, portraying the year 1520, during which Henry was still very happily married to his first queen, Katherine of Aragon. In 2004, the festival storyline revolved around the first trio of Henry's wives, including the deaths of the first two and the betrothal of the third.[19] By 2008, Henry was once again married to wife number five, Catherine Howard.

The MDRF begins the weekend before Labor Day and runs on Saturdays and Sundays through October, with the addition of Labor Day Monday. According to Bakhtin, "The feast is always essentially related to time, either to the recurrence of an event in the natural (cosmic) cycle, or to biological or historic timelines."[20] The timing of the Maryland faire allows it always to be associated with the annual harvest festivals that occurred in Renaissance England as well as with the end of the King's summer progresses away from the London heat. Several other major faires run roughly concurrently with the MDRF, including ones in Kansas, Michigan, Minnesota, Ohio, and Pennsylvania. Other large festivals take place at different times during the year: both earlier and later. Some of these faires provide different rationales for their existence at a particular time of the year, while others supply no reason. The MDRF takes care to attempt to supply historically believable reasoning behind its practices. For example, the king and queen and their court come to this small country village because they attempt to escape London's summer heat and its attendant illnesses.

Just as I was finishing this book, a surprising piece of information came to my attention. After twenty-four years at the Crownsville, Maryland, location, the MDRF is considering a move to a new locale. According to an article on *BaltimoreSun.com*, "Organizers of the Renaissance Festival — in its 32nd season of celebrating 16th-century English culture — recently undertook a location scouting effort across the region in order to expand their business, currently situated on 135 acres in Crownsville."[21] The importance of the

MDRF to the area and the impact it would have if moved is evidenced by commentary in the article by Robert L. Hannon, president of the Anne Arundel County Economic Development Corp., who said the reason behind the possible move relates to lease negotiations over the current site. Presidents of the county's Chamber of Commerce and Visitors Bureau also chimed in on the topic and expressed their hope that the festival would find a new location within the same county. The move, should it take place, could take several years before it is complete because of the building requirements to create a new village. Nonetheless, the impact on the community, wherever the MDRF occurs, is palpable.

The Smaller Renaissance Festival Circuit

While there are more than twenty "major festivals" in the country, there are more than six times that many smaller faires. Some of these are independent events; they are singular one-, two-, or three-weekend festivals with no connection to any other faire. Other small faires are part of a circuit owned by a single person or group. The first type of festival may come and go in a single season without ever having a chance of survival. Bad weather, poor planning, inexperience, and lack of funding can all cause a festival to fail. It can be many years before a faire breaks even or turns a profit. As Di Johnson-Taylor, owner of the small White Hart Renaissance Faire (that will be discussed further at the end of this section), elaborates: "If you start an event like this to make money, don't even start it, because it won't work. If it ever makes more than breaking even, you are very lucky. We do it because we love it and choose to invest ourselves in it more than any 'sane' person would dream of doing" (field notes). Love of the venue is the key, especially with the small Renaissance faire; profit as a motivating factor is a warning sign.

The second type of small faire, part of a circuit, often begins as a single festival and grows into a multi-event circuit. For example, Festivals International, co-produced by Gregory and Bonnie Schmidt, runs five separate events: the Des Moines Renaissance Faire; the Iowa Renaissance Festival (Amana Colonies, IA); the Lincolnshire Renaissance Faire (Decatur, IL); the Midlands Pirate Festival (Papillion, NE); and the Nebraska Renaissance Festival (Papillion, NE). All the faires with the exception of the Des Moines Renaissance Faire run for a single weekend in either the spring or the fall. Des Moines runs for three weekends in September. According to its website, Festivals International began in 1992 with the Iowa Renaissance Festival. The Nebraska faire followed just over a decade later in 2003, and, beginning a few years later, the organization has added a new festival each year: the Des Moines festival in 2006; the Lincolnshire faire in 2007; and the organization's first pirate-themed faire, the Midlands Pirate Festival, in 2008.[22]

Most small festivals are not nearly as successful. While various websites list over 180 different faires in the United States, by the time I went back to gather specific information on a particular faire, the link was often disabled. Many of these festivals were small, one-weekend, soft-site faires. Soft sites, which can include some of the larger faires, are created with period-style tents that are set up and taken down with each festival season. Hard sites, such as the MDRF, are faires in which all of the buildings are permanent, year-round structures. Yet, even some festivals with hard sites that featured multiple weekends fail to continue. Though it has now been reorganized as a soft-site faire, the Virginia Renaissance Festival was once a hard-site, which has since deteriorated into an abandoned ghost town, presumably waiting for development in the ever-growing area between Northern Virginia and Richmond, Virginia. The MDRF, the main faire at which I garnered most of the research for this book, had a sister site in Ontario, Canada, which did not survive to its tenth year, despite the strong success record of the Maryland festival owners. Therefore, any time a small, one-, two-, or three-weekend faire is able to survive multiple seasons, it is a success.

In 2008, information found on the World Wide Web indicated that more than forty states currently had active festivals. Of all the states, only Delaware, Hawaii, Maine, Montana, New Hampshire, North Dakota, South Carolina, West Virginia, and Wyoming, as well as the District of Columbia, did not have festivals of their own. Many people travel from Delaware, West Virginia, and the District of Columbia to the MDRF, and several of the other states which do not have faires of their own have accessible festivals in neighboring states, especially for those who live close to the border. California offered the most festivals, boasting more than thirty faires, all but two of which I classify as "small" festivals. More than ninety percent of these small California faires run for only one weekend. In California, February and December are the only months without a Renaissance festival entertainment to attend.

The mild climate which California offers undoubtedly makes it easier to run festivals in multiple months. Many small faires can survive for years in California because the risk of weather cancelling an entire weekend, which could be the full planned run of the festival, is far less than in other places. Small festivals in the Pacific Northwest, Northeast Corridor, and both upper and middle Midwest regions run only between the months of May and October, when temperatures are less likely to drop below freezing. Even then, however, the risk of rain is still an issue for many small faires, which fight from year to year to survive. One such festival, which has just finished its fourth season, is the White Hart Renaissance Faire.

The White Hart Renaissance Faire

In 2005, the year after I completed the initial research for this book at the MDRF, a small festival opened just outside of Hartville, Missouri, a small town situated amidst a large Amish community in which absence of electricity is not a temporary jaunt into the intrastice, but a constant way of life. This idyllic setting for the White Hart Renaissance Faire (WHRF) is nearly three hours from St. Louis, and more than three from Kansas City, Missouri. The closest "big city"— Springfield, Missouri, whose population is just over 150,000 — is located forty-five minutes away from the WHRF.[23] Nonetheless, the late Charles Taylor and his wife, Di Johnson-Taylor, veterans the Renaissance festival circuit on the west coast — including approximately twenty-five years Charles spent with the Living History Center/Renaissance Pleasure Faire, original festival opened by Phyllis Patterson — chose this location to open a new contemporary American Renaissance festival.[24]

Charles Taylor's resume reads like a "where's where" of festivals up and down the west coast. He was involved with faires in Arizona, Oregon. Nevada, and California from 1974 until his untimely passing. He served in capacities from performer to owner, from producer to director, from vender manager to entertainment director. Di Johnson-Taylor came to the festival scene in the late 1980s, worked as a court performer in numerous California faires, and then, with Charles, co-produced the San Diego Renaissance Faire (a soft site) before making WHRF their home. When Di came to Missouri in 2002 for personal reasons, she and Charles had already decided the time had come to find a site that could be become a permanent "hard" site. According to Johnson-Taylor,

> We decided when we were producing the San Diego faire to look for a permanent site, first in California, which turned out to be logistically and financially impossible on a limited budget. Then we started to look in Missouri after I had to move here to look after my parents in 2002. We found the area in southwestern Missouri when I read an ad for the sale of the Missouri Renaissance Fair in Mansfield. We fell in love with the area and started looking for a better site since her land was only eleven acres with limited parking. Our criteria included that the site must be no more than twenty miles from an Interstate with good roads and access, no local building restrictions or costly code processes, at least eighty acres, with about two-thirds for parking, and a level site with lots of trees. There is more, but it involves a number of intangibles about the "feel" of the site. It took us about a year and a half to find this place [field notes].

With their west coast experience firmly under their belts, they found the site they were searching for in Missouri, and the White Hart Renaissance Faire was born.

Part of the reason the Hartville locale is so ideal is that patrons begin to enter the intrastice long before they reach the gates of the WHRF. The rolling hills and surrounding countryside are reminiscent of the countryside in Dorsetshire, where the WHRF is ostensibly set, in the village of Hart Grove, which in reality exists to this day in southern England. More than ten miles from the closest highway, the trip back in time begins with the view from the car/carriage, especially when passing the Amish buggies which are prominent upon the country roads leading to the WHRF site.

Upon reaching the festival, it is obvious why Taylor and Johnson-Taylor chose this particular locale: it fit their requirements almost perfectly. There are one hundred acres total, with a house and barn located on one section, large areas of open field for parking, and nearly forty acres of woods which can be cleared as the festival grows. At the present (2009), only five acres have been cleared for the actual festival grounds, leaving thirty-five acres of woods surrounding the current village, which allows only small vestiges of the twenty-first century to remain visible. Because utilities are limited in the village — there are few electric poles or wires, and the water source is hidden inside a wooden tower — there are few modern sights that would normally pull a visitor from the intrastice. The site is a hybrid of hard site and soft site, with some permanent structures and many period tents and pavilions. Each year new permanent structures are added, as need mandates and funding allows. Often, structures may appear permanent, even though they are not. For example, in 2008, one of the key additions to the site of the faire was a beehive oven built by the woman who plays the village bakery mistress and her husband, who portrays one of the queen's guards. The baker, who along with her husband is a veteran of the southern California faire, utilized the oven to bake fresh bread on site each day. However, the base of the beehive oven is completely removable, and the oven itself, since it is built of mud, is easily replaced as the need arises due to the elements, etc.

The WHRF was founded not only on a specific site, but on a particular philosophy that will allow the faire to grow comfortably from small faire to whatever size it can achieve.

> We wanted to start an event that is valuable to the community as well as the faire community. Charles' dream was to eventually start a Performing Arts Camp to train the next generations of re-enactors, performers, artisans, and demonstrators. It will also train the people behind the scenes in how to build and maintain the infra-structure needed to keep the events running smoothly. His concept was that in the beginning, RPFN [Renaissance Pleasure Faire North in California] and RPFS [Renaissance Pleasure Faire South, also in California] were conceived in the same idea, but that when they went corporate, they lost the care for the cast and crew that made them a family. Our idea is to keep this "family" of all of us involved in Faire and when it starts to show a profit, start a profit sharing plan for all of the people who have given so much of their hearts to make this work [field notes].

At the vast majority of festivals on the west coast, and in the Midwest as well, cast members are not compensated financially for their efforts. Unlike the MDRF where every cast member is paid, at many of the faires in the rest of the country, "pay" can be anything from five dollars in company script good for purchasing food to two bottles of water. Taylor and Johnson-Taylor, having worked in the west coast tradition for nearly forty years combined, were well aware of the pay rates for the average performer, who spends the vast amount of his or her time in often sweltering heat and yards of fabric in an attempt to create the atmosphere that allows the intrastice to exist. Johnson-Taylor wants all involved to be paid, just as performers are at the much larger and longer-running MDRF.

With the opening of the WHRF, Taylor and Johnson-Taylor had a plan to change the way not only that cast is paid, but also the way that management handles interaction between various distinct aspects of festival. Johnson-Taylor explains:

> We want to compensate the performers at their actual value instead of squeezing out every penny of profit for the benefit of the owner of the faire, and eventually it will be set up as a foundation to keep greed out after I am no longer here. We feel that it takes three things to make an event successful: entertainment, fine artisans, and good food. All of these are of equal importance, because you can get the public to come to a show with the right advertising once, but without a good show, they won't return. The standard formula is that if you have a one-third return rate, you are doing it right [field notes].

Johnson-Taylor raises several important issues in the above quote. First, and foremost, she emphasizes the importance of paying performers for the hard work they do at faire. Second, she clearly outlines what is required for a festival to succeed, "entertainment, fine artisans, and good food." What is striking is her next statement that all three "are of equal importance." At most festivals, management places priority upon vendors and stage acts, leaving cast members largely unpaid. This has, in many cases, and even at festivals like the MDRF where the cast is well compensated, led to a "never the twain shall meet" attitude between performers and vendors.

One particular illustration of this attitude concerns an annual event held at the MDRF. In 2004, the Benefit silent Auction and Concert was in its third year. The announcement for the auction read:

> Once again we find ourselves in the position where we must reflect upon ourselves as a community. Regardless of our personal beliefs, we should recognize that we as a group are linked together, even dependent on each other in this life-style: what happens to one can happen to each and every one of us. And I have been here long enough to know that we do care. One of the main reasons, it seems, that most of us chose this life in the first place, was this very spirit of community, of connectedness to one another.

The announcement went on to explain that one of the MDRF's perennial vendors was undergoing cancer treatments, unable to open her booth that season, and was without health insurance. The proceeds from the auction and benefit would go to help this member of the festival community through a very difficult time. After seeing the announcement posted on one of the bulletin boards across from the festival office, I decided to attend. I was somewhat surprised that this was the third annual benefit of its type, and, yet, this was the first I had ever heard of it. I knew that many vendors and stage acts, who work and perform at multiple faires, do so without the benefits a regular day job provides, including health insurance.

I would also like to point out here that at the time I wrote this, I was living in a tent in the campgrounds site the festival offers for performers and vendors who travel from long distances for the MDRF. Up until about a week before the benefit, I had been maintaining two homes: a two-bedroom apartment in Naperville, Illinois, where I resided full-time with my son; and a one-bedroom garage apartment in Annapolis, Maryland, where I lived for the first three months of my research. When financial circumstances made it impossible for me to continue to maintain two separate homes, I bought a tent and moved onto the campgrounds. If I had not, I probably would never have seen the sign advertising the benefit. Living in the campground area, I had a far greater opportunity to interact with vendors and other workers than I had in my previous circumstances. I thought that attending the evening's festivities would provide an opportunity to see cast, acts, and vendors in a totally different way.

I was not mistaken; things certainly were different. Nonetheless, I was surprised by what I encountered at the benefit. My field notes, written immediately upon arriving home that evening, reflect my feelings at the time:

> The Fraternal Order of Police Lodge parking lot is usually empty when I drive by it on the way to the bank. Tonight, with lights glowing in the parking lot, it was difficult to find a place for my car. Inside under bright fluorescent lights I saw people for the first time with the aid of electricity. Usually it is only natural ambient light that allows us to see each other on the faire site. Soft music wafted through the open door out into the cool fall night. A bodhran set down the beat for the other musicians. Tables were alighted up and down the hall, donated goods displayed on them for bidding at the silent auction. The prices of original bids ranged from $1 to $100. Jewelry, mugs, pottery, clothing, and various forms of artwork were arrayed for perusal and auction. On a counter, a generous display of food lay: cheese and crackers, fruit, pate, pretzels, and soft drinks. There was a canister labeled "donations for food" by the counter. Everyone was on the honor system, just as with the "Donations" box by the front door. On that same table was a card for ... the beneficiary of this evening's event.
>
> I was the only member of the Company of the Rose present at the event. One

of the heralds [John Lasher], who is married to [Brenda] a member of the Fisher family [from whom the Smiths lease the land on which the MDRF takes place], was present. One of the members of Shakespeare's Skum [a stage act] was also there with his wife. Three of the Rogues [a bagpipe and drum band] were present.... Street act Jim Greene (Emrys Fleet, ratcatcher) was there. Otherwise, there were no performers. The rest of the aout sixty people were either vendors or patrons, or members of the Fisher extended family. The line between performer and vendor was never as clear to me as it was tonight. These were people who have little extra to give, but do so anyway [field notes].

The lack of cast members really struck me. It was only after I realized how few performers were present that I thought about where I had seen the flyer about the auction and came to the conclusion that if I had not been working in the office and/or living in the campground, I would never have seen it. By attending this event, I saw for myself, in a manner I never had before, the clear divide between performers and vendors. In an event with the sheer numbers of performers and vendors the MDRF utilizes, this is perhaps not a surprise, but it certainly is different when examined in juxtaposition with the small festivals such as White Hart.

While this separation between vendors and performers is not unilaterally true, it is often the case at larger faires. At White Hart, the before-fair-opens get-together is not called "cast call" as it is at the MDRF, but rather "morning meeting," and vendors and performers alike attend. At a large festival like the MDRF, it would be virtually impossible to have the vendors and performers all attending one meeting, but at a small festival like the WHRF, it is not only possible, it is deemed necessary to the mission of ensuring that all members of the festival feel equally included and important.

This leads to perhaps one of the biggest differences between the large and small festivals: the ability to maintain a "family" feel between everyone involved. Johnson-Taylor explains her views on the large versus small faire dynamic:

> I think that the larger faires tend to be run more with an eye on the bottom line before anything else. They lose the personal touch and sometimes become too corporate. People get to know each other when there aren't as many cast and crew members, and care about each other. It shows in the final production. As we grow, it is one of our primary missions to maintain that personal interaction. I'm not sure it will be easy, but it's worth it [field notes].

The difference Johnson-Taylor points out is the loss of "personal touch" and how people can "get to know each other" among smaller casts. The MDRF, despite its size, maintains that personal touch, if not necessarily between vendor and performers, then between the performers themselves. Furthermore, despite its success, the MDRF does not have the feeling that it has "become too corporate." Perhaps the ability to balance running a large faire and main-taining that non-corporate feel at the MDRF stems from the family-run nature of the business or the owners' origins over three decades ago at the Minnesota faire.

Another advantage of small faires is the ability to become well-acquainted with each and every cast member. As Brother William, who has performed as cast at both the WHRF and Oklahoma Renaissance Faire in Muskogee, Oklahoma, states, "I can play with the characters of small faires a lot easier than I can at the larger faires. It takes little time to be acquainted with them (at smaller functions)" (field notes). Brother William is known at many faires, and asked that he be referred to by his festival name. Even though he has worked as a vendor at the KCRF in the past and spent his free time in the streets performing one of his most-well known bits, carving flowers from twigs, he refuses to become a member of the cast there. Brother Williams states: "I have NEVER been cast at KCRF (I refuse to play their schedule games) and have worked full runs there paying my way in."[25] While at the MDRF a patron paying his way in the gates and then performing would be considered unacceptable for a variety of reasons (see Chapter Six for a fur-ther discussion of this issue), apparently at KCRF, since the performers are largely unpaid, this is not an issue, and Brother William walks the lanes carv-ing his flowers and handing them out to certain fortunate patrons.

Brother William has also visited the Bristol Renaissance Faire (BRF) in southern Wisconsin as a patron. Dressed in his usual costume, he approached the woman playing Queen Elizabeth at BRF and managed to introduce him-self as a visitor from another shire, conveying to her in the process his status as a cast member at one of the other Midwestern festivals. His decision to meet and greet the monarch turned out to be quite fortunate for the Queen. Brother William elaborates:

> At Bristol, it took waiting for the Queen to finish a "performance" and follow her through the lanes to the next performance location fast-talking all the way so she knew who I was and what I could do.... Talked to the Queen between [the] childrens' knighting [ceremony] and the performances down in the glen. It was dreadfully hot and sticky; the Archbishop had MS and had not made an appearance yet when his part came about. With that "dead air" space, the Queen asked if any of the patrons had any questions for her, and a man promptly stood up and said, "we would like to get married." The Archbishop CAN do that (*so could I by state law at the time), but he wasn't there.... She (Queen) without missing a beat, stating that the Archbishop was not yet pres-ent, scanned the audience, met my eye (at the BACK of the crowd), cocked her head to one side a little bit, and I nodded back, upon which she said, "but we have a visiting Monk with us this day...." and with the help of cast, we had a wedding five minutes later. (It turned out that it was really a renewal of vows

after 20 years, but at the time we did not know that ... we just went with the flow) [field notes].

At the MDRF, the concept of a performer from another festival simply appearing and taking major part in a show is unheard of, but in the Midwest, there appears to be a much greater mixing between festivals.

Another difference between performing at small and large festivals is merely a product of the numbers game. As a performer at the MDRF, it was not uncommon to create bits for the viewing pleasure of more than one hundred patrons at a time. The scenario that opened this book was often viewed by nearly that many visitors. At the WHRF, it was not uncommon for me to have single, private interactions with more one hundred different patrons. While personal interactions with single patrons or families is also one of my favorite parts of performing at the MDRF, with over twenty thousand patrons entering the gates on a given day, I never had the audacity to believe I could interact with every single visitor. At the 2008 WHRF, I played Elizabeth Talbot, the Countess of Shrewsbury, better known through time as "Bess of Hardwicke." I believe that on every day of the run in which I participated at WHRF, I at least spoke a greeting or a farewell to nearly every single patron who came through the gates. One day, I made it my particular goal to try to speak to every single patron I saw, and I did not see a visitor to the village without whom I had the fortune to have some interaction.

One particular patron interaction deserves special note simply because of the time and effort multiple cast members spent and exerted with her. As the WHRF monarch, Susi Matthews Cannon as Queen Elizabeth I, entered the village, a woman dressed in twenty-first century clothing stepped in front of her and for all intents and purposes stopped the queen's progress. She announced that she was Mary, Queen of Scots, and simply refused to let "Elizabeth" pass, hurling insults at the English monarch, including negative comments about Elizabeth's inability to produce an heir. After much wrangling, the queen, her guards, and her entourage managed to escape but left behind Sir Francis Walsingham, played by Mark Wickersham, to deal with this patron. [field notes] I was not in attendance to her majesty at the time of this occurrence, instead having spent the time preparing for her arrival at the royal pavilion. As she approached, I could tell immediately that something was wrong. After I greeted her majesty, she requested that I, "Bess of Hardwicke," please go meet Sir Francis and help him with the woman to whom he was speaking, "Mary, Queen of Scots."

Matthews Cannon's choice in sending me to help Sir Francis was twofold. First, and foremost, I was one of the more seasoned and veteran (read old) performers at the WHRF, and second, because in the particular moment of history we were portraying at White Hart, the Queen of Scots was actually a more or less permanent "guest" of my character's. In other words, "my husband," the Earl of Shrewsbury, and I had been tasked with being the jailors of the banished Scottish monarch, who at this time should have been safely under house arrest at one of "my" manor homes, either Sheffield or Tutbury Castle. By sending me, and using her known history of the relationship between Bess of Hardwicke and Mary, Queen of Scots, Matthews Cannon managed to remain firmly within the intrastice for any patrons who were looking on. I, of course, begged her majesty's leave and made great haste to Sir Francis, who was desperately trying to explain to the woman why she could not stand in front of her majesty, refuse to move, and demand to be recognized, despite hurling insults at the English monarch.

As I approached the situation, I stated loudly enough for anyone to hear, "Can my husband do nothing right? I have been gone from Sheffield but a week, and here he has let a member of royalty go unescorted about the countryside." By making this proclamation, I both validated the woman's identity and proffered my own interests in the situation. As I got closer I lowered my voice to speak personally with the woman, to try to help her understand why her course of action was inappropriate. It turns out that she was a history buff, and, in particular, a fan of Mary, Queen of Scots. While she had her own view of the history between the two monarchs, and thought she was rather well studied in Mary, she was nonetheless unfamiliar with the former Scottish monarch's time in my character's care. I was trying to explain the history of 1575 to her, with specific regard to the character she had chosen to portray in her attempt to enter the intrastice, when a *third* performer, Mistress Parsley Sage, joined in the conversation. After nearly a half hour of conversation between the patron and the three performers, all of whom stayed in characters, never breaking out of the intrastice, we managed to explain to her the issues of angrily confronting a monarch, pretending to be a character that is in the time period currently held under virtual lock and key several counties away, and doing all of this while wearing twenty-first-century clothing (which we merely called "inappropriate garment to meet and greet her majesty"). These actions and clothing provided no indication to the performers of her interest in "playing" at belief. Instead, she had entered the instrasticious state, where she had actively created her own belief, unfortunately without knowing enough to do so accurately. One of the main advantages of working a small festival is that *three* characters could take nearly *half of an hour* to educate and entertain *one* patron.

I should note that later that afternoon, now costumed in a newly purchased garnet velvet dress and accompanied again by the gentleman portraying Sir Francis Walsingham, the same woman approached her majesty, bowed, begged her forgiveness, and instead presented herself as a cousin of a young playwright named "Will," one of whose early works she was attempting to practice on the queen earlier in the day. Her veiled reference to Shakespeare made all the court members laugh, and her majesty graciously accepted the apology, welcomed the woman to Hart Grove, and wished her a most wondrous festival day. Sir Francis, who had obviously worked with her to help her find a better way to play in the intrastice, then gently guided her away. Again, she was able to experience her time in the intrastice in a non-combative, fun, and still carnivalesque manner only because of the time that three performers had spent with her. Examining the section on carnival later in this chapter will illustrate how those who wish to play within the intrastice and experience carnival do so, much as this patron learned in a difficult manner.

Michele Schultz, a graduate of the International School of Physical Theatre and a more than ten-year veteran of the Renaissance festival circuit, has performed at both small and large faires, primarily on the east coast and in the upper Midwest. Her views of the difference between small and large festivals initially focus on the financial and managerial aspects. She recounts,

> The biggest differences are the professionalism and lack of stress in larger ones for random things like weather.... Lack of stress, well, if it rains one weekend or even two at a 7–9 weekend faire, attendance can balance out. At a 1–3 weekend faire, that is most if not all of your income. Especially at hat pass faires for the stage acts, if you are in for one weekend and it rains, you are rather screwed as you depend on that money to survive. One bad weekend can break the faire's budget. Smaller faires need to be much more concerned with the short term bottom line. Larger faires have a bigger picture.
>
> There are more "themed" weekends at longer faires, more acts that can come in and out throughout the season. Sales can be much better for T-shirts and CDs as there are just more bodies coming through the gates and people can come back multiple times before they decide to go ahead and purchase [field notes].

Financial factors, like a single weekend of bad weather perhaps causing the failure of a small festival, are easy to overlook when examining the differences between small and large faires. White Hart lost nearly a full weekend of patrons in 2007 due to severe weather. Since WHRF is only a three weekend festival, that loss was a severe blow. Some small faires would not have survived such a scenario, as evidenced by the number that come and go each year.

Schultz also discusses the professionalism she feels is different between small and large festivals as well. She comments:

Professionalism at a larger faire means a better rehearsed cast, more interactive
and more accurate in history (at least on this side of the country). A clearly
defined staff with positions so you know who to go to with which issues. A
deeper and more ingrained crew of people. More permanent structures for vendors and a more complete village feel. Shorter faires are usually throw up/tear
down villages and tents and have the transitory feeling of a county faire in some
strange setting rather than stepping back in time more fully [field notes].

Having participated at both small and large festivals, I considered the first
sentence for quite some time. While WHRF does not have the number of
rehearsals that MDRF requires, at the smaller faire there are no scripted shows,
which take up a significant amount of the time allotted for rehearsal at the
Maryland festival. The WHRF training focuses almost exclusively on interactive immersion within the streets and historical context, so I initially thought
that perhaps Schultz's comment was slightly askew. Then I looked at the
caveat she added, "at least on this side of the country," and a new thought
process emerged. Coupled with Brother William's story of his impromptu performance at the BRF, I suggest that while there are certainly differences
between small and large faires, including the amount of time performers can
spend with an individual patron and the financial considerations, questions
of professionalism and what that means may have more do with the *location*
of the festival than with its *size*.

When I became part of the cast at the WHRF, many conversations ensued
about the difference between west coast faires, from which Johnson-Taylor
hails, and the Midwest circuit, at which such performers as Matthews Cannon have worked for nearly three decades. The introduction of my experience as an "east coast" performer brought even more varied and sundry
practices into the mix. There is also the question of pay. Johnson-Taylor's
plan is for the WHRF to be a cooperative effort in which all involved receive
pay. At the MDRF, all cast members are paid, but at many festivals in the
Midwest and on the west coast, there is little to no pay for characters unless
they are stage acts. Differences, therefore, between festivals may rest on several different issues: location, size, and professionalism (as determined by the
payment of members of the cast).

Faire a la Carte

In 2008, a brand new Renaissance festival venture began. Faire a la Carte
(FalC) is a new company designed to bring Renaissance faires on demand to
any location. Unlike a site-specific festival, this company is built entirely of
people: stage acts, musicians, cast, and vendors who are available for hire at
any site where an owner is willing to pay. According to the FalC website, the

company "was conceived as a travelling Renaissance road show, available to put on 'out of the box' Renaissance faires for organizations around the country. FalC is designed to bring a soft-format faire (tents and portable stages) to any location that contracts for one, complete with court and street players, stage acts, vendors and 'whatever.'"[26] Organizations can hire FalC to perform without needing to do any of the legwork or homework which planning a new faire normally requires. The brainchild of Matthews Cannon and her partner Becky Grotts, Faire a la Carte offers the opportunity for anyone with deep enough pockets to produce a festival by hiring the group, lock, stock, and Queen.

Matthews Cannon, who is a proud member of the Board of Directors for the WHRF, had previously been involved with a few now-defunct festivals, the Camelot Faire in Blue Eye, Missouri, and the festival in Mansfield which Taylor and Johnson-Taylor had originally considered purchasing. That work, combined with another horrendous experience at a small faire in 2008, left her "badly burned financially" (field notes). She recounts that many people ask her how much it would cost to start a faire, and when she and Grotts met with a businessman in Oklahoma who wanted nothing to do with the actual running of a festival, but merely wanted to finance it, they almost simultaneously thought of the idea that became FalC. Matthews Cannon recounts:

> We went to lunch and realized about simultaneously that "we could make a business out of this"; our knowledge was marketable, and our combined experience could enable us to start a new business, that of producing Renaissance themed weekends and other events. There will be another "arm" to this, called "Feasts a la Carte" when my other partner in this venture finally makes it back from England, hopefully this year [field notes].

Rather than working for someone else and depending upon that person for support, Matthews Cannon and Grotts were now in charge of the festival.

The company, which was formed in the late summer of 2008, had its first festival in November of the same year, the Heartland Renaissance Faire in Shawnee, Oklahoma. The sponsor of the first faire for the new company was a casino, the Sac and Fox. The faire took place not in the casino, but in a fenced-in area adjacent to the Sac and Fox, which features a large amphitheatre that the casino owners had built previously to hold concerts and other entertainments designed to bring business to the venture. While a casino may seem an odd venue for a Renaissance festival, the owner was willing to hire FalC in order to increase traffic for his primary business. He had no need to learn anything about festival management or entertainment. By hiring FalC, the festival came to him, and he could continue to concentrate on his venture and leave the festival details to the professionals, Matthews

Cannon and Grotts. Unlike so many festivals in the Midwest, small and large, FalC is a completely professional endeavor.

The company contracts with a variety of performers, including stage and street acts, musicians, and cast members, as well as vendors. All performers receive pay not only for their daily work, but also to compensate for travel and lodging. This professional, paid aspect makes FalC an even more interesting concept. Matthews Cannon explains that the decision to make the company a paid faire was based upon years of experience. She states,

> We know a whole lot of really fine performers who are tired of being jerked around or beggared in order to do their favorite thing: perform at faires. All of us have gone out-of-pocket time and again, whether on costuming or travel expenses. Remember the copious rennie jokes such as: "how can you tell a rennie? When they have costumes worth more than their cars!" All of us have built wonderful "families of choice," whom we only see, usually, while performing at faires. When this idea burst into our heads, we realized that we had the opportunity, finally, to both use our knowledge and the knowledge of our friends to build a professional organization, based on "No drama, no politics, no bullshit, no kidding!" The board members of FalC collectively have about 140 total years of involvement in faires; a pretty impressive number [field notes].

Taking that experience into account, it seems ridiculous that the performers would *not* be paid. However, at many festivals around the country, experience equal to that of the FalC board would not guarantee payment of any sort.

The Heartland Renaissance Faire featured Queen Elizabeth I (played by Matthews Cannon) and her court, villagers, several musical groups including Capt'n. Black's Sea Dogges and Queen's Gambit, comedy ranging from storytelling to fractured Shakespeare skits, sword fighting, and jousting. Since there are no scripted cast shows, and all the performers are professionals with prior Renaissance faire experience — many of them at the same faires — the need for an extensive rehearsal process disappears. Unlike the long preparation periods at both the MDRF (for both scripted and improvisational performances) and the WHRF (highly focused on interactive improvisation), the first time these cast members and stage and street acts came together was at the morning meeting, one hour prior to the festival opening. Previous experience replaced the rehearsal process, and it remains to be seen how well this new venture will work. However, if the first event is any indication, this may be the new wave in Renaissance faires.

Matthews Cannon is confident about the company because of the members' prior experiences with each other. According to Matthews Cannon, "We've done some pretty intensive training of actors at both White Hart and the other faire so we know we have a good pool on which to draw. We literally have enough professionally trained friends and friend-of-friends on whom to call, to populate almost any size of Renaissance event" (field notes). FalC does have many qualities of the traveling faires of the Renaissance, some that are part of other festivals, some unique: soft site, general knowledge of each other without repeated rehearsals; and emphasis on improvisation. Nonetheless, one constant — despite size and location, hard site or soft site, mobile or stationary casts — is the essence of the carnivalesque which pervades the sites and the opportunity it provides for entrance into the intrastice.

The Heartland Renaissance Faire was a resounding success. With no prior festival history and a soft site, several thousand patrons came through the gates. Many of them had never been to a faire before but saw the local advertising and ventured inside the gates. With nearly three stages featuring acts from Indiana, Kansas, Missouri, Oklahoma, and Texas, there were near continuous performances from 10 A.M. to 6 P.M. In addition, a cast of villagers and courtiers entertained the patrons as they wandered from stage to stage, through the vendors, and to the jousting field. The Royal Pavilion was also a beehive of activity featuring Her Majesty's morning entrance, the Royal Feast, and the Children's Knighting Ceremony. Another event in the lanes which drew a great deal of attention was the rat pucking competition. I explained it to a patron as "peasant golf." Rat pucking is a game played on a nine-"hole" course in which contestants attempt to toss fabric rats at a target with sticks. The immersive interaction from all of these events created an intrastice, even without hard buildings. Furthermore, there was no alcohol at the event, so it was not a matter of people seeking escape through imbibing.

Perhaps the most poignant experience of the weekend, which illustrates how the intrastice forms, came from the participation of a single patron, an elderly blind woman who was accompanied by her daughter. When she first approached the Royal Pavilion, Matthews Cannon as Elizabeth I had the daughter bring the woman up so she might feel Matthews Cannon's clothing. Another member of the Royal Court allowed the woman to touch some of the bobbin lace that she was creating. Later, the family went to listen to Capt'n. Black's Sea Dogges perform and purchased one of their CDs so that they would be able to hear some of the sounds of the festival at home. After the band finished playing, members of Capt'n. Black's Sea Dogges came down to the front row where the blind woman was sitting and allowed her to feel their various costume pieces. She marveled at the differences in the brocade, leather, linen, and velvet. She even fingered the manacles worn by Lord John Hamilton, the quartermaster of Capt'n. Black's Sea Dogges. I also approached the woman, and she felt the various beads on my clothing, pearls and small rose cut metal beads. She was particularly tickled, literally, by my feather fan.

She was experiencing everything at the festival in a completely tactile way, and her immersion into those moments allowed her to enter the intrastice, where she could play at belief. Without sight, she was not troubled by the world beyond the fence or cars that could be seen beyond it. Instead, she was able to immerse herself in sound and touch, and with the food she ate there, taste and smell. (For further information on the overall sensescape festivals provide, see Chapter 3.) All of these elements of the sensescape contribute to the overall spirit of the carnivalesque that pervades the faires around the country.

Carnival: Then and Now

How do these festivals continue to illustrate carnival in the Bakhtinian sense? Contemporary American Renaissance festivals continue to provide the opportunity — unlike television or movies — for patrons to openly participate

The patrons in the circle are the gentleman on the far left and the woman to his right, visitors from Wisconsin who normally attend the Bristol Renaissance Festival. The performers (from left to right) are Geoff Thompson as Friar Tuck, Jeff Bryant as Will Scarlet, and Laura Ingalls as Maid Marian. Photograph by Carrie J. Cole.

by donning costumes, creating personas, affecting accents, and then turning the tables back upon the performers by making comments of their own. There is, as the above-referenced situation between the queen at WHRF and the patron who did not understand the spirit of carnival illustrates, a limit to the way the tables can be turned. Nonetheless, faires continue to celebrate the Bakhtinian "lower bodily stratum." In 1976, after traveling to Patterson's Northern California faire, Blazer illustrated the continuation of carnival. He writes, "Then the sheriff of the shire appears in the thatched tower above, just to the (audience) right of the box office. The dialog between that worthy and the M.C. is marked by sexual innuendo, low comedy material dealing with the human anatomy."[27] Open laughter at ribald jests otherwise considered inappropriate — as one performer asserts, "If your children get the joke, it's not my fault" — is rampant at the festival. Of the carnivalesque laughter, Bakhtin writes,

> For the correct understanding of these carnivalesque gestures and images we must take into consideration that all such gesticulations and verbal images are part of the carnival as a whole, infused with one single logic of imagery. This is the drama of laughter presenting at the same time the death of the old and the birth of the new world.[28]

This laughter exists as part and parcel of the history of contemporary American Renaissance Festivals, and though the majority of patrons would never consider acting on a stage, they willingly perform in the streets of Revel Grove. They mingle — sometimes visually and vocally indistinguishably — with the actors.

This intermixing of patron and performer illuminates the carnivalesque nature of both the historical faire and contemporary festivals like Maryland's. Bakhtin writes, that "carnival does not know footlights, in the sense that it does not acknowledge any distinction between actors and spectators."[29] Faires are built upon this premise of interaction and sometimes even the inability to distinguish between actor and audience. These patrons often portray characters vastly different from their own personalities, allowing them to turn the world upside down and experience the carnivalesque in a visceral manner. They encounter the rebirth of a new world in the old world of the sixteenth century. It is a new world order for them, even though it has been lived before, because they have never personally experienced it. Patrons know it is only temporary, so they are free to enjoy this new world order as long as it exists. Bakhtin writes, "While carnival lasts, there is no other life outside it. During carnival time life is subject only to its laws, that is the laws of its own freedom."[30] It is this freedom that allows patrons to behave contrary to their actual identities.

Successful businesswomen with high powered careers outside of faire dress as wenches and openly celebrate the carnivalesque body. Men who wear business suits all week suddenly appear in kilts, often with nothing underneath, a practice known colloquially as "going regimental." They are also known to wear codpieces which exaggerate and emphasize their lower body, just as the constraint of a tightened bodice will embellish and accentuate a woman's bosom. Bakhtin writes of the relationship between carnival rebirth and overstated bodily factions, "the old world that has been destroyed is offered together with the new world and is represented with it as the dying part of the dual body. This is why in carnivalesque images there is so much turnabout, so many opposite faces and intentionally upset proportions."[31] As the historical knowledge of sixteenth-century England and the actuality of twenty-first-century America merge to form the intrastice, patrons experience the carnivalesque. This dying of one world is truly an inversion as patrons see the old worlds as those outside the gates of Revel Grove, and the new world as the pretext of Tudor Oxfordshire. Victor Turner writes that the relationship between mundane life and cultural performances is "reciprocal and reflexive — in the sense that the performance is often a critique, direct or veiled, of the social life it grows out of, an evaluation (with lively possibilities of rejection) of the way society handles history."[32] This particular type of inversion of temporal-spatial society offers a strong opportunity for patrons both to celebrate the carnivalesque and to critique their own society by setting it aside in favor of one nearly five hundred years past. It is a critique that requires no words, as merely stepping into the other society conveys the message of a longing for what patrons imagine to be a simpler time.

The visitors to Revel Grove celebrate — in the case of the MDRF — nineteen days of this freedom, and Bakhtin explains that it is the temporally bounded nature of carnival that allows its excesses. He writes,

> The feast was a temporary suspension of the entire official system with all its prohibitions and hierarchic barriers. For a short time life came out of its usual, legalized and consecrated furrows and entered the sphere of utopian freedom. The very brevity of this freedom increased its fantastic nature and utopian radicalism, born in the festive atmosphere of images.[33]

It may seem odd to characterize these modern festivals as a kind of utopia, but for many they offer an opportunity unavailable in any other setting. Furthermore, the festival has a limited run, so in the end all involved know they must eventually return from the intrastice to the reality of modern America. Also, the MDRF runs only on weekends (and Labor Day Monday), so in between the spurts of carnival utopia, patrons and performers alike must return to the mundane world, which seems so safe with its hierarchies and prohibitions. This draw of carnival — the time of a temporary suspension of social mores — is one way that Rabelais's world is brought to the twenty-first century.

There appears to be no difference between the smaller and the larger festivals with regard to level of immersion in the intrastice, nor with experience of the Bakhtinian carnival, the temporary suspension of mores, and the ribald laughter of the marketplace. The number of visitors through the gates seems not to affect whether the carnivalesque atmosphere is present. People who seek the atmosphere the contemporary American Renaissance festival provides can find it during the nine weekends of the MDRF, the three weekends of WHRF, or the single weekend of the Norman Medieval Faire. Whether the number of patrons is counted by the hundreds or the thousands, on a five-acre faire site in the infancy of its growth or a twenty-five-acre site of a festival that has been established ten times as long, the spirit of the marketplace is alive and available for those who want to step outside the normalcy of the mundane world and into another century, to varying degrees of intrasticiancy.

However, when the contemporary reality of the world is on the brink or experiencing profound change, and the safe haven it offers is threatened, people also seek the safety that carnival provides. Though the societal norms may be reconfigured, carnival offers an opportunity to escape from the harsh realities the twenty-first-century world may pose. In the next chapter, I examine just this experience: what happens at a festival when the conditions of the real world change in such a drastic, dramatic, and disastrous manner that they generate a need for the carnivalesque experience based on patrons' desire for revival and renewal.

2

Carnival Setting, Cultural Work

"Entertainment is always a national asset," President Roosevelt told the National Conference of the Entertainment Industry for War Activities in 1943. "Invaluable in time of peace, it is indispensible in wartime."[1]

The World Turned Upside Down

While the first chapter of this book provided a brief history of forty-five years of contemporary American Renaissance festivals and their relationship to the carnivalesque, in this second chapter I will examine in detail one specific weekend during that forty-five-year history to illustrate how the carnivalesque adapts to the ever-changing nature of the world order it inverts. On the morning of 15 September 2001, when the performers at the MDRF gathered for cast call, they prepared to adapt to a new world order. Life for many in the United States had changed irrevocably on the preceding Tuesday, 11 September 2001, when terrorists flew hijacked planes into both towers of the World Trade Center in New York and into the Pentagon in Arlington, Virginia, and crashed another jet in a field near Shanksville, Pennsylvania. At that time and in intervening years, the media attention has focused upon the attacks on the World Trade Center towers, where the vast majority of lives were lost, and upon the heroic efforts to retake control of the plane by the passengers on the aircraft which crashed in Pennsylvania.

However, for those who live in the Washington, D.C. metropolitan area, the attack on the Pentagon was more than an issue of national security; for many it was very personal. Parris Glendening, who was governor of Maryland in 2001, writes that

> the tragedy directly affected numerous Marylanders. Many Marylanders died or lost loved ones on September 11th. Maryland surrounds two-thirds of the District of Columbia. Many of our citizens work in the Pentagon. Fire and

rescue personnel from Montgomery County, Maryland, were among the first responders to the plane crash into the Pentagon. Our National Guard Units were some of the first called up by the president.[2]

In the District of Columbia, Maryland, and Virginia, numerous people had friends or family who worked at the Pentagon. Countless more lived or worked close enough to be within hearing or feeling distance of the explosion as Flight 77 crashed into the westernmost side of the building representing the United States's military superiority. Workers evacuated buildings in and near the nation's capital. The cast at the Maryland Renaissance Festival was a segment of that community which had experienced the attack in a personal manner. Even four years after Flight 77 crashed into the Pentagon, another terrorist attack — the train bombings in London in July 2005 — evoked memories from 11 September 2001, as MDRF cast member and U.S. government employee Paula Peterka recounts: "That [injury from 9/11] isn't a scab; it's still an open wound" (field notes). On 15 September 2001, that emotional wound for many of the cast members was not just still open; it was bleeding, as it certainly was for many Americans in the area and throughout the country. The owners of the MDRF made the decision to open the festival, and the cast was preparing for a day in which no one had any idea what to expect.

The decision to open was made by Jules Smith, Jr., the General Manager of MDRF. According to Carolyn Spedden, Entertainment Director at MDRF, "Jules made the decision to be open, and the staff all agreed. Entertainment is a diversion in times of stress and hardship, and we thought it would be a place where people could take their minds off the horror" (field notes). For the many people who had spent the past five days watching and re-watching the media images, the festival could provide a brief time of safety in a realm where televisions did not exist. In the usual tradition, the nature of the Bakhtinian carnivalesque became a place and time which presented an inverted view of the everyday world. On this particular weekend, the MDRF provided a carnival space in which patrons could avoid the horrors of the reality of twenty-first century America by entering the pretext of Tudor Oxfordshire where the only York was rather old, the only Washington was young Master Kenneth, and the only tower to which anyone ever referred was the one in London that you wanted to avoid.

The phone calls that flooded the office phones that week indicated that most people were seeking an escape, or at least wanted to know if the possibility of one existed. There is no record of who these callers were or if they ever did attend the festival, but their interest in the faire and whether it would be open was certainly tremendous. Mary Ann Jung, Royal Court Director and Historian at the MDRF, states:

I remember the overwhelming positive response from callers that we would be open when everything else shut down. I would say one hundred calls to one were in favor and glad. The ones who were not happy and felt it was disrespectful were very angry and vehement, and I did my best to sympathize, which I did, and provide understanding for their upset. Some were distraught that we were not doing more in the way of a memorial [field notes].

Undoubtedly there was a faction that disagreed with the festival's decision to open, but the phone calls seemed to illustrate a greater need for the escape than not. Jung references some phone callers' ire that more of a memorial was not planned. The festival did donate a significant amount of money from box office receipts for the rest of the season to the Pentagon Relief Fund. Furthermore, at the end of the day a change was made to the *Pub Sing*, the final show of the evening. (I will treat this in further detail later in this chapter.) However, for some these efforts were clearly not enough.

Homefront USO

Spedden emphasized during the cast call on Saturday, 15 September, that we would make no mention of the events of Tuesday, 11 September 2001. She explains her decision:

While some of the cast members absolutely disagreed with me, I was insistent that they keep to the Renaissance theme — no American flags, no black bands, etc. My thought was that if people choose to attend a Renaissance Festival during times of stress, they are looking for an escape and relief from their woes. If every performer made reference to the event, it would not give the customers the opportunity [to escape] [field notes].

Some cast members had prepared red, white, and blue favors to wear on their costumes, but upon hearing of Spedden's edict removed them. At least one other festival management issued the same order, but apparently it fell on deaf ears. According to Susi Matthews Cannon, who was a veteran performer at the Kansas City Renaissance Festival,

One of my fellow performers made little lapel ribbons out of red white and blue ribbons and was handing them out to other performers to wear. He's a veteran himself and although [he] doesn't say much about such things, it is obvious that he was feeling a lot very deeply; we all were. We did ask people not to wear black armbands as that was too distracting from our work. The idea was to DISTRACT people from their fears and troubles, not to continuously remind them of the situation [field notes].

Fellow KCRF cast member Elizabeth Cole comments, "Many cast had made minor changes to costumes to have small pieces of red, white & blue showing, despite having been told by management not to do so. Personally, I had a blue skirt, a white chemise & a red shawl" (field notes). Cole was able to choose exactly what she wore that day because of a change in the weekend's theme, which I will discuss in detail further on in this chapter. That change allowed her the opportunity to pick her costume, and she chose to dress in red, white, and blue as a personal statement of patriotism.

Mark Wickersham, who gave fencing and swordsman ship demonstrations at KCRF in 2001, remembers that participants at the festival went out of their way to find a manner to show patriotism while not defying outright the entertainment director. According to Wickersham, "The ED had declared no display of the American flag would be allowed, so the Blackarchers made up a bunch of arrows fletched in red, white and blue and embedded them into a bunch of booths at flag height" (field notes). There was obviously a disconnect between what the KCRF management requested and what the cast actually did, despite Matthews Cannon's emphasis that the idea was to "distract people from their fears."

At the New York Renaissance Faire (NYRF), commonly referred to as "Tuxedo," there was no attempt to hide patriotism even as performers worked to create the carnival world the contemporary American Renaissance festival provides. Melissa McGinley, a MDRF cast member in 2004 when I performed the bulk of the research for this book, was performing at Tuxedo in 2001. She recalls:

> There was a big "show must go on" thing happening. A lot of our actors (myself included) were living in NYC at the time, and more than one worked at the World Trade Center. I remember the email chain trying to find everyone and make sure that everyone was alright. Luckily, our cast experienced no losses. At the joust, Robin Hood rode out with an American flag to thunderous applause, and most of us had red, white, and blue ribbons on our costumes for the remainder of the run. A lot of the vendors also hung flags from their booths. I also remember a lot of red, white, and blue garb on playtrons [field notes].

Apparently, the management at NYRF had no illusions of attempting to prevent illustrations of patriotism, most often found, as referenced by McGinley above, in the omnipresence of flags and the traditional American colors of red, white, and blue.

At the MDRF, cast members and acts largely followed Spedden's edict on lack of red, white, and blue ribbons or any other form of reference to the twenty-first century. I will explain in detail the major exception later in the chapter. I argue that maintaining the illusion is important to situating the festival in its carnivalesque and intrastician contexts. People needed more than to simply turn off the television; they desired an opportunity to suspend disbelief, play at belief, or create belief so that for a few hours the world which had been so safe and had now been turned upside down melted away into a world where there was a different sort of order. Spedden had a precedent for her decision to avoid mention of the outside world. She states, "that's why movie sales were so huge during the Depression — people need escape, and that is an entertainer's job" (field notes). According to musical theatre scholar John Bush Jones, quoting the 12 June 1943 *Billboard Magazine*, in the same speech in which President Franklin D. Roosevelt gave the quote which opens this chapter, the President continues, "All those who are working in the entertainment industry ... are building and maintaining morale both on the battlefront and on the homefront."[3] In her book *Women at War*, historian Brenda Ralph Lewis focuses on the importance entertainment had in building morale. She writes,

> Keeping morale high in wartime has always been seen as crucial to victory. During World War II, this need to boost people's spirits was the cue for famous stars of the entertainment industry, as well as lesser-known performers, to do their part to divert troops, and also civilians under the extraordinary pressures of wartime.[4]

In a way, the performers at MDRF became a sort of USO for the civilian population in the area.[5] Festival street act performer Bill Wood recalls: "We had just been attacked and so on some level, we were all now in the middle of the war zone, and the function of USO is to support the troops; to boost morale by providing diversion, levity and entertainment" (field notes). In the tradition of the USO and other performers during the wars of years gone by as a way of attempting to lift morale, the festival performers at the MDRF hit the streets and stages of the faire the Saturday following the terrorist attacks, determined to offer a distraction from the week's events.

The impact the performers had on patrons that weekend is similar to the effect actors and actresses had on the citizens of London during the Luftwaffe bombing at the beginning of World War II or on troops on leave in the United States. While entertainment may seem a minor event during such tragic times, letters from the earlier time period illustrate that entertainment was an important part of citizens' lives. Sgt. Keith Laidler of the Royal Australian Air Force was killed when his plane was shot down on its way back to England following a bombing run over Germany. Before he left for England, Sgt. Laidler had been in New York. A letter he wrote on 13 January 1944 details some of his time in New York, and focuses on the entertainment available for serviceman and civilian alike:

> I traveled around and saw Radio City which occupies a whole block and also the Music Hall which seats 6,000 people. Also saw the only theatre that has an ice show on the stage: it was "Stars on Ice." New York never seems to sleep as the shops don't close till near midnight and the theatres at 3 o'clock. So you can see that when we went out to see the shows in the night we wouldn't get home very early. Sunday is late also except that the main shops are closed. At the the-

atres you would see a film followed by a stage show which had different well-known personalities as Tommy Dorsey and his orchestra, Kathryn Grayson and Rags Ragland, both M.G.M. film stars.[6]

It is obvious from Sgt. Laidler's letter that both the cinematic theatre and the appearance of live actors were important as diversion.

The way people describe the difference between the time before 11 September 2001 and after, that the world changed that day, is reminiscent of the speeches given following the attack on Pearl Harbor. Maxine Andrews, one of the members of the extremely popular singing group The Andrews Sisters, recalls in her memoir focusing on World War II, "Suddenly the empty sidewalk outside the theater symbolized a stark reality: The world was different now and would be for the rest of our lives."[7] The number of times that sentiment has been echoed since the terrorist attacks in 2001 is countless. However, many of the performers in World War II had slightly longer to prepare to retake the stage than did their 2001 counterparts. A week after the attacks, on 18 September 2001, Christine Ebersole, who was at the time starring in *42nd Street* on Broadway, made an appearance on *The Rosie O'Donnell Show*. She recounts her return to the stage:

> I went back on Thursday night, two days after the attacks, and it was nerve-wracking. I was afraid.... When we got there it was so meaningful.... I was so afraid, but I thought: "I need to express courage and I need to be strong, not only for my fellow cast members but for myself too to show that we're not going to be bullied...." When I got there you could feel the energy; It was just like you were in a war zone. It was so bizarre.
>
> We had a lot of fireman's families that were there that night, and it really gave new meaning to the show. I felt like I was in the USO, entertaining the troops because in a sense I think we're all soldiers really and because of this thing that has happened we really have to brandish our weapon, our weapon of spirit, and that is the weapon that we have to brandish, and that can never, ever, ever be destroyed, never; that's impossible; that's not the nature of spirit. [8]

Ebersole clearly evokes the feelings of needing to be strong for her fellow cast members despite her fear over returning to the stage just two days following the attacks. She also clearly invokes the same USO comparisons as the MDRF performers.

Festival performers in the New York area experienced similar emotional reactions to the event, while still maintaining their professionalism at work. McGinley remembers:

> For myself, I needed faire that weekend. I worked in Times Square in the advertising industry. We specialized in Broadway. Work sucked. People were afraid to come into Manhattan. One of our consultants had lost her husband. I'd get off the subway from Astoria every morning, and as I walked through the subway stations, there were hundreds of posters looking for people who were "missing."

When I got back onto the street, the air stank. Of decay and burnt metal. The sky was always gray. It took days to find everyone you knew and cared about. It was hard to get cell signals. Everyone was so depressed all the time, no one wanted to socialize. We all felt an acute sense of loss all the time in the city [field notes].

Despite the desperation and feeling of loss, McGinley and her fellow performers, like those at the MDRF, appeared on Saturday and performed. Though all the performers at the MDRF were given the option of taking the weekend off, not a single cast member did. Interestingly, this was not the case at the KCRF, located over a thousand miles from the scene of the attacks. Brother William, who was working for a vendor (ironically called Somewhere in Thyme), recounts, "I remember that leading up to it there were strong feelings expressed (via AFR, Alt.Fairs.Renaissance) that it (the faire) should NOT go on that weekend; that it should close. There were several cast who refused to attend when they did not close" (field notes). Alt.Fairs.Renaissance and Alt.Faires.Renaissance are Internet sites devoted to Renaissance festivals. Though many who formally frequented these sites have since moved on to Live Journal on the Internet, in 2001 AFR was the main on-line meeting ground for Renaissance festival performers and patrons alike. Back in Maryland, however, the AFR conversations had no impact as the entire cast had appeared. Spedden and the members of that cast encouraged each other to take care of themselves, doing whatever was necessary to maintain their characters onstage and their personal health off-stage, and to take frequent breaks if needed. This became for many a difficult exercise in negotiating the intrastice.

Backstage/Frontstage

Crossing the line between backstage and onstage was different for performers that day at the MDRF. Backstage most of the cast tried to keep up each other's spirits or attempted to wheedle information out of those on cast who held government positions in which they might have more information than the general public. Jim Frank, who works for the Office of Naval Intelligence, was among the most pestered by cast members who wanted to know if everything was going to be alright. In addition to constantly checking his work phone backstage, that weekend Frank spent a great deal of time reassuring cast members not to worry even as he spent time considering "where someone could do something to the faire and made sure to check on strange events" (field notes). Such a short time after the attacks, not knowing what, if anything, was going to happen next, most of the cast had realized that a space where the potential to injure or kill more than twenty thousand people in one fell swoop would hold allure for anyone attempting to commit terrorism. Unlike football and baseball stadiums which re-opened the following week to extra security, the festival was guarded merely by men with swords. Sociologist Randall Collins writes,

> Major league baseball, at the resumption of play the seventh day, prominently publicized their new procedures: increased numbers of police and security guards; inspection of all bags at entrances; investigation of stadiums for bombs; and prohibition of parking within 100 feet of the stadium. Some stadiums banned backpacks or bags of all kinds. Thus, the first experience of spectators entering these events was to be surrounded by emblems of authority, imposing delays and intrusions into personal space.[9]

At the Renaissance festival, however, no such "impositions" occurred, and the protection of the village was left largely as it would have been in the Renaissance: to the monarchs' guards and the others on site who were permitted to carry bladed weapons.

Frank, in his position at Naval Intelligence, probably realized this to a far greater degree than the rest of the cast. He was also performing that weekend after losing co-workers both at the Pentagon and on two of the planes that crashed. So, while backstage, he was in a completely different mode than he was onstage. He knew that when he was onstage he had to perform for the audience that "needed to get out and were very happy to be out. Entertaining them was easy. They wanted to laugh and be happy" (field notes). The heightened emotions greatly amplified the normal switch a performer must make from backstage to onstage that weekend as the mere assumption of the character would not be enough. Figuratively, performers had to leave their twenty-first century selves — with their knowledge of the terrorist attacks — behind in order to be able to do their jobs effectively. Performers had to take care of themselves in order to take care of patrons. McGinley, a 2001 Tuxedo cast member, explains:

> I needed to go up to Tuxedo and be someone else for a weekend. I needed that little village that sat "out of time." I needed to escape and put on a court dress and have my biggest problem be trying to keep a secret marriage and pregnancy from Queen Elizabeth, if it was only from 9 to 7 Saturday and Sunday. Of course I knew everything was different, for me it was. But for my character, Bess Throckmorton, it wasn't [field notes].

Performers had to prepare themselves to be their characters in order to be able to properly interact with patrons. Unlike performers such as Ebersole on Broadway, the performers at the contemporary American Renaissance festival personally interact with the patrons. Onstage does not necessarily refer to being on a stage, but rather may simply mean being out from behind the scenes, in the streets and lanes of the village portrayed. Performers felt an

increased sense of responsibility to be completely in character while onstage
or in the streets because of the audience's deep need for laughter and release.
Wood expressed the resulting difficulty of moving between backstage and
onstage:

> I remember Saturday as being about the loosest, most open, ready to have fun
> crowd ever in fifteen years that I've worked the faire. Backstage, however, was a
> different matter. I do remember many cast members talking about 9/11 with lots
> of anger and vitriol. So while onstage I saw nothing but professionalism, clearly
> at least some cast members were feeling quite a bit of strain. I guess I felt a bit
> of that as well. It was somewhat surreal to walk backstage for a quick break.
> Crossing the line going past the wall of the village is always a bit like stepping
> from one world into another, but that day I felt as though the boundary was
> much more real and physical [field notes].

The movement between backstage and onstage, which always requires a festival performer to make a shift, was more prominent that weekend, and
Wood's description illustrates the sometimes corporeal nature of the threshold. So, despite Spedden's offer to performers that if they felt they could not
perform under the circumstances they could go home or take extra breaks as
they needed them, in some ways, it was probably easier to remain on the
street as much as possible, rather than to continuously have to move from the
twenty-first-century into the intrastice.

Personally, I experienced the transition between backstage and onstage
to be extremely difficult. I was required to go backstage in order to prepare
for several shows which took place literally upon stages. Those times when
I had to cross the threshold, waiting backstage for my entrances, were among
the most difficult times I spent that weekend. I found myself avoiding
the backstage area as much as possible. In one particular instance, I was
required to disrobe down to my chemise, hose, and shoes alone for the
show *Dress the Duchess*. I would normally disappear behind a wall and have
someone help me remove my outer garments. I would then appear, fresh
from my afternoon "nap," and the ladies of the household would proceed to
dress me in the fashionable Tudor clothing. (For more information on this
show, see Chapter 4 and the discussion of the show, re-named after 2001 to
Dress for Excess.) During the weekend following 11 September 2001, I requested
that the ladies of the household undress me in the pavilion, out in the open,
before beginning the process of redressing me. I simply did not want to cross
back out of the intrastice; it was just too hard.

Continuing to perform in the street, however, required that patrons
also choose to enter the intrastice. Living history scholar and ethnographer
Stephen Eddy Snow has written about the actor-audience relationship
at Plimoth Plantation, and he explains that there exists an informal contract

between the two groups that allows the experience to succeed. According to Snow,

> The actor-audience relationship is based on what each party brings to it. The best relationship occurs when both parties are sincere and want to play the game together: the actor/historians want to do their best to embody and communicate historical information, and the visitor/audience wants to allow them, even encourage them, to do just that. The situation breaks down if either or both groups behave cynically.[10]

At the MDRF this contract also exists as performers attempt to embody their sixteenth-century characters in order to facilitate the patrons' ability to cross the threshold into and linger within the intrastice. Never was this more needed or evident than on the weekend following the 11 September attacks as patrons sought to participate in the sixteenth-century world the MDRF portrays. Patrons for the most part did not seek, in Snow's words, to "behave cynically." During this difficult time, they came to escape the reality of the twenty-first-century American world and sincerely did not wish to make it more difficult for those creating the pretext of Tudor Oxfordshire.

The actors, therefore, despite the difficulty involved, believed they had to work as hard as possible to maintain the intrastice. As cast member Diane Wilshere comments, "We were the USO. I honestly believe that I now know how Bob Hope must have felt after going into a war zone and entertaining the troops. It was emotionally draining to keep up the spirit, and I remember being exhausted at the end of the Saturday" (field notes). Despite the emotional difficulty, the performers worked hard that weekend to bring the crowds what they wanted. Over 45,000 patrons came through the gates of Revel Grove that weekend, a much larger number than normally visits the village that early in the run. The festival also set a season record for attendance in 2001 that has yet to be broken.

Other faires experienced a similar phenomenon. According to stage and street performer Ken Silkie, "as a friend of mine said at the Pennsylvania faire that same 9/11 weekend when they broke all attendance records, 'It wasn't where people were, but when.' In other words, any place but the present was just fine" (field notes). Silkie's recollection of his friend's words is a poignant reminder of the intrasticiancy that visitors to the MDRF and other festivals can find. In Maryland, Revel Grove was the place, but the time —1527 — was far more important. The village was open, and people came, stepped into the intrastice, and experienced the carnivalesque atmosphere the pretext of Tudor Oxfordshire offered.

At Tuxedo, so close to New York City and the epicenter of the attacks there, patrons also came to find comfort within the past/present overlap. McGinley recalls, "The crowds were large; there wasn't a drop off that was noticeable in numbers. I think that our patrons really did need that escape into another world that a Ren faire provides. Especially since the vast majority of our patrons came from the suburbs of NYC [field notes]. The driving distance between the site of the World Trade Center at Liberty and Church streets in New York City and Sterling Forest, New York, where the Tuxedo festival is located, is just 45.89 miles, with an estimated travel time of only one hour and fourteen minutes.[11] However, on the weekend following 11 September 2001, the distance between the two sites was more accurately measured in years than in miles. According to McGinley, their entertainment director told the cast much the same thing that Spedden had on that Saturday morning. According to McGinley,

> I remember our entertainment director saying it was really important that we go on doing what we had done, because we were an escape for our patrons. In our village it was the 1500s (I think it was 1587), and that is what our patrons needed, so apart from the obvious shows of affection when we saw our regulars and each other, not much changed in the performance [field notes].

She specifically recounts the importance that it was around 1587, some four hundred plus years away from the horror of 2001, and she acknowledges the lack of change and attempt to "go on with the show" except for the "obvious shows of affection" as people saw each other for the first time since the attacks. The display of the American flag and the pins apparently only served as temporary nods to the twenty-first-century side of the intrastice.

In the Midwest, at KCRF, though some performers (as previously noted) refused to participate that weekend, most did. Lady Niniane, a musician and Midwest faire circuit veteran who was working as a vendor in 2001, remembers that many of the cast performed with heavy hearts amidst fears arising from remembrances of the Cold War. She recounts,

> Kansas City had a history of being a focus point for tension during much of the Cold War (because of the proximity of the ICBM silos in Kansas and Nebraska, and being within driving distance of several armed forces bases in the Midwest), so anyone who was from that area knew that it would not take much for things to "go down" in a hurry there. And we found out early on Saturday that a member of the International Rogues Guild was in one of the towers when the planes hit, and had not been heard from since that day (he was later confirmed as a casualty). While I did not know him personally, I knew of him; that was my own "first contact" with anyone who died as a direct result of the attacks, and it was very sobering [field notes].

Lady Niniane's statements bring into focus the concern in the Midwest, far away from the sites of the attacks, because of memories of a war gone by, the Cold War. It is a reminder that on that weekend citizens still had very little knowledge of how much danger the country might still be in. Nonetheless, performances went on at KCRF because the patrons needed the intrastice as a place for escape, and, as with MDRF, PARF, and NYRF, there were significant numbers of patrons who visited that weekend. Lady Niniane recounts, "Our sales were actually up from the first weekend by a small amount, which was very unusual for the second weekend of faire" (field notes). This fact is much more compelling when taken into account with the memories of Elizabeth Cole, who was a contracted theme weekend performer at the 2001 KCRF. According to Cole, "One of the most vivid memories (or drab, depending on your point of view) was the fact that it rained solidly the entire day on Saturday. It was cold and wet, and my feet hurt" (field notes) Despite the horrid weather, sales for the weekend were still up, indicating a drastic need on the part of the patrons to visit and spend money, perhaps in a show of patriotism in an attempt to keep up the economy.

Patrons did visit KCRF that weekend. Brother William offers another possible explanation: "I felt it should stay open because folks were going to need an out, a vent, and those who were not comfortable in going to a church for such, needed a place to go" (field notes). Perhaps it was the desire for a place to go to commune. It is interesting that Brother William, who is an ordained minister in real life, makes a correlation between church and the Renaissance festival as places for people to go for "an out, a vent." Brother William experienced that need for an out/vent in one of the most personal ways possible during that weekend. He recounts:

> I had a general unease about the two days, and the feelings got worse through Sunday Noon. I had a feeling that there was something that was going to happen (to or about me) that built till it did happen. I had spent some of the time from 9/11 to that weekend working (carving) on a new flower, a lily. I carried it about during my wanderings on the first day and showed no one. I did hand out quite a few of the ribbons we had made for the occasion, ⅜" black ribbon backed with a red-white-blue one doubled around on itself (like the pink breast cancer ribbon) sewn on to a safety pin — probably 30 or so from my basket and there were 3 other folks with them that weekend. I got down to about booth 552 (Olde North Bramble) and someone came out to me and told me I was needed. One of the boothies there's brother was in Tower #2 and had not been heard from (and never was again). I went in back of the booth, pulled out the lily, a ribbon and handed it to him, and they stood and shook for a while, then we hugged for a while, and about two hours later we wandered back out from behind the booth. Such a nerve-wracking, heart rendering counseling session I had not had in quite some time [field notes].

Despite the knowledge by the vendor (boothie) that his brother was missing from the World Trade Center, he had still come to work at KCRF that weekend, searching perhaps for that out/vent. With Brother William, he found it. Ritual, at the heart of Turner's liminality, is often associated with religious services and practices. For some, on the weekend following the terrorist attacks of 11 September 2001, that ritual translated instead to the intrastice of the contemporary American Renaissance festival.

Patrons Through the Gates

One of the more emotionally grueling tasks performers faced as visitors swept through the village at MDRF that day was a direct result of the nature of carnival, where "masks" protect the identity of the participant, who often leaves his or her true name unknown. According to re-enactor Kellie Hendley, "We all watched and wanted to make sure that all of the same old familiar faces still showed up" (field notes). While festival employees knew that some of their co-workers or friends would not be able to attend the faire that weekend because "of their weird government jobs" or "they were being sent out of the country" or "were on call indefinitely," there were many more people whom the performers know only by their festival personas. Though these are paying patrons, they introduce themselves by their "faire names," such as Sir Black Fox or Lady Dawntreader. Though festival employees see them nineteen days each fall, every fall, for years in a row, and may speak with them for hours over the course of those days and years, it is not uncommon never to learn the patrons' real names and to continue the pretense of communication between two personae. So, amidst the enormous crowds that weekend, performers sought out those familiar faces that should be among the throng. McGinley commented that the same search occurred at Tuxedo: "We asked about regular patrons we didn't see, and vendors as well. We knew everyone who came through those gates, at least in some way, needed the same escape we did, and we tried to give it to them. We carried on as best we could" (field notes). McGinley's commentary shows that alongside the desire to check on those who were not readily recognized as being in attendance, the attitude of attempting to carry on was always present.

Unlike at heritage sites such as Plimoth Plantation or Colonial Williamsburg, or in the conventional theatre, it is common for patrons at the festival to attend in costume. Most of the stage and street performers with whom I spoke recall the crowds — including those in costume — being larger than usual. Spedden relates that Smith Jr. told her "he remembers more people in costumes than ever before. Obviously the need to escape was huge" (field notes). The more involved an audience member becomes with the faire world, often the more pieces of "garb" or period-like clothing he or she will acquire. Patrons flocked to the many stage shows, and every line that was supposed to get a laugh got one, often much louder and longer than usual. Stage act performer Spencer Humm states, "I recall the Hack and Slash crowds being extremely enthusiastic that weekend. We got an ovation the second we hit the stage, and that's rare" (field notes). The standing ovation is illustrative of the overwhelming appreciation throughout the festival that spectators showed for the performances the entertainers were continuing to present despite the difficult circumstances.

The crowds at MDRF were also extremely "well-behaved," according to every performer with whom I corresponded about this issue. No one remembers anyone getting out of hand, being overly drunk and loud, or requiring removal by security. This is remarkable if for no reason other than the accompanying rise in beer sales that weekend: according to Spedden, Smith Jr. told her "it was the biggest beer selling weekend EVER" (field notes). Despite this greater consumption of alcohol, the patrons at the festival maintained a level of decorum otherwise unknown at the faire. The attendance that weekend was much closer to the number of spectators the festival usually draws during the final weekends of the run, but the beer sales of 15–16 September 2001 were the largest of any weekend, including those extremely well-attended days later in the season. The world turned upside down of carnival had again been achieved within the intrastice as the normally loud and rambunctious crowds imbibed in greater amounts than ever; yet, with their world outside in upheaval, they participated at the festival in the most orderly manner, seeking safety in a co-created world removed by entrance into the intrastice from the horrors repeating on the television.

The festival offers opportunities for patrons to enter different levels of intrasticiancy, depending upon their personal needs. That weekend, as with most others, some were perfectly happy to work within the intrasticial moments of suspension of disbelief or intrasticive instances of playing at belief. According to living history cast member Laura Kilbane,

> I remember one lady who came up to talk to us after *Dress for Excess* [actually the aforementioned *Dress the Duchess* at that time], and she said that she worked at the Pentagon, and that her husband and kids had dragged her out of the house and away from the TV to come to the faire. And she said how much she appreciated what we did, and how it was the first time she had laughed in days [field notes].

This woman was participating in the intrasticial state, willingly suspending disbelief during the show, but returning to the knowledge of the twenty-first-century section of the overlap when it was over. Her talk of laughter during the show, however, is reminiscent of the laughter of the marketplace so common in the Bakhtinian concept of carnival. He writes of this laughter, "Rabelais and his contemporaries were not afraid of humor in their rendition of history: they were afraid only of petrified narrow seriousness."[12] Festival is much the same, especially on that weekend of 15–16 September 2001. As performer Jennifer Silverman recounts in a *Washington Post* article from 9 October 2001,

> After the attacks ... the [Maryland Renaissance Festival] got numerous pleas from patrons to stay open. Walking onstage for my first show the following weekend, I was aware of an electricity in the air. You could tell that the audience was with the performers, cheering extra loud, pulling for us. I practically danced off the stage. What an amazing high. Knowing that I can be part of a magical place that allows people to escape from their everyday lives, if only for a short while, has helped me through this sad time.[13]

The festival wishes to historically inform its patrons, but it simultaneously attempts to avoid the utter sorrow that relating that history can convey. Dancers danced; musicians played; actors performed. The living history component of the festival presented the show *Dress the Duchess*, designed to convey how Tudor women achieved their fashionable shape, from their undergarments outward. It certainly was not intended as a comedy, though the performers — myself included — did highlight the light-hearted aspects of the dressing process, thus bringing laughter to history and providing an opportunity for patrons like the woman who worked at the Pentagon to watch the show, willingly suspend disbelief for a half hour, and engage in laughter with fellow beings.

It is also interesting to note that once people had come to the festival, they took advantage of all the faire had to offer in way of escape. They laughed raucously and applauded loudly. They drank beer in record amounts and still showed a sense of decorum. And they had their fortunes told in record numbers. According to festival Tarot reader Trivia Prager, "When I checked my book to see who was doing tarot readings at our booth the weekend after 9/11, the first page I flipped to showed that I made more money 9/15 than any other day the whole season" (field notes). Over the course of the 2001 festival run she averaged twelve readings a day. On 15 September she performed nineteen readings, an increase of over 58 percent. Her patrons were searching for answers in larger numbers than usual, a reaction to the world turned upside down.

Changing Performances/Performing Changes

In deference to the increased sensitivities that weekend, the performers at the MDRF also made slight changes to some of the shows. One duo removed a "bullet catch" from their show; in the *Chess Game* a death shot by a pirate was turned into a mere wounding. The performers tried to be responsive to the perceived desires of the audience while maintaining the integrity of the show and observing Spedden's charge to avoid mentioning the attacks.

According to stage and street performer Bob Garman, "We changed [removed] one part of our intro, the bit when we have the audience kill the person next to them. Crowds were large and responsive, if a little odd. We felt that a comedy show is no place to deal with a national tragedy" (field notes). As these examples illustrate, most of the changes to the shows revolved around removing performative acts of violence that ended in death. The world could be turned upside down in the carnival space of the MDRF, but there was a self-imposed limit as to how far that reversal would go. During that weekend, one half of the temporal-spatial intrastice — the reality of twenty-first century America — was already in a temporary state of reversal. It melded with the other half — the historical knowledge of sixteenth-century England — to create a pretext of Tudor Oxfordshire, which aimed to provide a sense of safety and security.

During the weekend of 15–16 September 2001, there were a few other very specific changes made that address the intrasticiant nature of the festival. Prior to 11 September, Bill Huttel, who portrayed King Henry VIII for over a decade at the MDRF, would end the main in-house stage show of the day, *The Grand Event,* with the following speech:

> And to this royal throne of kings, this sceptred isle,
> This earth of majesty,
> This other Eden,
> This fortress built by Nature for herself
> Against infection and the hand of war,
> This happy breed of men, this little world,
> This precious stone set in a shining sea,
> That doth serve in its office as a wall
> Against the envy of less happier lands;
> This blessed plot, this earth, this realm, this England.[14]

Spedden had adapted this from William Shakespeare's *Richard II*, and Huttel, who died shortly after the end of the 2001 season, finished the monologue with a rousing "God save Revel Grove," during which time he would point his finger to the sky, and the crowd (both actors and patrons) would echo the line. Beginning with the show on Saturday, 15 September 2001, Huttel added the additional line, "And God bless [*pause*] us," as he spread his ample arms wide. By saying "us" instead of "America," Huttel maintained the illusion of Renaissance England and followed Spedden's counsel.

Unless someone had previously seen the show, it is doubtful the difference in the final speech would be noted. However, the enthusiasm with which that day's audience reacted to Huttel's speech — and here Spedden's choice of the piece from *Richard II* becomes somewhat eerily prophetic — was beyond any that had occurred before or that transpired after. People were truly in the

intrastice, caught between a reality they wanted to forget and a pretext they
were trying to believe. Many patrons strongly associated Huttel with Henry
VIII. His presence on the stage and streets of Revel Grove was regal and com-
manding. His six-foot seven-inch frame towered above almost everyone, and
his booming voice was unparalleled. When the King asked for God to save
Revel Grove and to bless us, patrons and performers alike could believe for a
time that he truly was part of the Great Chain of Being, Defender of the Faith,
and one of God's Intercessors here on earth. Cast members and visitors to the
village for a time found safety in the intrasticious moment of belief, deeply
immersed in the pretext of Tudor Oxfordshire created by the collision of contemporary reality and sixteenth-century history.

Both the NYRF and KCRF faced an additional challenge with regard to
storyline changes. At both festivals, characters of Middle Eastern heritage
were to be a focus, at least on that particular weekend. The two faires handled the situations in completely different ways. At NYRF, according to
McGinley,

> We didn't change aspects of storyline (we had Suleiman the Magnificent as a
> character, and I believe there was some concern as to how a Middle Eastern
> character would be received in the aftermath), but our story that year involved a
> summit of world leaders (Sultan, Ivan the Terrible, Henri of Navarre, and an
> African Queen as well), and it was a very inclusive kind of thing, so we made
> sure to play up the inclusiveness. It was what a lot of us as cast members needed
> as well. We didn't play ignorant, but we didn't mention it either, if that makes
> sense [field notes].

Despite the proximity of Tuxedo to the World Trade Center attack site, the
management decided not to change the storyline and to focus on, in McGinley's words, "the inclusiveness." In the Midwest, a very different decision was
made.

KCRF features different themes on each weekend. The weekend following 11 September 2001 was to have been a Middle Eastern theme, but the management changed it entirely. Cole recalls,

> That weekend was supposed to have been "Arabian Nights," and I was to have
> been the Head Wife in the Sultan's Harem. There had been a great deal of con-
> fusion about the costumes we were to wear, so I had emailed the office 4 differ-
> ent times in the previous two weeks regarding the costumes, with no response.
> Finally, on September 13, they responded, saying that the decision had been
> made to change the theme to The Great Harvest, and that we would wear stan-
> dard peasant garb [field notes].

Despite the distance between KCRF and the sites of the attacks, in the heartland of America, the Middle Eastern there was cancelled, though some of
the entertainment scheduled for the weekend continued. According to

Wickersham, "It happened to be the weekend of the 'Middle Eastern invasion,' i.e., the belly dance weekend ... but, boy, was it muted" (field notes). So even those performers who had even the tiniest link with the Middle East, including, as Wickersham notes, the belly dancers, were quieted if not completely removed.

Despite Spedden's warning not to draw attention to the twenty-first-century part of the intrastice, an unsanctioned event highlighted the present American condition. The members of the Rogues of Scotland, a popular bagpipe and drum band, performed their last set of the day at the Dragon Inn, which is on the far side of the festival grounds from the entrance gate. As patron Mark Peters describes it:

> Their evening set at the Dragon Inn was unique [on 15 September 2001]. They erected a small flag pole and had a flag raising ceremony, complete with Marine Corps honor guard (kilted). Half way through the set, a line of patrons processed up to the flag pole to lay roses at the base [field notes].

Craig Rhymer filmed the event and sent me a copy of the DVD to review. The vast majority of the Rogues's set had its customary party atmosphere, during which children and adults danced in the aisles. People's voices can be heard chattering despite the intensity of the pipes and drums. However, when the piper played "Amazing Grace," there was a reverent silence in the crowd. However, afterwards, the Rogues played more of their Scottish dancing music with the American flag still atop the hastily erected pole. This unauthorized performance — Spedden only found out about it after it had occurred — brought the reality of twenty-first-century America directly into conflict with the history of sixteenth-century England. Collins offers a possible explanation why cast members both at the MDRF and at other festivals found it necessary to show some form of patriotism, despite warnings to the contrary. He writes, "The most intense expressions of solidarity are the most ephemeral. These occur at gatherings where crowds are assembled, sharing a contagion of emotion from body to body, with a mutual awareness of focus of attention that makes the feeling of belonging to the group palpable and sometimes overpowering."[15] Perhaps the show of patriotism emanates from the sheer numbers of people gathered together, at one moment dancing and a few seconds later crying.

The contrast between the solemnity during "Amazing Grace" and the exuberance afterwards created a moment within the intrastice in which patrons were alternately and abruptly faced with first one and then the other of the two worlds forming the pretext of Tudor Oxfordshire. Merely watching the video of the performance, nearly five years after the event, I had a gut-wrenching reaction to the sudden change between the ceremony referencing 11 September 2001 and the usually joyous musical entertainments the Rogues provide. I cannot say what those who were in attendance that day felt, but I can attest that my own response was visceral and unpleasant. Switching too quickly from one level of immersion in the intrastice to the another can be a jarring occurrence.

As evening draws near, it is customary in Revel Grove to gather in the White Hart Tavern for the final show of the day, the *Pub Sing*. At the White Hart on 15 September 2001, an attempt was made to produce a functional transition across the threshold from the intrastice back into twenty-first-century reality. The *Pub Sing* normally generates a form of *communitas* as patrons and performers join in singing together a mixture of rollicking sea shanties, bawdy ballads, and sorrowful love songs. Even for those not actually present at the pub that day, the music was touching and emotional. According to performer Denise Ringhold (not her real name), who was back stage during *Pub Sing*, "I am usually [busy] during *Pub Sing*, but I remember the songs really affecting me.... I had someone spray me in the face with water to get me back to the real world. I was wiped out at the end.... One of the hardest shows I've ever been a part of" (field notes). For Ringhold, who spends her entire day in character on the street interacting with patrons, the sense of *communitas* was carried in the sound waves that flowed to her position some 100 feet away. For those who were gathered together in the White Hart Tavern, there was a great deal of hugging, laughing, and, eventually, crying. The sense of *communitas* was heightened.

Following the end of the day's singing, the king usually addressed the assembled patrons and performers. On that day, Huttel chose to reprise his speech from *The Grand Event*. It was obvious from the reaction of those in attendance that many had not previously heard the monologue. Without the context provided by *The Grand Event*, the speech became a prime example of intrasticiancy within the carnival setting as the anguished reality of twenty-first-century America melded with the history of sixteenth-century England to facilitate the pretext of Tudor Oxfordshire, the safe haven that was Revel Grove. Following Huttel's speech, two trumpeters played "Taps," the most overtly-sanctioned reference to the preceding week's events. Because of the absence of reference to the events of 11 September throughout the day, Huttel's speech provided the necessary transition for the audience. As Huttel spoke the words of Shakespeare, he continuously referenced England, but the assembled audience could fill in the gaps and substitute America in his words, thus preparing them for the playing of the non-sixteenth-century "Taps," which served as an effective yet minimalist memorial.

When the *Pub Sing* concluded, the Royal Court led visitors and performers alike towards the front gate. The procession serves as another transitionary period preparing the patrons to step through the gates and back to the world of their waiting automobiles. Members of the cast stand outside the gate to wave goodbye to the visitors and ask them to return. The genuine gratitude the patrons showed was beyond compare, and most seemed to leave with a renewed sense of the ability to laugh and smile. According to performer Cybele Pomeroy, "we did spiritual work that weekend, and for the rest of the season. If memory serves, the weather remained as bright and beautiful as it was that previous Tuesday when stolen airplanes drove into the country's most iconic buildings" (field notes). That spiritual work happens in the intrastice, a place within which boundaries shift and open and close depending, hopefully, upon individual needs and choices.

Conclusion

The spirit of the carnivalesque and the laughter of the marketplace were alive that weekend, just as they had been at the MDRF for twenty-four seasons before and seven seasons since. Just as the sensescape I describe in the following chapter provides the physical environment against which the final three chapters should be read, the carnivalesque nature of the faires illustrated here imparts a historical backdrop against which to examine chapters 4, 5, and 6. Analyzing the way carnival informs festivals in general illustrates the intrastician nature of this theatrical event, while examining the carnivalesque during the weekend of 15–16 September 2001 at the MDRF offers a deeper understanding of the way intrasticiancy exists within a given cultural moment.

3

A Stroll Through the Sensescape of the MDRF

The colors, the people, the fabrics and garb, the twinkling leaves rustling in the breeze, the sunlight streaming down through the colored leaves, the signs, the stages, the walkways, the vendors, the pubs, the performers and street characters, the fountains and landscaping, even the ground and the mulch is a beautiful thing. Everywhere you look are wonderful and unforgettable visions. It truly is sensory overload sometimes [field notes — patron Elizabeth Marcus].

While most theatrical venues primarily engage the senses of sight and sound, the Renaissance Festival immerses performers and patrons alike in an atmosphere that also features smell, taste, and touch as part and parcel of the experience. Patron and performer conduct and their interaction with and within the sensescape at the festival illustrate their immersion within the intrastice of the pretext of Tudor Oxfordshire that the MDRF provides.

While sight and sound are certainly important elements of the theatrical experience at the MDRF, as Elizabeth Marcus's commentary opening this chapter attests, she continues on about smell and taste:

One smell that always sticks out for me are the cinnamon roasted almonds. I don't even like nuts, but I love the smell of the cinnamon roasted almonds. Even in a mall it reminds me of faire. There's also the smell of being downwind from the elephants ... but, that's not quite as pleasant. When we're really missing the faire season, we go out for soup in a bread bowl. There's also no cider quite like the first taps from the top of a keg on opening day. It's the best sip-o-cider around [field notes].

As these details of smell and taste indicate, the manner in which performers and patrons interact with the various media that create the sensory elements reveals information about the MDRF culture. Anthropologist Victor Turner writes,

66

Each culture, each person within it, uses the entire sensory repertoire to convey messages: manual gesticulations, facial expressions, bodily postures, rapid, heavy, or light breathing, tears, at the individual level; stylized gestures, dance patterns, prescribed silences, synchronized movements such as marching, the moves and "plays" of games, sports, and rituals, at the cultural level.[1]

Turner writes about the manner in which a society's members convey meaning through their sensory repertoire, and he establishes that senses beyond sight and sound convey important meaning. Within the combination of all the senses, the culture of the MDRF is revealed. For the purposes of this study, I use sociologist Wendy Griswold's definition of culture: "Culture refers to the expressive side of human life — behavior, objects, and ideas that can be seen to express, to stand for, something else."[2] The participants at the MDRF constitute a culture, and, as recipients of the sensory messages about which Turner writes, *create meaning* based upon their personal framing of the event in which they are participating. According to Marcus:

The hand-kisses are nice, too. What a sweet, lovely gesture that is. It can be impish and playful, a sign of deep respect, or a simple greeting. Too bad that's not done anymore in the boring world. I think more men could stand to kiss a few hands and more women could stand having their hands kissed [field notes].

Marcus's description of touch illustrates her understanding of the distinction between daily life in contemporary America and temporary existence within the intrastice. The addition of touch to the theatrical event provides an opportunity to become more deeply immersed in the intrastice.

Scholarly attention has focused upon landscape and soundscape, which largely treat the way a culture experiences sights and sounds of its environment. Landscape scholar Paul Groth explains that even landscape involves more than mere vision. "For writers in cultural landscape studies, the term *landscape* means more than a pleasing view of scenery. *Landscape* denotes the interaction of people and place: a social group and its spaces, particularly the spaces to which the group belongs and from which its members derive some part of their shared identity and meaning."[3] Thus, landscape is more than the visual background of an environment; it is also the people who populate that locale. Music sociologist Otto E. Laske has written that soundscape is the "sonic habitat in which people live."[4] Laske further takes this somewhat tautological definition borrowed from R. Murray Schafer and elaborates: "the soundscape is a projection of man's biological and intellectual capabilities into the ecological environment."[5] In other words, the soundscape encompasses all noises in a particular location, including those made by man and those made by nature. By combining the ideas of landscape and soundscape and adding in the way a culture also experiences taste, touch, and smell, I create a definition which serves to include all five components. I term this

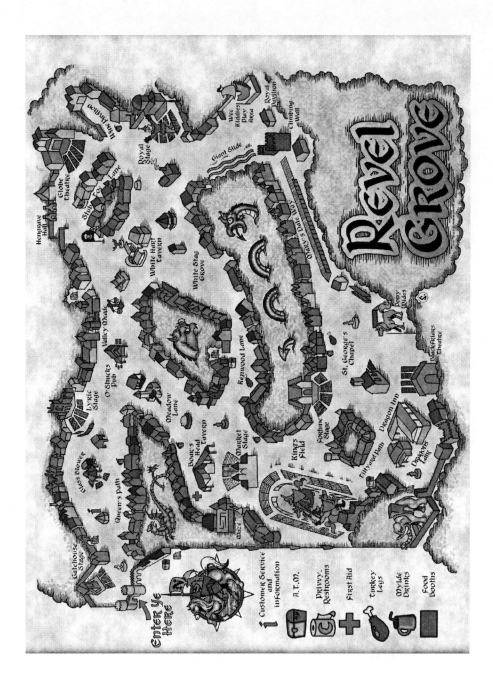

phenomenon a "sensescape" and define it as *an environment in which sight, sound, smell, taste, and touch combine to create an overall atmosphere distinctive to that particular type of theatrical event.*

Theatre theorist Elinor Fuchs, in her chapter "Reading for Landscape: The Case of American Drama," writes: "every dramatic world is conditioned by a landscape imaginary, a 'deep' surround suggested to the mind that extends far beyond the onstage environment reflected in the dramatic text and its scenographic representation."[6] At the MDRF, the dramatic world is not suggested to the mind; it is realized. The patron does not merely see a representation; the patron interacts with constructed as well as natural scenographic elements. Moreover, patrons and performers are not constrained to sight and sound as in a traditional theatre setting, but are able to experience the environment with complete visceral reaction through all five senses. There are certainly instances in the legitimate theatre in which senses beyond sight and sound have been engaged, most notably in naturalist plays. However, even when the sense of smell is invoked — as in August Strindberg's *Miss Julie*— it is rare for taste and touch to be vigorously activated. Smell is directly related to immersion in the intrastice. As biologist Lewis Thomas comments, "The act of smelling something, anything, is remarkably like the act of thinking itself."[7] Through patrons' activation of their differing olfactory senses and historical knowledge, they frame their experiences in diverse ways and therefore enter into different levels of intrasticiant immersion.

I argue that the sensescape at a theatrical event can influence greater participation in the intrastice. Patrons experience the sensescape in many venues. The MDRF is not an amusement park, but it shares sensory similarities with that theatrical event. Marie Laure Ryan writes,

> If there is an environment in which you can literally take your body with you into worlds of the imagination, it is the amusement park. We may dismiss this culturally invasive avatar of the faire as an attempt to recreate the communal

Opposite: A map of Revel Grove. It is important to note that the map is not to scale. The arrow at bottom center indicates the gates to the village. My walking route of the village begins on the *Queen's Path.* I make the U-turn and head towards *Meadow Lane* and then down *Tiltyard Path*, circling back around to the Royal Pavilion and the *King's Field and Joust Field.* Next I move up *Kenwood Lane* through White Stag Grove and down *Stub Toe Lane*, again making a U-turn and then heading toward the Wine/Brewers Pavilion. The giant hill I describe is next to the area at the top of the map where the slide is located. I then follow *Mary's Dale Way*, also known as *The Boardwalk*, before returning to the Joust Field and the White Hart Tavern. The final procession again follows the Queen's Path to the front gates. (Note: Italics indicate section headings within the chapter.) Map courtesy of International Renaissance Festivals, Ltd.

street life of earlier days in a fenced-off and fully commercialized space of three-dimensional postcards, but with its multiple offerings, diversified geography, parades and masquerades, and mosaic of sensory stimuli, it also stands as a testament to the postmodern fascination with the playful spirit and protean nature of the carnivalesque.[8]

It is within that multiplicity of sensory stimuli — the combination of all the sensory elements — that the people at the theatrical events can experience intrasticiancy. Ryan also invokes the spirit of carnival, another theatrical event which utilized the entire sensescape to create an intrastice. In this chapter I will explore the various elements of the sensescape that is Revel Grove by providing a tour of the village and examining how the senses interact at various points.

For many patrons, the day's entertainment at MDRF begins before they even enter the gates. The visitors arrive early, turn off the paved street onto the gravel driveway, drive across the field cleared to serve as a parking lot, and park. The village is surrounded by a wooden fence, though roofs of the taller buildings, flags, and standards peak out over the top of the graying wall. To the right of the entrance is a Tudor-like building with windows where patrons may purchase tickets. The visitors' entrance consists of three wooden doors which swing open when it is time to go in. These doors are part of a cream-colored stucco façade, resembling a castle right down to the turrets upon which actors tread to address the gathering throng.

Opening Gate Ceremony

Once the movement into the village begins, spectators' paths converge and diverge with each step. The choices each patron makes take him or her on a unique journey through Revel Grove. Though the boundaries of the village are stable, every step provides a different experience. Michel de Certeau's writing on "Walking in the City" provides a framework for this chapter, as I "Walk the village" as my character, Elizabeth Seymour (Lady Ughtread). De Certeau was careful to elucidate that the city changes as a matter of form with each pedestrian's footsteps. He writes, "walking affirms, suspects, tries out, transgresses, respects, etc., the trajectories it 'speaks.' All the modalities sing a part in this chorus, changing from step to step, stepping in through proportions, sequences, and intensities which vary according to the time, the path and the walker."[9] So, while I attempt to illuminate the overall sensescape at the MDRF, because the choices of time and path were mine, I only illustrate one of an infinite number of possible ways to experience the village. Nonetheless, this methodology provides a foundation upon which I build the ensuing chapters, and the patrons and performers I encounter during my walk tell their own stories.

When the gates finally open, amidst warnings from the knowing performers to unsuspecting patrons to "cover your ears," a loud cannon blast marks the beginning of the festival day. After the cannon is fired, the crowd pushes forward, funneling from a large uncontrolled mass into three semi-organized lines that press through the doors. Patron Ryan Waters comments, that "the throng of people just as the front gate opens and everyone is trying to get into the faire as quickly as possible is one of my favorite times. Everyone crowds together, but the rush seems tempered by politeness" (field notes). That hurried yet polite movement through the gates signals the patrons' voyage across the threshold of intrasticiancy. With the feeling of bodies in close proximity, but without the rudeness that might ordinarily accompany such a swell, patrons and performers are likely to experience a feeling reminiscent of both festival and carnival atmosphere of the sixteenth century which fosters a spirit of *communitas*. As Turner writes,

> The passage from one social status to another is often accompanied by a parallel passage in space, a geographical movement from one place to another. This may take the form of a mere opening of doors or the literal crossing of a threshold which separates two distinct areas, one associated with the subject's pre-ritual or preliminal status, and the other with his post-ritual or post liminal status.[10]

The festival gates are the Turnerian threshold which visitors cross, separating the reality of twenty-first century America and the recorded history of sixteenth-century England from the pretext of Tudor Oxfordshire. As patrons enter the intrastice, they may change from spectator to participant as the spirit of carnival offers the opportunity to engage intrastically, intrasticively, or intrasticiously by "*plunging* into the realm of the non-visual senses."[11]

The Queen's Path

As the masses pass the gates, costumed performers greet them and offer to help guide visitors to various sites within Revel Grove. Immediately, patrons are immersed in the sights and sounds of the faire, as the sixteenth-century costumes on the actors and many of the visitors are accentuated by the various buildings and shops along the wooded path. As living history scholar and ethnographer Stephen Eddy Snow comments in his work on Plimoth Plantation, "The contradictions, of course, are constantly present. The illusion of the seventeenth-century setting is broken the moment the visitors enter, looking like inhabitants of the twentieth century and carrying equipment such as Instamatics, video packs, and Walkmans."[12] The same thing happens at the MDRF at times. While the cast members are supposed to be in costume at all times, to use only period implements for drinking and eating, and to refrain from acknowledgement that it is indeed the twenty-first century, it is

The morning dance. In the foreground, at left, my character's brother, Sir Edward Seymour (Christopher Ellison); left center, my character's sister, Mistress Jane Seymour (Brittney Sweeney); at right center, Anne Boleyn's musician, Master Mark Smeaton (J. Adam Wyatt). Photograph by Carrie J. Cole.

true that the festival's king for eleven years, the late Bill Huttel, who was an avid Washington Redskins fan, would acknowledge visitors who brought with them hand-held televisions during football season by asking, "And how do they fare, our knights of the burgundy and gold?" (field notes). However, a major difference exists between MDRF and Plimoth Plantation or Colonial Williamsburg in that many of the patrons visiting Revel Grove are dressed like the performers. Patrons can rent costumes immediately upon entering the festival gates, and many will buy parts or entire costumes from any number of vendors throughout the day. Many patrons are completely dressed for the sixteenth-century before they enter the village. (I will discuss these particular visitors to the village in detail in Chapter 6.)

Vendors begin to hawk their wares, and the sounds of instruments from the Musical Merrymaking performance that opens each festival day just a few hundred feet from the front gate waft in all directions. Moving to the sounds of the music, village dancers swirl in a colorful array of costumes. One of the strongest senses of touch for the performers and patrons alike is the fabric they wear as part of their costumes. According to Marcus:

> I love touching fabric because it is interesting to me. Leather, wool, velvet, cotton, brocade, embroidery, feathers, fancy ribbons and trims ... there's always things to touch and admire at the faire. Especially when someone with a well-made garment comes by, I have often stopped people to ask how they made it, what it was made of, and then ask if it's okay to touch it [field notes].

Marcus not only wears her own costume, she is fascinated with the costumes others wear, especially those items which are unlikely to be worn in the twenty-first-century world. Cast dancer Theresa Olson described one of her most connected feelings of touch as "the swish of my skirts while doing a dance move" (field notes). The skirts serve as a reminder of the sixteenth-century history that helps to form the intrastice, and the dances are in themselves strong senses of touch.

Many of the actors embody history by performing the physical movements their historical counterparts would have danced nearly 500 years earlier, and the dance patterns offer a tangible link between present and past. According to Alice Rayner, "With or without the sense of mimesis, representation is a kind of repetition that generates the phantom of a double."[13] By actually performing the dances, I produced the repetitive patterns, and brought myself further into the intrastice, that space that is the "phantom of a double." Not even one hundred yards from the village gates, the actors form two circles: a smaller inner circle of courtiers and local nobility and a much larger outer circle of peasants. Immediately a feeling of cultural difference is established as a hierarchy of courtiers and villagers is clearly marked by the inner and outer circles. According to Eowyn S. Ellison, who in years past had served as assistant dance mistress at the MDRF, "We set it up so that the court and high-ranking villagers dance in the inner circle to prevent the courtiers from being mixed up with us lowly villagers" (field notes). While in the twenty-first century we discuss class differences that are both overt and covert attempts to fight the first and unearth the second, in the sixteenth century represented by the created intrastice created that is Revel Grove, it was openly demarcated who was who and where people belonged. This was a society that still believed in the Great Chain of Being, a vertical chain with God in Heaven at the top, in which there was no such concept as an "equal." The dance quickly illustrates the cultural difference, and Ellison's self-definition as a "lowly villager" is representative of the English class system at the time. This historical record of sixteenth-century England combines with the costumed performers and intricate dance steps to draw the patrons into the intrastice.

Almost all the actors participate in this particular morning ritual. As Thomas Luckmann writes, one of the "adjustments that are required in the coordination of social interaction ... consists in the synchronization of two streams of consciousness."[14] This interaction is exhibited as visitors watch and confront the actors, who are dancing. If the visitor allows himself or herself to experience the intrastice, he or she will achieve the harmonization of which Luckmann writes. "Once synchronization of two streams of consciousness is achieved, actions originating with different individuals can be geared into one another so as to form a unitary course of social interaction."[15] As I performed the morning dance, "The Promenade," I came to think not about performing, but rather about how I, as Elizabeth Seymour, a recent widow, could use my movements to attract a potential suitor. I also found myself judging the flourishes, hand placement, and lightness of foot of actors whom I had known for years not as themselves, but as their characters, assessing whether each would be a suitable match for a woman of my station (field notes). In the movements and touch of the dance, within the sensescape of tall trees, Tudor-style buildings, and music performed on lute and flute, even I entered an intrasticious state. The synchronization of these streams of consciousness between what is the reality of twenty-first century America and the historical record of sixteenth-century England occurs within the intrastice, the pretext of Tudor England that is the village of Revel Grove. As the visitors enter and watch the dancers, they are faced with this melding of two worlds, this repetition that presents the phantom of a double. Of course the visitors are not in 1536, but they are confronted with its phantom.

In years past, the patrons also participated in many of the dances. Performers in the MDRF dance troupe would teach period dances to any visitor who wished to learn. When the village dance mistress retired just prior to the 2004 season, the ensemble was disbanded for the year, and the patrons lost the option to actually take part in the dances. Physicality is part of the faire, and patrons like to participate actively in various events that incorporate the sense of touch, such as the dances. If that is taken away, they express their displeasure. For example, one patron was quite vocal on one of the comment cards that visitors may fill out as they depart Revel Grove. On one of these "Royal Registry" cards, a spectator — a woman who described herself as a returning patron over age 61— stated that she really felt the lack of participatory dances this season. The actual participation in the dances, moving in a manner unfamiliar to the twenty-first-century sensibility, allows patrons to understand and experience the sixteenth-century pretext in a physical way. The dancers touch each other, but that is only one aspect of the physical connection to the sixteenth century. Their feet come in repeated contact with the earth in patterns unfamiliar to their twenty-first-century sensibilities. Performance Studies scholar Margaret Thompson Drewal writes, "In its formulations of time, space, and dynamics, dance transmits a people's philosophy and values; it is thought embodied in human action."[16] By immersing themselves in an action that privileges touch, the visitors to the village are able to receive that transmission of sixteenth-century philosophy. In experiencing those values and thoughts through action, dancers move from the willing suspension of disbelief (intrasticial state) to either playing at belief (intrasticive) or active creation of belief (intrasticious) in the pretext of Tudor Oxfordshire.

The melding of two or more senses creates an environment more likely to entice the visitor to enter into the intrastice. A smell many performers and patrons signal as important to the festival sensescape is incense. As I walk past a gypsy vardo, an aroma, not quite familiar but not quite foreign, greets me. A visitor explains how sound is added to the smell. According to long-time patron Lisa Rockport, "the gypsy calls from her porch to let her read your palm to see what fortunes are bestowed upon you" (field notes). The sound, like the scent, is both familiar and foreign. Because the "gypsy" is not English, her accent is unusual, even among other performers, adding an air of intrigue and mystery. Yet, because of the twentieth- and twenty-first-century stereotype of the gypsy, which is often indicated in contemporary films by a not-quite-distinguishable Eastern European accent, there is a familiarity to her call. If a visitor to the village approaches the gypsy and pays for a palm reading, then touch also becomes a major factor as the fortune-teller will grasp the patron's hand in her own to perform the reading. As Mikhail Bakhtin writes, "in the popular marketplace aspect of the feast a substantial place was held by games (cards and sports, as well as by various forms of fortune-telling, wishes, and predictions)."[17] The fortune teller is just the beginning of the games a visitor may experience through the senses, games which have been part of festival culture for hundreds of years, and which draw the patrons further into the pretext of Tudor Oxfordshire by providing a context drawn from the historical record of the sixteenth century.

Leaving the fortune-telling gypsy's vardo behind, I pass the pipe organ of the Lyric Stage. This organ can be heard throughout the village playing sixteenth-century tunes, some of them of Henry VIII's own composition. The deep, resonant tones of the organ follow me as I approach the first available pub, O'Shucks, which is known as much for its proximity to the front gate as it is for its unique contribution to the festival fare: oyster shooters. As Daphne Bridges, a multi-year MDRF attendee, explains: "My group traditionally starts our annual trip to the Faire with a round of oyster shooters at the oyster bar. The chorus of thankful cheers for another year of celebration at the festival is mixed with 'yucks' and 'euws' of those companions who do not enjoy the slimy spicy slide of the oyster down the throat and into the tummy" (field notes). This patron privileges the taste and touch of the oysters as firm benchmarks of entrance into another year at the festival. It is important to note that the oyster shooters are traditionally accompanied by an ale chaser. Even early in the morning, just after the gates have opened, the beer and cider flow freely. According to Bakhtinian scholar and theorist Caryl Emerson, "Remarkably, Bakhtin — a chain smoker and tea addict — attends almost not at all to the chemical side of carnival, that is, to intoxication, addiction, and drunkenness, although any practical understanding of holiday bawdiness or vulgarity is unthinkable without it."[18] At the MDRF, there is also a chemical side — usually ale, cider, mead, or wine — and it does have an effect on the way people experience the faire. Unlike Bakhtin, I will attempt not to be so sightless as to ignore this particular part of carnival, and I shall treat the presence and consumption of alcohol along with its attendant effects throughout this chapter.

After the first round (or two) of oyster shooters, visitors have many more entertainments to experience. It may be a musician whose wafting notes of the flute draw the patrons away from the pub. Sometimes a performer redirects the visitor by engaging in a conversation and imparting juicy gossip about the Royal Court. Describing basic found environments in which performances take place, theatre scholar Brooks McNamara writes: "There is no rigid separation between spectators and the performer as there is in orthodox theatres, and their relationship is fluid and informal. The audience is free to watch the performance or ignore it as they please, to retreat when the hat is passed for contributions, or to drift away to a more interesting performance somewhere else in the street or marketplace."[19] Likewise, at the MDRF patrons may engage with a particular musician or actor, or the visitor may simply ignore performers and move along at his or her own pace. The visitors make the choices from the ample options the festival provides for the patrons to engage with every sense.

Meadow Lane

While chatting with visitors finishing a round of oyster shooters, they hear a strange sound, one not quite familiar. I move with them as they investigate, and we find one of the many games available for patrons to play at the festival. Erin Kelly, who has participated for more than fifteen years at the MDRF as patron, vendor, and performer, reports, "one sound I always associate with the festival is the Thor's Hammer Game — y'know what I mean, that distinctive 'thunk ... clang!!!'" (field notes). In Thor's Hammer, a patron uses a heavy mallet to strike a padded target which moves a piece of metal up a wide pole in an attempt to sound the bell at the top. Both sound and touch are privileged at this particular part of the venue. During the 2004 season, one gentleman rang the bell fifty times in a row, a truly amazing feat considering that many stout and hearty young men can not ring the bell even once. It was indeed the repetition in quick succession of the distinctive "thunk ... clang" that drew me and many spectators to watch this patron's prowess.

A few other performers were nearby, and soon we had all the patrons cheering in unison, encouraging the modern-day Hercules in his test of strength with hearty rounds of "Huzzah" after each successful attempt. When he had completed his record-setting run of rings, Lady Rochford (played by second-year festival performer Sonia Motlagh) and I congratulated this visitor and bestowed upon him small trinkets to illustrate our admiration: a badge from Lady Rochford and a small hand-made bracelet from me. He seemed truly amazed by our fawning and fussing, and he very quickly learned the proper way to kiss a lady's hand and exhibit reverence. I explained to him that wearing my bracelet would be like carrying a lady's favor at the joust and hoped he would forever be my champion. Later in the day, when I saw him preparing to leave, he held his hand high in the air and proclaimed in an English accent he had not used when we first spoke, "I am the Lady Ughtread's champion" (field notes). He was willing to play at belief and had entered into the intrasticive state through his gaming and interaction with the performed historical characters.

Standing by Thor's Hammer after our Hercules had left, the spectators and performers hear instrumental music, which may emanate from a nearby tavern, or glen, or open meadow area. Often patrons gravitate toward the new sound. According to music theorist Paolo Prato, "Music has always been a part of street life."[20] Patrons wandering through the festival lanes are almost always within earshot of some form of music, whether it be the upbeat sounds of fiddlers and drummers who provide the accompaniment for the dancers or the sonorous melodies that emanate from the pipe organ. These sounds, however, are often an accessory to so many others in the streets of Revel Grove.

Patrons do not attend the faire solely to hear music, but almost everyone mentions music when talking about the festival, so it is indeed an important part of the sensescape. However, whether performing on stages or in the streets, musicians must often compete for attention with the other sounds of the marketplace, including the patrons' own conversations. According to Prato, "To compensate for the deficiencies of distracted listening and to appeal to a flowing stream of passers-by, street musicians oscillate between two solutions: virtuosity and familiarity."[21] Prato explains that virtuosity signifies its "*presence within* the contingent spatio-temporal coordinates," while familiar music "tends to relate to *absent* elements of the socio-cultural code rather

than to the present materiality of the performance."[22] These descriptions of
the mixture of virtuosity and familiarity are indicative of intrasticiancy as six-
teenth- and seventeenth-century compositions and/or instruments mix with
modern tunes upon the streets of Revel Grove. For example, wandering away
from Thor's Hammer in the hot sun, I am drawn to the raucous tones of multiple instruments that radiate from the jousting field, where the musical group
Wolgemut is playing its first set. Wolgemut plays period instruments including bagpipes, shawm, lute, fiddle, harp, and flute. They play compositions
which date from thirteenth- and fourteenth-century Spain, Italy, and Germany. However, they are also well known at the faire for adding to their music
by playing, on their Tudor era instruments, rollicking verses of modern rock
songs including "We Will Rock You" and "Tequila."

Tiltyard Path

Past the jousting field and down a dusty hill, I encounter a pungent
smell as I approach the elephant ride, which is just past a set of privies. When

**The Blessed Scents booth is in the background. From left to right, John Lasher
as Master William Trent, Scott Sophos as Sheriff Reginald Sharp, and Tim
McCormick as Guy of Guisborne. Photograph by Dr. Carrie Jane Cole.**

speaking of smell at the faire, almost everyone comments upon the privies and the elephants. The area in which the elephants are kept is also next to the stable area that houses the jousting horses during performance days. On the warmer festival days, this olfactory overdose may signal one of the moments closest to sixteenth-century living, at least by the standards of how contemporary people believe Tudor England smelled. As performer J. Adam Wyatt, who portrayed Mark Smeaton and Allan Adale for the 2004 season, comments, "even the smells of the privies on a warm day add to the fact that this is an old English village" (field notes). The odor contributes to moving a patron into the intrastice and to deeper immersion within it. As David Howes comments, "*there is a connection between olfaction and transition.*"[23] Add in the animals — horses and elephants — and it can sometimes become difficult to discern from which area a particular aroma originates. Unlike Colonial Williamsburg, the festival does not have animals roaming in the streets, so at least patrons are spared the inconvenience of stepping in dung, even if the smells linger in some areas.[24]

In a shaded area around one of the festival's taverns, the Dragon Inn, patrons and performers must be wary to avoid tree roots and slippery mulch, which provide tactile feelings under the feet that elicit connections to the sixteenth century. As patron David Thompson — a professor at a large Midwestern university — elaborates, one of the strongest sensations of touch is "the squishy feeling underfoot of walking on the duff, even when it hasn't been raining — this is woods, not dirt under trees" [field notes]. The feel of unstable ground mixes with the other senses and contributes to the feeling of intrasticiancy. Walking on uneven ground, with grooves and ruts created by nature, is part of the overall ambiance of the faire, and the owners have resisted all requests to put in any sort of pavement.

Once I negotiate the hill from the elephants past the Dragon Inn and back down toward the Fortune Stage, I am greeted by one of the most pleasant and recognizable smells of the festival. The Blessed Scents shop sells an extremely wide variety of herbs, spices, and oils, and a good breeze can carry the smell from the shop almost far enough to mask the scent of the jousting field. As performer Lisa Ricciardi-Thompson commented, "the smell that stays with me is the splendid mixture that emanates from the Blessed Scents booth. Each scent alone is wonderful, but as you walk by they blend into something exotic and mysterious" (field notes). That scent is tied to the intrasticiancy of the faire, as it is not quite placeable as a twenty-first century odor. When all of the senses are affected, the result can be overpowering. As Ricciardi-Thompson further explains, "My mother was so overwhelmed by the village itself, she said she felt as if she were time traveling" (field notes). Ricciardi-Thompson's mother has seen her perform in numerous conven-

The Royal Pavilion. Sonia Motlaugh (left) as Lady Jane Parker, Viscountess Rochford, and John Kelso (right) as Master Andrew Stewart. Photograph by Carrie J. Cole.

tional theatre venues, but the sensescape at the MDRF caused a reaction different from any she had previously experienced. She entered the intrasticious state.

King's Field and Joust Field

Leaving Blessed Scents behind, I perambulate through Revel Grove and pass the Royal Pavilion en route back toward the jousting field. The pavilion is at the edge of the tree line, and as I walk into the sun that covers the jousting arena, the change in the climate is palpable. Waters comments,

> As Revel Grove is primarily hewn out of a woods, and I tend to attend in late September to early October, you get the crispness of an early fall morning.... At some point one moves onto the Meadow Lane area which up to the Jousting Field is the only totally exposed area. As the morning clouds have burned off later in the day, you get the sudden warmth of the sun at some point. To me it just feels like you are entering a different part of the "country" [field notes].

Mike Martin as Master Hamish Stewart (left) fights in hand-to-hand combat with Casey Severn, portraying Gronk. This fight is staged combat as part of the *Human Chess Game* in which pieces win or lose based on the outcome of the choreographed fights. Photograph by Carrie J. Cole.

In this case, the sensescape serves to move within the intrastice from one pretext of Tudor Oxfordshire to another based upon this particular patron's framing of the space. While there is no physical difference between the MDRF site in which this visitor participates and that in which others partake, since he has framed it as a movement to a different part of "England," he will have a different experience.

Taking a seat on the wooden benches at the jousting field, I watch a game of Human Combat Chess. This Renaissance custom comes alive each day at MDRF. Bakhtin wrote, "In his 'Poliphila's Dream' Francesco Colonna describes a game of chess; the chessmen are represented as live people, wearing conventional costumes inspired by that game. Here chess is transformed on the one hand into a carnival masquerade, on the other hand into a grotesque image of military and political events."[25] In the case of the chess game at Revel Grove, held on the same sandy field as the jousts, the smells of sweat and horse and horse sweat are often strong, creating a mixture of all the senses unparalleled elsewhere in the village. As one performer comments, "The scent of horses, often wet horses, and a wet jousting field, probably the less said, the better" (field notes). The strong olfactory sensation created upon the Joust Field is absolutely overwhelming. The dampness of the jousting field might well be welcomed by those who actually have to perform the stage combat in the arena. As Mike Martin, who portrays Hamish Stuart, notes,

> another sensation that could be classified as less than pleasant is the dust effect at the MDRF. With dry spells that last for weeks and tens of thousands of people marching through the same paths, the dust can be pretty intense. There are weekends when I have to drink cups of water just to wash out the taste of dust from my mouth. The sensation of a dusty mouth is like having sandpaper for teeth. The more you rub your tongue over your teeth, the more they feel like they are covered with 150- [or] 200-grit sand paper [field notes].

Amidst either the wet or the dry sand, the stage combatants take the field of honor and perform complex fight choreography with weapons ranging from bullwhips and broadswords to quarterstaffs and fists. As fight choreographer Jim Frank notes, two of his strongest senses of touch at the faire are "the weight of a sword" and "punching a friend" [field notes]. And though the fights are choreographed, risks do exist. Bruises, bumps, and cuts are routine, though broken limbs have also been suffered during the *Human Chess Game*. Patrons watch the chess game from almost all sides, seated on wooden benches, often in the blazing heat of the midday sun. Vendors hawk pretzels and nuts, so the sound of the hawking follows them even there in the joust arena, and the salty flavor of the foods purveyed adds taste to a cool drink perhaps brought into the jousting arena. Following a half hour in the bright sun watching the chess game and cheering loudly along with the patrons seated all around me, I seek out a cooler, shadier area as well as food and libation.

Kenwood Lane

Walking down the shade of Kenwood Lane in search of something to eat, I am surrounded by those hawking their wares, from turkey legs and ale to jewelry and wall hangings. Musicians play in the middle of the path. Dancers jump to a lively tune, and so that I may purchase something to eat, I sneak by several actors nearby who are engaging in a rather loud disagreement over the next queen. This soundscape of Revel Grove is reminiscent of life in the Renaissance as Bakhtin describes it:

> We must recall that not only was all advertising oral and loud in those days, actually a cry, but that all announcements, orders, and laws were made in this loud oral form. Sound, the proclaimed word, played an immense role in everyday life as well as in the cultural field. It was even greater than in our days, in the time of the radio. (As for the nineteenth century, compared with the era of Rabelais it was silent.) This fact should not be ignored when studying the style of the sixteenth century and especially the style of Rabelais. The culture of the common folk idiom was to a great extent a culture of the loud word spoken in the open, in the street and market place.[26]

Vendors hawking their wares, actors promoting their shows, musicians playing spirited melodies, and trees rustling in the autumn breeze contribute to the overall pretext of Tudor Oxfordshire. Amidst this noise, the need for the "loud word" becomes apparent as what should have been an intimate conversation between performers develops into a well-seen piece of street theatre as they shout secrets to each other from fifteen feet apart. MDRF invokes this spirit of the street and marketplace by producing, in close proximity to each other, the contiguous performances of these elements of sixteenth-century life.

In this same area is one of the festival's sets of privies, and sometimes on especially hot days the smell of privy mixed with the smell of ale and food carried on a warm summer breeze also provides for a non-twenty-first-century aromatic experience. Kenwood Lane is often quite crowded, and negotiating the area between the two rows of booths on the street often requires jostling and close contact with those both known and unknown. This close physical proximity, with women wearing corsets that prominently display their breasts and men wearing codpieces, is also quite reminiscent of the world of Rabelais to which Bakhtin refers. Waiting in line for the privies, one patron spoke of how he found himself in discomfort. Frequent fairegoer Mike Dowling, who dresses in a Scottish kilt while at the MDRF, comments, "the closeness is not as pleasing, my feet are being stepped upon,

someone nearby is in need of a shower, and the privies begin to smell. In
the press of humanity, someone finds me a tempting target for an anonymous
'kilt-check,' and now I find myself feeling assaulted and brutalized when
I should be flattered" (field notes). Dowling did continue to say that it
was the end of the day and that contributed to his feeling of being assaulted
rather than flattered. It is a frequent joke among festival performers and
patrons that there are official "kilt inspectors" within the village. According
to Emerson, "the suspension of everyday anxieties during 'holiday time'
and 'carnival space' — the specific locus being the vulnerable, yet superbly
shame-free, grotesque body — rids both me and my most proximate neighbor of the excessive self-consciousness that keeps both of us lonely, our
words insipid, and our outreaching gestures timid."[27] Obviously, the
kilt-checker was in the carnival space and failed to exhibit self-consciousness
with regard to the Bakhtin's grotesque, transgressing boundaries and creating an awareness of another's carnivalesque body while maintaining personal
anonymity.

   When patrons wear costumes — such as Dowling's kilt or Marcus's brocade — they signal their participation in at least the intrasticive state, a desire
to play at belief. Despite Dowling's negative reaction to the late-day "kilt
check," he admits that under other circumstances he would have been
flattered. He indicated his choice to enter the intrastice by wearing his costume, which conveyed a desire to play within the rules of carnival. Bakhtin
has written,

> The mask is connected with the joy of change and reincarnation, with gay rela-
> tivity and with the merry negation of uniformity and similarity; it rejects con-
> formity to oneself. The mask is related to transition, metamorphoses, the
> violation of natural boundaries, to mockery and familiar nicknames. It contains
> the playful element of life; it is based on a peculiar interrelation of reality and
> image, characteristic of the most ancient rituals and spectacles.[28]

Dressing in Renaissance garb for the contemporary festivals serves the same
function as wearing masks did for the carnival world Bakhtin describes. Various costumes of widely diverse colors swirl through the streets, maintaining
a visual landscape that is in constant motion. Silks, brocades, and lace, more
often seen as upholstery or curtains than as clothing in the twenty-first century, march past in a dizzying array. One patron told me his costume was the
greatest sense of touch he had at festival. This patron, Mark Peters, explains,
"When you're used to wearing T-shirts and jeans or a suit to work every day
wearing garb at faire alters your whole perspective with every move you make."
He describes his costume in detail:

> My garb is Sandlar boots, laced up the calf on the outside as opposed to shoes
> or sneakers tied on the foot; long sleeved shirts from the House of Dra, no but-

tons or fasteners of any kind except for draw strings on the front; doublet from Moresca, laced up the front; pants are wrap pants from Purple Unicorn [with] no pockets or zipper, legs are tucked into boots [field notes].

When I asked Peters how it made him feel to have all those different sensations of touch, he answered, "That's easy — normal" (field notes). Peters participates within the intrastice in such a manner that there is no sense of being out of the ordinary for him when he wears his garb.

I watch as a patron raises a garbed arm to bite into one of the turkey legs and follows it with a swig of ale; the visitor is listening to the vendors hawking their wares as he stands next to the privy line in which people eat and drink, talk and sing, hug and kiss, and he observes the costumed patrons and performers walking past. Through his "observations and actions" he has experienced each and every sense simultaneously, and in interpreting them this visitor becomes part of the overall culture of the faire and enters into the intrastice as a result of the overwhelming signs communicated through his perception of the sensescape.[29]

As I leave this patron behind and continue to walk the village, passing by more food vendors on one side (selling everything from peasant bread to pork chop on a stick) and crafters on the other (purveying wooden swords, cloaks, and pewter wares), an unusual smell arises. It is the smell of heat; not summer heat, not warm breeze, but fire-hot heat as the blacksmith's forge is in full operation. Frank comments on the smell of the "brimstone of the blacksmith," and Denise Ringhold, adds that her most memorable scent is "Rorik's coal forge starting up for the day — the smoke, the sooty odor — throwing a few oak leaves in the fire" (field notes). Once the fire is in sight and the sound of metal on metal at the forge is heard, the various senses mix to create a strong sensation of the sixteenth century. Pre-electric England was a realm lit only by fire, and in the pre-industrial age the smell of smoke and burning wood was common for both peasant and noble. This is a smell that pulls performers and patrons alike back in time.

Stub Toe Lane

Moving down Stub Toe Lane, a group of madrigal singers serenades a crowd of visitors with melodies written over 400 years ago. Unlike a concert hall performance, these singers must vie for attention just like everyone and everything else at the MDRF. According to musicologist Shai Burstyn, "an imaginative reconstruction of the soundscape in which past listeners lived could provide useful clues about the outer limits of their dynamic world."[30] The festival's intrastiancy provides a rough reconstruction at least of street music, as musicians must deal with not only competing sounds from nature, but also with multiple contiguous performances affecting all five senses, which draw the attention of the audience. Actors perform nearby, handing out small tokens to the children. The massage garden is directly across from the singers, and those taking advantage of the special touch of the masseuses hear sounds from the trees above, the singers behind, and the Globe Theatre ahead. They smell the fragrant incense and candles from the massage garden as their bodies receive relief from a long day of walking the unpaved paths. As patron Steve Jamison comments, "I usually get one or two short massages a year; it's expensive, but if I could get a good massage in the late afternoon every faire day, that would be incredible" (field notes). Touch again becomes an important element of the overall sensescape in Revel Grove, whether it is brought to fruition or merely manifested as a kinesthetic desire.

Beyond the massage garden is the Globe Theatre, where many of the most popular acts at the MDRF perform. At this time Shakespeare's Skum is appearing on stage with one of their popular shows. In 2004, the troupe performed *Tag Team Romeo and Juliet, Henry the 'V,'* and *Richard III*. The festival's Artistic Director, Carolyn Spedden, writes these fractured Shakespeare pieces, which are perennial visitor favorites. The Bard's stories and language along with period costumes provide a sixteenth-century backdrop even as modern anachronisms in speech and clothing creep in, both raising the hilarity of the performance and becoming self-referential reminders that the intrasticiancy at the faire does indeed cover here and now as well as there and then.

Climbing up a rather steep hill near the Globe leads me to one of the favorite shaded spots in the village: the Wine Garden. There is a covered area here in which performers and patrons alike may choose to have their lunch in relative privacy. Many take advantage of the wide variety of wines offered at this particular pub. According to Bakhtin, "Certain feasts acquired a specific tinge depending on the season when they were celebrated. The autumn feasts of Saint Martin and of Saint Michael had a bacchanalian overtone and these saints were the patrons of winemaking."[31] Without a doubt, the festival has its bacchanalian overtones. Members of one group comprised of both performers and patrons have made the Wine Garden a "Home Away from Home." They proudly proclaim themselves as the ODS, Order of the Drunken Sots. I admit here my own culpability in participation with this particular group. One weekend in 2002, after performing two different characters under the blazing September sun, I found myself being spirited away to the Wine Garden at the end of the performance day by three gentleman of the cast. The tradition of frequenting this haven was just beginning, and I soon found myself the welcome recipient of a bee-sting, a drink made of cider and mead. By 2004, when I returned to perform the ethnographic research for this study, the ODS had swelled to nearly 100 members (perhaps more, since some refuse to admit their participation). That year, the bartender at the Wine Garden even created a drink and named it "The Dizzy Lizzy" after my character, Elizabeth Seymour. In addition to the drinking, there is much hugging and clasping of arms, significant forms of touching, as people greet each other at this haven. The body is privileged here, in both touch and taste, in direct contrast to the Aristotelian hierarchical order which ranks these two as the lowest senses and labels them animalistic.[32] Perhaps it is the theatre's devotion to Aristotelian principles — which have been reiterated for millennia — that leads it to privilege sight, hearing, and sometimes smell, while often ignoring taste and touch. Unlike conventional theatre, MDRF provides a taste of the autumnal feasts that exalted the animal sensations.

Most of the people who imbibe at the festival do so in a responsible manner. As patron Greg Dennis explains, "Renn Fests have much more senses involved [sic] in the experience than traditional theatre due to the fact that food/drink is not only available, but an integral part of the entire experience" (field notes). Many partake of the alcohol available simply as another part of the sensescape, but some are exasperating when drinking, as I wrote in the following excerpt from my field notes:

> I also had a problem this weekend with that particular brand of patron, the drunk who wants nothing more than to get you out of character. He followed me for several hours from venue to venue, from show to show, and insisted upon asking me questions attempting to break me out of character. I thought I had finally lost him when he stopped to get yet another beer, but he quickly showed up at my next stage show [field notes].

This brand of drunk is annoying, but tolerable. Unfortunately, it seems that at least once each season, there is a patron who imbibes too much and acts in an irresponsible and dangerous manner. I chronicled a particular example from 2004 as such:

> This year's drunken story was not quite so bad. An obviously intoxicated patron pulled my eating knife out of my basket and showed it to his friend. "It's not really a knife," he said. "It's not really sharp." He was about to run it across his arm when I said, "Halt. Sir, indeed 'tis sharp otherwise I should naught have opportunity to eat meat. To defile my eating dagger with human blood would be most inappropriate." He paused, looked at me, and seemed to be considering what I had said. He grabbed my hand and went to draw the knife across my wrist. "Sir," I said, "I must warn thee, that knife is sharp, but it is not the sharpest item in my basket. If thou wilst hold for a moment, I will show thee something much sharper." He stopped and let go of my hand so I could dig in my basket. I pulled out my two tined forchet. "Sir, thou canst surely see," I said holding up the pointy fork, "there are two tines on this and only one edge on

the knife. It will poke through even the most thickest of meats to hold them whilst I cut." He contemplated the forchet, something he was unfamiliar with, and I managed to exchange the knife for the fork. Safely tucking the knife away in my basket, I explained that the forchet was so sharp that we only used it to hold the meat, but that to place the meat in our mouths we would rather use the eating dagger, only one chance to stab ourselves instead of two. I then made him an offer he could not refuse. "Sir," I said, "I have something even more sharper than the forchet thou dost hold. If thou does return it to me, I shall reveal that most sharpest thing that I have." By now he had forgotten his urge to cut anything and was obviously dying to find out what else I could pull out of my basket. He gave me back the forchet without a fight and asked what I could possibly have upon me that was sharper than both the knife and fork. With a wink at his friends, I smiled as I turned to walk away, and tossed over my shoulder, "Well my Lord, of course, that which is the sharpest be my wit!!!" I quickly walked away and left his laughing friends to explain to him how he had just been had [field notes].

With that I hurried away as quickly as possible to find someone from security to watch this particular patron on his way out. His desire to indulge in the taste of mead, ale, or wine had turned into a potentially dangerous situation because he additionally desired the sense of touch, which in this case involved the use of a bladed utensil. While Bakhtin may have largely ignored the mere presence and along with it the inherent dangers of alcohol within the carnival setting, I wish to illustrate that though the vast majority of our patrons imbibe with requisite restraint, it is not always the case. The laws and mores of the twenty-first century contribute to patrons' belief that the festival is a site in which they are safe, while their sixteenth-century counterparts were probably well aware of the true lawlessness that ensued during carnival.

Mary's Dale Way/The Boardwalk

Leaving the wine garden area and heading to the most heavily wooded and coolest section of the faire also requires navigating the most treacherous hill the festival offers. When it is hot and dry, the ground gives way far too readily, and it is easy to slip on the loose uppermost layer of dirt and mulch. When it is wet, the mud can suck you in more quickly than you can imagine. Part of performing at the festival means performing in every kind of weather, and sudden summer/autumn storms are fairly well known within Revel Grove. Kelly speaks of rain days and their results: "The cold that seeps into your bones while walking around in the mud in skirts soaked to your knees can only be described as insidiously brutal" (field notes). Martin, who has been working at the MDRF for seven years, describes the "insidiously brutal" feeling Kelly mentioned:

You find that when you are out in the rain for six hours or more that your whole body becomes hyper-sensitive. I can feel my shirt rubbing against my skin, the socks in my boots, and the wet kilt around my neck. It is a kind of uncomfortable feeling that only the insane would want to experience year in and out. I assume it is akin to what life would have been like in that specific time period, but I'm not a history major [field notes].

I contend that Martin's assessment that the heightened sensitivity to the senses may bring about a greater understanding of the sixteenth century is key to grasping the intrasticiancy at the MDRF. Through visceral moments of sloughing through mud while being chilled to the bone by wind and rain and scratched by drenched clothing, participants — performers and patrons alike — in the rain-day atmosphere at MDRF experience deep levels of immersion into the intrastice. It is in this case, and in many others, this added element of the sensescape, touch, that facilitates the active creation of belief in the pretext of Tudor Oxfordshire.

Once one has successfully traversed the hill, the beautiful boardwalk area awaits. On one side there is a row of vendor booths offering crafts: leather goods, cloaks, magician's implements, French Hoods, ceramics, and musical instruments. On the other side is a boardwalk with a railing that overlooks a pastoral scene straight out of Sherwood Forest. Musicians play on the boardwalk, and magicians perform their tricks. At a specific time of day, a fight breaks out between two actors who swing at each other with quarterstaffs, seemingly with abandon, though the scene is completely choreographed. Martin comments on the overall sensescape of the faire, especially with regard to this particular area.

One sensation that is pleasant is the earthy, or more accurately, the tactile-ness (for lack of a better word) of the village. With every step your feet feel the rocks and mulch beneath you. You see and smell the smoke preceding the roasting of turkey legs. The structured and ridged support of the boardwalk in stark contrast to the earthy and wild forest it butts against. And the warmth of a friendly hug as you walk the path. With all of this is mixed fantasy, the loss of one's perceptions and timely duties. Where on Monday I have to file, report to bosses and focus groups, on Sunday I am walking through time and my only duty is to live one single festival day. A day where me (my character) has no boss and I wander aimlessly enjoying my time with the visitors. Of course, I do have duties there and I do have a schedule that I have to follow, but on those precious days where all of these things melt away and reality mixes with fantasy, I can truly say that the greatest feeling overcomes me: escape [field notes].

Martin's recollections of the ground upon which performers and patrons tread — a part of the landscape most ignore until a sprained ankle or a fall in the slippery mud forces awareness — provide the foundation figuratively and literally for his overall evaluation of the sensescape and the intrasticiancy created at MDRF. The sensescape is indicative of the subculture at the festival which experiences all five senses en route to creating a society that exists in the intrastice within the reality of twenty-first-century America and the recorded history of sixteenth-century England.

Not all of the adventures on the Boardwalk are tied to pastoral sensations. While the background is bucolic, there are also games of skill and chance, including "Drench a Wench" and the "Axe Throw." In the first game, a young woman dressed in peasant attire sits in a cage as patrons pay for the privilege of lobbing a ball toward a target. If the spectator's aim is true and the ball hits its mark, it triggers a mechanism that releases her bench and sends her falling into water of an undetermined cleanliness and temperature. Bakhtin's lower bodily stratum and the world of Rabelais are well at work here in this sixteenth-century wet bodice event. Next to the tank is the even more testosterone-laden game of the Axe Throw, where men (and a few women) attempt to hoist a throwing battle axe above their heads, then hurl it through the air towards a target some twenty feet away. Patron Ryan Waters comments that one of his strongest memories of touch at the faire is

> an axe leaving the hand, there is the heft of the axe, the feel of my hand on the wood or tape, swinging the axe with one hand a couple of times, then joining the second hand on the shaft as I pull it overhead and let it go on the forward stroke. This is then followed by the dull thud as the axe hits the target wall and slides down or bounces back. And, occasionally, you get the excitement of the thwack as the axe sticks in the wall [field notes].

The memories of the axe throw for this patron involved the physical sensation the feel of the axe provides as well as the auditory indication of successful versus a failed fling. Though the Axe Throw as well as the Drench a Wench tank back up to the forest area and are always covered with shade as only thin beams of muted sunlight press through the leaves, it is not the pastoral setting which provides the primary sensory perceptions of these events. Other elements of the sensescape, auditory and physical, take precedence for Waters, who experiences the kinesthetic response to the axe only because the spirit of carnival allows the spectators to participate as active agents.

The Boardwalk area is a classic example of the way that the festival utilizes the natural scenery of Revel Grove. Other venues often completely change the landscape when they create an entertainment site. Unlike MDRF, the created environment of Disneyland in California left none of the original topography. In "Bayreuth, Disneyland, and the Return to Nature," Matthew Wilson Smith writes, "Walter Elias Disney (WED) Enterprises had quietly bought up 160 acres of property. WED Enterprises bulldozed the land, burning orange, walnut, and eucalyptus trees, in order to create a stage upon which to manufacture an entirely new landscape of hills, valleys, and lakes."[33] Conversely, the MDRF does all it can to work within the natural physical milieu, with benches often built around trees. One of the pubs, The Dragon Inn, features several giant oaks which emanate from its floor, as the entire tavern was built around the existing forestry.

Completing the Walk

Leaving the Dragon Inn to head to the White Hart Tavern for the final event of the day, the *Pub Sing*, a patron again passes by the Joust Field, just in time to experience the final joust of the day. The jousting at the MDRF — unlike at many festivals, competitions, and other performances such as Medieval Times Restaurant — includes actual, unchoreographed combat. One long-time jouster explains the tactile feelings of full combat jousting. According to Barchan,

> Touch-wise is where I get the strongest sensations (duh). Like getting clobbered by professional stuntmen in the joust. Like getting knocked off a horse, hitting a post, then the ground, and not getting hurt! Like finishing a joust with a six-inch long lance tip stuck in your groin area (that fell there the first pass). Like feeling a stone in your boot that turns out to be a nail through your boot. Like getting an eye infection from dirt kicked in your face by a horse jumping through your legs. Or cracked teeth from holding the reins there. Or broken teeth from badly fitting armor [field notes].

Without question, the jousters experience the sensations of touch like no one else at the faire. It is precisely because of their actual feats of combat that I will treat them in detail in Chapter 4.

Following the final joust, Their Majesties — in 2004 King Henry VIII and Queen-to-be Jane Seymour — process through the village to the White Hart Tavern for the *Pub Sing*. This nightly gathering again encompasses the entirety of the senses as the pub is filled to capacity with patrons and performers alike, mingling amidst songs from the Pyrates Royale, Wolgemut, and other musicians. Beer and cider flow freely, and the taste of the libations as well as the smell is heavily in evidence. The taste of anything from a pewter mug is also quite a different sensation and part of the overall sensescape. Many cast members have commented on how anything tastes different out of a pewter mug, though they were not quite sure exactly how to explain the taste. In this physicality of taste, however lies an important aspect of the festival, illustrating the theoretical understanding of the shifting dynamic of performance when embodiment becomes foregrounded. Performance studies scholar and ethnographer Dwight Conquergood wrote of this metamorphosis, "[Victor] Turner shifted thinking about performance from mimesis to poiesis. Now, the current thinking about performance constitutes a shift from poiesis to kinesis."[34] This transition privileges more than just imitation; it illustrates how a kinesthetic response leads to embodiment, and then how that same embodiment of the past at the MDRF in turn produces more kinesthetic response in a continuous cycle of intrasticiant behavior.

Pub Sing is also an opportunity for nightly goodbyes, hugs, and kisses, the physical manifestations of a long day spent in intrasticiancy. These hugs are given between patrons, between performers, and between patrons and performers. The ritual nature of this exchange becomes clear as Steve Jamison comments, "lots of hugs from faire friends you only see that time of year. It almost feels like a church fellowship at times to me" (field notes). The nostalgia of looking back upon those moments is not tempered even by the close quarters at the end of a long hot day. According to actor J. Adam Wyatt, "the way that the costumes feel after a long day out in the sun I think adds to the experience of the performer. Just heavy and wet with sweat gives an idea of what it must have been like to move and exist in that time" (field notes). Performer Melissa McGinley chimes in on the way smell pervades the end of the day. "I seriously think that a Renn Festival has its own distinctive smell. At least anything you wear to one does. It's a mix of dirt and sweat and horse and food. It's probably mainly sweat, but nothing I wear to the gym smells like anything I have worn to a festival. It's also unmistakable once you've smelled it" (field notes). The camaraderie of knowing that everyone else smells too may provide the impetus to continue with the hugs and kisses amidst the music and hawking of wares. Although, according to actor Timothy McCormick, the village's evil deputy, not everyone smells exactly alike. "The Renn Faire is unique in that aspect.... You can kind of get an idea of the bustle and smells and cacophony of sound at an Elizabethan market. Why we even have the drunks and the tarts. And believe me, drunks have a particular smell. Especially when they've been drinking all day" (field notes). Despite the various odors, the hugs, kisses, singing and drinking continue.

When it is nearly time to go, Jim Frank usually heralds the coming of the final song by blowing a fireball into the sky above the tavern. Much like the traveling jongleurs of the Middle Ages and Renaissance, Nymblewyke provides another entertainment reminiscent of years gone by. The performers and patrons sing a final song together, and then Their Majesties urge the patrons to follow them to the front gate. As the season goes on, this admonition takes on greater meaning since it is quite dark by the time the festival closes, and the torches carried by the king's guards to illuminate the way to the front of the faire provide the safest way to traverse the grounds. Following the king's farewell, Brad Howard of the Pyrates Royale then calls for the sounding of the evening cannon. As Bakhtin writes, "The end of festive freedom is clearly heralded by the ringing of the morning church bells; while earlier in the play the bells of the marching harlequins begin to tinkle as soon as the monk has made his exit."[35] As with the cannon that opened the festival, this one signals its closure. The booming sounds bookend the faire day.

Most of the over 250,000 patrons who grace the festival each year enjoy all that the sensescape has to offer. They eat, drink, and sing to their hearts' content without overstepping boundaries. They greet old friends and meet new ones. They enter in jeans and t-shirts and leave in brocade gowns. Their first drink of the day is from a plastic cup; their last comes from a pewter mug. As they walk through the line of torch holders into the darkness, they seek their carriages to go home, and in the field in which their cars are parked, they suddenly find themselves facing the twenty-first century again as they search for both cars and keys. Right behind them, however, and, in many cases, inside of them, remain the sights, sounds, smells, tastes, and touches that form the sensescape of Revel Grove. As museum scholar Barbara Kirshenblatt-Gimblett writes of Plimoth Plantation, "The Pilgrim village is a homunculus of history, fashioned not from clay, but from the living tissue of twentieth-century actors. More than an embodiment of history, the village is an imaginary space into which the visitor enters. Gone is the fourth wall. Immersed in a total environment, the visitor negotiates a path through the site, both physically and conceptually."[36] Barbara Kirshenblatt-Gimblett's "imaginary space" is the intrastice that exists in the sensescape, the total environment of Revel Grove.

Furthermore, the people who are acting in the village — the members of the cast, the street acts, and the stage acts who engage in a first-person style of interpretation through interactive improvisation — help to bring all of those senses to the forefront. There is a great deal to be learned from the details of the period which the living historians described in the next chapter portray. As museum scholar Kirshenblatt-Gimblett writes, "Forfeiting third-person omniscience for the partiality of the first person seems a small price to pay, for what is lost in historical comprehensiveness is gained in immediacy and detail, in the completeness and penetrability of a small virtual world. Immersed in an experiential situation, the visitor uses all her senses to plot her own path, at her own pace, through an imagined world."[37] Walking through the village of Revel Grove, visitors' experiences will be different depending upon the path they take, the activities in which they engage, and the performers with whom they interact.

If landscape is a "way of seeing," and soundscape is a "way of hearing," then the sensescape is a way of experiencing, for at the theatrical event that is MDRF, performances are not merely seen and heard, they are smelled, tasted, and touched. The visceral connection between performer and patron, between what is happening and what is being experienced, stems from the overall immersion into the sensescape, an environment that does not merely privilege sight and sound, but one rather that incorporates them with the other, lesser theorized and written about senses of taste, touch, and smell. The total impact involving all five senses generates greater opportunity for immersion into the intrastice at its deepest level.

4

Living History at the MDRF: Performing Embodied Knowledge

Standing at the top of the hill between the Chapel and the Dragon Inn at the Maryland Renaissance Festival and looking down to the right of the Jury Rig Stage, visitors see a small pavilion brimming with activity. A dozen or so people clad in bright yellow accented with black bustle about as they prepare the day's mid-day repast. From afar, the activity resembles busy bees as the colors swirl around, caught in an improvisational dance that has an end goal and steps necessary to reach it, but no completely choreographed pattern. The motion continues until two members of the gentry—their employers, Sir Thomas and Lady Kytson—approach, and the assembled bees drop as one in deep bows or curtsies in whatever spot they are currently occupying. One of the workers, a man clad in black with gold trim bows deeply and booms: "God save Sir Thomas." The others respond: "God save Sir Thomas." When the apparent leader of the bees then calls out, "God save Lady Kytson," the others repeat in kind. Only when given leave to rise by the man addressed as Sir Thomas do the yellow and black clad performers return to their previous positions.

This group, known as St. George, or the Household of Hengrave Hall, is the part of the festival cast specifically tasked with performing living history. In this chapter, I examine in detail these living historians, along with two other re-enactment companies, *Das TeufelsAlpdrücken Fähnlien* and The Free Lancers. These three groups are by no means the only portrayers of living history at the MDRF. Other displays include a working forge and a bow-making clinic. However, The Free Lancers, the Household of Hengrave Hall, and *Das TeufelsAlpdrücken Fähnlien* (The Devil's Nightmare Regiment) are larger groups performing at faire which represent three different types of living history. I have either been a member of, worked with, or rehearsed with each of these organizations, so I have an insider's understanding of their practices and philosophies. Two questions are paramount in this chapter: what types of intrasticiancy do living history performances facilitate?; and how does the pedagogical aspect of living history affect levels of intrasticiancy? By examining these three living history groups, I seek to explicate the relationship between intrasticiancy and the performance of living history.

Folklore and museum studies scholar Jay Anderson defines living history as "an attempt to simulate life in another time."[1] The word "simulate" in Anderson's definition is problematic with regard to theatre scholarship, calling to mind Jean Baudrilliard's work on the simulacrum. Baudrilliard writes that in its final state it "has no relation to any reality whatsoever; it is its own pure simulacrum."[2] Since the overlap of two realities (twenty-first-century America and sixteenth-century English historical record) help to create the intrastice at the MDRF, Baudrillard's description of the simulacrum is inappropriate. The dictionary definitions for simulate only contribute to the confusion. According to the *Encarta On-Line* Dictionary, to simulate means to: (1) "reproduce features of something: to reproduce an essential feature or features of something, for example, as an aid to study or training"; (2) "fake something: to feign something, or pretend to experience something"; and (3) "mimic somebody or something." I think the second definition of simulate, which describes the action as faking or feigning, and the third definition, which relegates simulate to fakery, are inappropriate for this work. The first definition is most apt for this study. Folklorist Rory Turner defines living history as "the broad label for the mimetic performance of past events in the contemporary world."[3] I think that Turner's construction of living history as a performance is an important addition to the definition. I also prefer his more specific temporal and experiential description "past events in the contemporary world" to Anderson's "life in another time." To Anderson's characterization, I substitute the first dictionary definition of simulate, which indicates the reproduction of an "essential feature" for the purposes of "study or training." I argue that for reasons of "study or training" is equivalent to educational or pedagogical purposes. By combining this more precise language with the components of both Anderson and Turner, I define living history as *a performative attempt, for pedagogical purposes, to reproduce the essential features of past events in the contemporary world*. While this definition is still imperfect, it is workable within the boundaries of the present study as all three units I focus on subscribe to this definition for their particular area of reenactment.

The MDRF provides a distinctive opportunity to examine living history because of its sensescape. Many living history and reenactment locations are site specific, including the well-studied Plimoth Plantation, Colonial

Williamsburg, and Gettysburg battlefield. In England, Kentwell is a site that features living historians enacting the Tudor era. The performers at each of these sites stage history in the physical locale in which the history actually occurred. The MDRF creates the intrasticial site physically far-removed from the actual location (Oxfordshire, England) upon which it is loosely based. Also, many historical sites have museum status, which thus confers upon them a level of expectation regarding accuracy and authenticity. As theatre and living history scholar Scott Magelssen writes, "The way museums make their presented history 'real,' however, is through their very authority as educational institutions."[4] The MDRF obviously does not have this advantage since it is not a pedagogical institution. The living history groups' authority and ability to make the information they present "real" must instead come from their capacity to perform tasks at a high level of competency, allowing spectators to confer confidence upon them. While each group at the MDRF employs similar methods of research and preparation, and all perform embodied knowledge, they utilize different presentational strategies.

The Company of St. George, the Household of Hengrave Hall

St. George's motto, "God is in the Details," reflects the definition I have synthesized for living history, equating the details of the St. George motto to the "essential features." Much like a quilt in which each individual square is a piece of artwork in and of itself but only when sewn together does the full design emerge, the small pieces of history the Household of Hengrave Hall impart have distinctive meaning, but when they are linked together they create a more complete view of the pattern of early-sixteenth-century life. When so many anachronisms abound (some within a proximity so close as to be seen or heard at the living history pavilion), there is a concerted effort amongst some performers to compensate for this by focusing upon the details. Magelssen denigrates the use of detail as a strategy of living history. He writes, "Indeed, for the tourist, the symbolic value accorded the minutiae on display at historic sites, preserved or re-created for public display, seem to be the very elements that guarantee *real* history, despite the fact that many of these details are often the most conjectural elements."[5] Magelssen calls the details, the essential features of the period, conjectural elements. However, primary source documentation containing details regarding cut and fabric used for clothing, embroidery patterns, and recipe ingredients are hardly conjectural. Perhaps it is not the details themselves with which Magelssen should take issue, but rather the manner in which certain historic sites employ them.

The members of the Household of Hengrave Hall use the details as the building blocks of their performances in accordance with the guidance of their directors, Larry and Paula Peterka. Combined, the Peterkas have a total of more than forty years experience working at Renaissance faires in Maryland, Virginia, and California. They have both worked at the festival originated by Phyllis Patterson and have played characters ranging from village militia to reigning monarch. However, neither of the Peterkas has an advanced degree in history. They are not members of the scholarly academy. They have not been published on the topic of Tudor history. Nonetheless, I posit that it would be academic arrogance and pedagogical elitism to discount their knowledge for these reasons. As performance studies and ethnography scholar Dwight Conquergood has written, participation that leads to knowing how and knowing who is an intimate, active, and, ultimately for those reasons, legitimate form of scholarship. The Peterkas have taken their interest in the Tudor era and transformed it to a form of study similar to that in the academy. They conduct research with primary documents in several languages and artwork from multiple countries. They read critical sources and evaluate them against their primary evidence. However, they then embody that knowledge by performing it, testing and re-testing whether it is feasible and viable knowledge, thereby creating a form of ethnohistorical research. My own participation in living history was also in this vein, in accordance with the pre-scripts Conquergood provided. I maintained a personal connection that stressed understanding the manner in which the Peterkas and the members of St. George researched and disseminated information and knowing who they were as people and performers. Rather than studying their work from above and from afar, I rehearsed and performed with the members of Hengrave Hall, having had a lengthy personal connection with this group which allowed me to understand their research and performance strategies well.[6] The Peterkas' passion for history drives St. George into an ever-evolving state as they continue a quest for more specific details to provide greater historically-driven educational performances.

The group has experienced a significant metamorphosis since its inception in 1998, when it operated not as the Household but as the separate guilds of St. George (court characters) and St. Genesius (village characters). The primary focus of these guilds was to increase the number of performers either attending upon the royalty or filling in the streets when the village actors were on stage. The guilds began to take on a living history focus because the Peterkas were chosen as directors. In 1999, the Guilds of St. George and St. Genesius became the Household of Hengrave Hall. According to MDRF Artistic Director Carolyn Spedden, "I suggested a manor house from top down, and she [Paula Peterka] did the research. I thought it would make sense if the focus wasn't just supernumerary, but a little more focused on living history."[7] The Peterkas chose to portray Sir Thomas Kytson and

Margaret Donnington (Lady Kytson), the owners of Hengrave Hall, a grand manor home in Suffolk, which is extant and recently sold its archive of documents dating back to the sixteenth century to Cambridge University. In 2000, the Guild of St. Genesius became an actor-training program separate from St. George. Spedden's letter to returning actors explained St. George's concentration: "The Guild of St. George will focus on living history, daily life activities at the festival.... Members of the Guild will still be a part of the Household of Hengrave Hall. But the focus of the guild is history."[8] With smaller numbers and a physical location designated for their use, the Peterkas and the members of St. George began to focus even more heavily on daily life activities where they could perform certain essential features of sixteenth-century England.

Paula Peterka illuminated the purpose of St. George in a 2002 e-mail sent to the group's listserve:

> One thing I can definitely say that we are not is a LARP (Live-Action Role-Playing Game), in its most common context, even though we are live action, and we are certainly playing roles, because not everyone we come in contact with is playing roles, and we are not doing this solely for our own enjoyment (although it is enjoyable). We do this to educate and entertain the public, who pay us to do so. I firmly believe in both aspects, education and entertainment, and to put a finer point on it, education through entertainment. History is not dull boring dry stuff, the way it's taught in most schools. It's colorful, vibrant, interesting, gritty; the stuff soap opera writers only dream of putting in their scripts but can't because no one would believe it. It is the story of all of us.[9]

Peterka emphasized the importance of the pedagogy that St. George provides for the visitors to the MDRF. She was also careful to explain that it is possible to provide that information because they are doing so in an entertainment venue. This concept of "education through entertainment" is critical to understanding the nature of living history at the MDRF. Entertainment is everywhere throughout the twenty-five acre site, but only in specific places is pedagogy the *raison d'être*. Peterka continues in the same e-mail:

> I can entertain an audience by stepping outside the historical context of the festival. I can sing 18th Century Sea Shanties instead of 16th century drinking songs; I can put on a silly wig and a bad French accent and prance around insulting people instead of putting on a silly period mask and dancing around as a Commedia dell'arte character; I can do a show with no accent at all and talk about modern cultural differences for laughs instead of doing a show in the right accent and talking about period cultural and social differences as expressed through dress (and undress) for laughs. The question is why would I, and who am I serving by doing so?[10]

As Peterka points out, anachronisms abound at the MDRF. The Household of Hengrave Hall — as well as *Das Teufels Alpdrücken Fähnlien* and The Free

Lancers — attempt to perform aspects of the time period with as few anachronisms as possible. In the case of St. George, Peterka points out that the group endeavors to complete its pedagogical mission by using information on sixteenth-century music, accent, and clothing.

The MDRF's equivalent of a playbill lists the Household of Hengrave Hall as a Living History entertainment and the location as The Living History Pavilion. The workers at Customer Service as well as actors direct patrons to the Pavilion and the members of St. George if the visitors express an interest in learning more about the time period, the history, or particular areas in which the Hengravians have expertise. Patrons search out the members of St. George to ask them pertinent questions precisely because the festival — and now the spectators — have framed Hengrave Hall as a repository of historical knowledge. Thus, since the patron has already established that the purpose of the encounter with the members of St. George is pedagogical, a particular frame has been created.

The cast of St. George uses fewer anachronisms, pays greater attention to historical detail, and undertakes research using primary documents from libraries including Johns Hopkins University, UCLA, and the Folger Shakespeare. The standards of costuming, properties, and dialect are different for the Hengravians than for the Company of the Rose, the members of the cast who act as village and court characters on stage and in the streets of Revel Grove. For example, all costume pieces must be approved by either Paula Peterka or Laura Kilbane, the assistant director of St. George, who has an M.A. in Tudor History from the University of Maryland. According to Paula Peterka there are specific requirements for the costumes any of the members of Hengrave Hall might wear. For example, Peterka described the fabric and style of the clothing worn by the members of St. George:

> The women of lower station are required to wear, in addition to the plain white linen chemise, two skirts and an overbodice with either integral support built in or a supporting underbodice. They must have a white linen cap to cover their hair and a hat or hood to be worn over. They must also have sleeves to be pinned on as needed or not needed. They may not show their shoulders. They may not show their hair [field notes].

These choices are different from the Company of the Rose in several ways. First, fabric worn by those in the general acting company is often made of polyester and nylon, anachronistic products which are less expensive to purchase. Furthermore, women in the acting company portraying characters of questionable reputation may wear their hair down without covering, while women of lower station in the Company of the Rose frequently wear their chemises off their shoulders. If either group sees Peterka's Lady Kytson character heading toward them it is not uncommon for them to quickly cover themselves — hair or shoulders — knowing that she will question their morals for improperly displaying parts of themselves before God, King, and whomever else may be watching (field notes).

Considering properties, the standards are similar. Peterka explains a simple difference between St. George and Rose:

> We allow fans for the women in the household to carry. I do not allow folding fans because folding fans [which Rose members frequently carry] did not appear in England until late in Elizabeth's reign, and we are in the middle of Henry's. Women of lower station may use woven fans. Upper class women have to carry either flag fans or feather fans, the kind you see in the portraiture [field notes].

In addition to the differences between the properties allowed for the actors and the living history performers, St. George also displays properties in a far greater volume. The group is very props intensive, according to Peterka. Because the Hengravians have a specific space in which to work and do not move throughout the festival grounds like the members of the Company of the Rose, there is a place for all of the properties which include drop spindles and wool, butter churns, wood carving supplies, cooking utensils and food, and herbs and soap-making ingredients. Why are properties and costumes so important to the creation of the living history mission? According to Rory Turner,

> The items are tangible objects that embody the world of the past. They are the props that re-create the past as a lived context, a creation central to the reenactment experience. Tactile, sensual, aesthetic, the material culture of reenacting persuades the experiencing body of the reenactor that he can participate in the Civil War world.[11]

These same physical elements of clothing against the skin and properties with which the living history performers at the MDRF work operate in a similar manner, invoking an embodied experience of a past none of the participants ever actually lived. Yet, through the tactile experiences, the members of St. George gain an insight into the world of sixteenth-century England that does not exist if one merely pretends to use an item rather than actually employing it.

A major difference between the conventional theatre performances and living history presentations exists in this concept of "doing." While an actor on a stage may pretend to spin wool, embroider a shirt, or prepare a medicine, the performers from the Household of Hengrave Hall actually create spun wool, embroidered clothing, and efficacious potions. Peterka explains the importance of the properties to the members of St. George, many of whom have no formal actor training:

> We are prop intensive because the people we have in our group are not actors per se; a lot of them would have trouble approaching someone and just striking

up a conversation. By having the props, people come to our space and ask questions, and we don't have to start the conversations. It makes the interactions much more effective. I really want every patron who walks through my area to come away having learned something or at least to have a better appreciation for what life was like in the sixteenth century [field notes].

Therefore, unlike re-enactors who are performing for themselves, the members of St. George are also charged with educating the patrons. According to Peterka, "People like stuff; people are in love with the material culture of a previous culture. 'What is that?' 'What's it for?' 'Can I see?' 'Can I try?'" (field notes). For those who seek out the members of Hengrave Hall it is almost a mantra.

The spectators are there to learn, to gain knowledge that the living history performers exhibit through their use of the items representing the material culture of the sixteenth century. As Stephen Eddy Snow writes of Plimoth Plantation, "For the truly interested, workshops are sometimes given in the village on how to cook over an open hearth or how to rive a piece of oak. A few individuals are enthusiastic enough to study the historical texts and re-create tools, weapons, or clothing on their own."[12] At the living history pavilion the workshops also disseminate knowledge, with specific shows on period cooking, defense, and daily diversions in addition to the activities which are constantly taking place. The frame of the encounter for the visitors is thus pre-established with the patron as seeker of knowledge and the performer as supplier of information. During the 2004 season, one of the living history shows, *Dress for Excess*, moved to the Market Stage. The switch to the larger venue allowed greater numbers of patrons to witness the performance, which has continued to grow in popularity since its inception as *Dress the Duchess* in 2001. Paula Peterka explains, *Dress for Excess* demonstrates how to "get that fashionable Tudor shape — a cone on top of a cone" (field notes). Because the Peterkas cannot dress themselves in the Tudor-style clothing, the show also demonstrates the hierarchy of early sixteenth-century England.

Embodiment for the Hengravians does not end with the outer physical accoutrements, however. Peterka also attempts to guide the members of St. George in slightly different pattern of accent than the Company of the Rose. Handouts given to the general acting company describe the basic accents used by performers. In the Company of the Rose, the members of the Royal Court and nobles use Received Pronunciation (RP), while the peasants use Cockney. Even though the directors at the MDRF know that the accents they use do not sound at all like sixteenth-century speech, they make a theatrical choice based upon spectator perception. According to handouts and language classes during the rehearsal process, "since most people think of the British in terms of those two distinct accents, that is what we will concentrate on" (field notes).

Peterka, on the other hand, works with the Hengrave Hall people on a broader, more flat sound. She explained the speech pattern in the following manner:

> It's an accent and a way of speaking based on English before the Great Vowel Shift or during the early parts of the Great Vowel Shift. We have some indication that what we are doing is somewhat accurate. We know it's more accurate than Cockney because we know when and where Cockney developed. It's a broader and flatter type of pronunciation, further back in the throat in some ways. All the Rs are hard, there are no dropped Hs. It sounds to some people like it has traces of the Irish or Scottish accent, some of the brogue, but if you listen carefully it bears more resemblance to some of the dialects spoken in the Appalachian and Ozark areas of the United States where people lived for generations in a fair amount of isolation [field notes].

The members of St. George are applying recent scholarship on the Great Vowel Shift (GVS), including work by Melinda J. Menzer at Furman University, and attempting performance based upon the theoretical writings.[13] Peterka admits that the performers succeed to varying degrees. Nonetheless, the undertaking is another component of the embodiment of historical research that marks the living history performance. It also provides the opportunity to test knowledge. Kilbane, who has Bachelors of Arts degrees in History, Anthropology, and French from the University of Wisconsin-Madison, acknowledges that portraying characters at the festival has been a unique prospect for her. "The most important aspect for me has been how my knowledge of the period has increased so vastly. It is not just a matter of names and dates and battles fought anymore. I now have a sense of the look of the period, of its people and their lives, that I think I would never have been able to acquire any other way" (field notes). In essence, Kilbane is positing that through living history re-enactment, the members of the Company of St. George are able to test their knowledge of the sixteenth-century record. She is not privileging performing at the festival over historical research. Rather, much as with St. George's attempts at the pre–GVS language Menzer is studying, she is using both the archive and the repertoire, an approach advanced by performance studies scholar Diana Taylor.[14]

When questioned why it was so important to focus as much as possible on the details that are known about the sixteenth century, given the constraints of the twenty-first, Paula Peterka is quick to explain that the desire to tell the truth, as much as it is known, comes largely from a belief that the history itself is more interesting than any fictional account. She explains, and I quote here in length because I believe this is a strong explanation of how popular culture utilizes historical elaboration far more than living history:

> You can see this in popular culture. *The Other Boleyn Girl, The Tudors, Elizabeth, Elizabeth: The Golden Age*. They all could have been marvelous movies

with fascinating stories that were historically accurate because the real history is fascinating and dramatic and stuff good writers dream about being able to write. Because a director didn't think a story was exciting enough or they didn't want to confuse they audience, they had the writers hack the history all to pieces.

Take *The Tudors*, I was really excited about *The Tudors*. I was really looking forward to it. Henry VIII had a sister named Mary and a sister named Margaret. He also had a daughter named Mary. The five most common names in Tudor England for women are Mary, Katherine, Anne, Margaret, and Jane. They're all saints. The director/producer/writer, whoever was in charge, decided that to have a sister named Mary and a daughter named Mary would be just too confusing to the audience, so they say Henry only has one sister and her name is Margaret, and instead of having her marry the king of Scotland the way Margaret actually did, or instead of having her marry the king of France which princess Mary actually did, in the show, she marries the king of Portugal and then kills him. Absolutely ludicrous. Especially when the real story is ever so much more interesting.

Margaret's husband James gets killed at the battle of Flodden by troops sent to the North by Henry's wife, Katherine. Then there's the part where Princess Mary marries the really, really old King of France, who dies after a couple of months because he can't keep up with his young wife, and then, while she's locked in a tower in France until they can determine whether or not she's pregnant, the heir apparent, Francois, has to be knocked up side the head by his mother, Louise of Savoy, to keep him from going to Mary and trying to seduce her, and thus potentially cutting himself out of the succession in favor of his own bastard. I mean, that's drama and comedy right there. You couldn't make this up, and you shouldn't have to, and you shouldn't try [field notes].

Peterka explains here how the living history has dramatic tension equal to or greater than the historical elaboration portrayed in *The Tudors*. I believe it is insulting for producers, writers, or directors to even imply that an audience would be so confused by a sister named Mary and a daughter named Mary. Furthermore, as Peterka illustrates, the living history — the historical truth as we know it through the details — is just as interesting, if not more so, than the completely elaborated storyline. Using fact should not have to relegate something to The History Channel. Mainstream television, film, and theatre arts sources could benefit from it as well.

When the emphasis on details and corroborated research is taken into consideration along with abhorrence for anachronism and breaking character, the St. George members place themselves in a position of historical distinction. These performers are charged with the task of education by presenting living history, and their attempts to live that history often draw them deeply into the intrastice. Turner writes of similar occurrences with Civil War re-enactors and recounts experiencing the phenomenon himself:

The illusion of the Civil War frame can become so convincing that reenactors undergo what they call "time warps"— moments when the "as if" of reenacting becomes "this is." I experienced a "time warp" when I participated in the reenactment of Pickett's Charge. I marched abreast of more than a hundred men up the long green field in the hot June sun, the first row sent to the slaughter. It was hard to think clearly about anything in the tumult, until I lay dead and still on the ground and the lines pushed forward past me.[15]

St. George members have had experiences similar to what Turner explained, moments where they were so deeply immersed in the intrastice that they had entered the intrasticious state. During these times, the performer is not simply attempting to remain in character for the benefit of the spectator, he or she may not even realize that the other self exists. This experience is critical to understanding how the intrastice functions based upon the performer-patron dynamic.

One of the preeminent and least ambiguous examples of these types of moments occurred for one founding member of Hengrave Hall on the weekend following 11 September 2001. A patron approached Phil Wujek (in his character of Bartholomew Barwick, the household marshal for St. George) on Saturday, 15 September 2001. After establishing Barwick's position, the spectator continued to ask questions. As Wujek recalls:

> One patron inquired about my position in the Household. Explaining that I was a Household Marshal, in charge of security, keeping the household members safe from dangers, and that my men and I were charged with keeping not only intruders out, but keeping our belongings within the walls of Hengrave, I was asked the following question: "Are you good at protecting tall buildings?" Being the oldest naïve re-enactor around, I carefully explained that "Hengrave be but two stories tall in the main, and access to the chapel bell tower and the various lookout towers be limited, thus that aspect of my duties are fairly easily carried out." It was not until about ten minutes later that I realized she was alluding to the World Trade Towers in New York City [field notes].

In attempting to carry out Spedden's edict not to mention the events of the preceding week, and in immersing himself so deeply in his character's portrayal, Wujek had inadvertently entered into a slightly different space in the intrastice than had this patron. She was either willingly suspending disbelief or playing at belief by not mentioning the World Trade Center towers by name and asking about his position at the household, placing her into either the intrasticial or the intrasticive state. Wujek, in performing his character, had a moment where he failed to realize that she was invoking her twenty-first-century knowledge, and he was actively attempting to create a belief in his position at Hengrave Hall, more in the intrasticious state. According to Wujek, he was "in full costume, in character, in Revel Grove. I was completely 'in the zone!'" (field notes). This "zone" is equivalent to what Turner called the "time warp."

Wujek added that the woman looked confused as he continued explaining the guarding of Hengrave Hall. Since the patron and Wujek were experiencing different levels of intrasticiancy, I suggest that her difficulty existed as she tried to filter his answers from one frame (sixteenth-century England) to another (twenty-first-century America). The patron had also framed the encounter as a pedagogical experience, one in which she would gain information. Wujek's knowledge of essential features of the period — both of his position as a household marshal and of the layout of Hengrave Hall — combined with his embodiment of the character through costume and accent throughout the day allowed Wujek to enter the intrasticious state. The details are the mode by which the pedagogical information is exchanged. However, this very commitment to living history creates an important distinction.

A Landsknecht guard and a camp follower, who provides support for the guards, pose with two ladies from King Henry's court. Left to right, the author as Lady Elizabeth Ughtread; John Machate as an unnamed Landsknecht; Katherine "Dru" Robinson as Hildegarde, the German camp follower; and Lisa Ricciardi-Thompson as Margaret Wyatt, Lady Lee. Photograph by Carrie J. Cole.

Because the spectator was seeking information and had framed the encounter as a pedagogical one, she could not understand that Wujek was in a different state.

As patrons come seeking information from the members of St. George, they acknowledge their place in the intrastice as one that will rarely go beyond intrasticial. If the spectators were deeply immersed within the intrastice, they would already have the knowledge they are trying to obtain from the Hengravians. Once the spectators have garnered these particulars from the members of St. George, they may come back to participate intrasticiously, but during the exchange the very nature of the interaction precludes deeper immersion.

"Das Teufels Alpdrücken Fähnlien" (The Devil's Nightmare Regiment): The Landsknechts

If there was ever a question of how "real" the participants at the MDRF can seem to visitors, the Landsknechts, as they are fondly known, provide a perfect example. In 1994, ten years before I undertook my ethnography of the Maryland site, the festival was on its first round through the six wives of Henry VIII. That particular year featured the German princess, Anna of Cleves. Wandering about the village in preparation for her marriage to Henry, Anna — played by Paula Peterka — was accompanied by several German Landsknecht guards. That day, a very important and unusual visitor was in Revel Grove, a young princess of the American political scene, Chelsea Clinton. The daughter of then-president Bill Clinton spent the day touring the village with several of her Secret Service detail. According to Larry Peterka, the teenaged Chelsea began to approach the Princess of Cleves, but members of her Secret Service detail stopped her, refusing to allow Ms. Clinton to move toward Henry's newest bride-to-be. Apparently, as Paula Peterka terms it, "Her Secret Service detail didn't like the looks of my Secret Service detail" (field notes). In other words, Ms. Clinton's bodyguards would not allow her to approach the woman who was "playing" a princess because she was surrounded by men "portraying" German mercenaries holding halberds. I contend that when the Secret Service detail purposefully steered Ms. Clinton away from the intimidating guards, they had not entered into the intrastice; therefore, I can only draw the conclusion that they saw in the Landsknechts the real potential of a threat to their charge's safety. Perhaps they were only being overly cautious, but the security for Ms. Clinton saw something in the German guards that was historically alive enough to prevent her from approaching the unintimidating Princess Anna of Cleves.

While the women the Landsknecht men guard usually appear to pose

no physical threat, the female members of the Landsknechts are an entirely
different story. Historically, the German camp follower's position was one of
military support, sixteenth-century style. They provided water for their soldiers who walked in heavy armor, tended to their wounds when they were
injured, prepared food, sewed clothing, and provided diversions. At the festival, the camp followers perform many of the same duties. They carry large
jugs of water to provide hydration for the Landsknecht soldiers. They prepare food and sew, as well as play chess and cards in the German camp. They
often also offer support for the members of the Royal Court. When an eight-
plus hour performance day in ten-plus yards of velvet, silk, or brocade on an
autumn afternoon during which the temperature hovers near one hundred
degrees begins to take its toll on a performer, it is often one of the Landsknecht camp followers who is there to offer a steadying hand, a cool com-
press to the back of the neck or the wrists, or a refill of water.

Over the years, the Landsknecht soldiers and camp followers became
casually known among the performers as the unofficial security at the festival. As one actor stated, "the people in actual security are not there to protect the performers; they are there to protect the Smiths' [the festival owners]
property" (field notes). The security staff at the festival is not deployed in a
manner conducive to protecting the cast members. Finding a member of the
staff in his or her dark blue t-shirt marked with SECURITY across the back
is not as easy as finding a Landsknecht guarding the King and/or Queen,
walking in full armor, multi-colored parti hose, and carrying a large weapon,
often a halberd or *zwiehander*, a two-handed long sword. The unarmed members of security are also far less intimidating than the well-armored and well-
armed Landsknechts. Furthermore, to have actual members of the security
staff constantly hovering about the cast would serve as far too great a reminder
of the twenty-first century. Aesthetically, it is more pleasing to have the informal sixteenth-century form of protection for the King and Queen. Indeed,
that they merit guards with weapons is an illustration of their royal status.

The Landsknechts, who no longer perform as an entire group at the festival but rather as individually-hired guards only, exist separate and apart
from the MDRF, unlike St. George, which functions only during the faire
season. The members of the group participate in several other venues throughout the year, including a Winter Campaign and Marching Through Time at
Marietta Mansion in Greenbelt, Maryland and Military Through the Ages at
Jamestown, Virginia, where the troupe has won several awards. They use
many of the same research techniques as St. George, which is not surprising
since the Peterkas were the founders of the Landsknechts. Like the members
of Hengrave, the German guards and camp followers again embody the history they research, but, unlike St. George, they do not solicit patrons. The

Landsknecht guards surround and protect Queen-to-be Jane Seymour. From left to right, the author as Lady Ughtread; Katherine "Dru" Robinson as Hildegarde; John Machate as an unnamed Landsknecht; Ray Partenheimer as Hans Partenheimer. Photograph by Carrie J. Cole.

Landsknechts will engage with the patrons if the spectators approach them, but in portraying their characters' parts, they blend into the background. They become, like the Secret Service, part of the scenery until they are needed.

If there is a threat — real or perceived — to the royalty, the Landsknechts will do whatever they can to stop it. For example, performers who have no right to be close to the King and Queen may have planned to try to approach them for something as benign as "begging a boon," which is the MDRF manner of asking for a favor. However, if the cast members have not previously cleared the meeting with the King and Queen, the Landsknechts will step forward and keep the potentially offending parties from approaching the royals. If the actors resist, the Landsknechts have been known to physically remove them from the presence of the royal court (field notes). Thus, the Landsknechts actually guard the King and Queen, embodying the practice of their historical antecedents.

Sometimes, however, it is not the performers who are the potential dangers. When spectators approach, the German guards must work with greater care. While they can "manhandle" a performer, they certainly cannot do the same with a patron. While the Landsknechts may physically remove an actor from the presence of the Royal Court and place him or her in the stocks, that option does not exist with a spectator. When a threat from a member of the audience is perceived, how do the German guards react? According to Larry Peterka, "they will physically interpose themselves between the offending party and whoever they are guarding" (field notes). Often merely the placement of the German guard between the royal and the patron is enough to deter the visitor. Whenever Anne Boleyn is queen, there is always great potential for patron interference, Larry Peterka explained, and the 2004 season was no exception. He recalls:

> Some "gentles" [Peterka utilized the festival term in a sarcastic manner] decided that they were going to rescue the queen and basically told people they were going to do it. The guards interposed themselves between the patrons and the queen. People were trying to get to the queen and they had to be physically stopped from doing so. They had to be blocked. You never know if you hadn't stopped them or gotten in their way what they would have done. You don't know because you didn't let it happen [field notes].

In the role of Landsknecht guard, an essential element is to play the part so well—*to embody the historical information in such a manner*—that his mere presence is a deterrent to errant behavior.

Most of the time, that is an effective tool, and the Landsknechts use the embodied performance and German accent and language to assert their positions. There are, however, always exceptions. Paula Peterka recalled a particular incident which had escalated to a level where the potential hazard caused one of the camp followers to react:

> Janice [Partenheimer, who plays camp follower Maria] had to once show a guy that she was carrying bladed roundels to get him to back off. The guy was in Ray's face saying, "What would you do?" [Ray Partenheimer both plays Janet's Landsknecht husband Hans and is married to her in real life.] Janice had to show him that she was carrying weapons and told him he was her husband, and he finally backed down [field notes].

In this case, the patron was not participating in the intrastice, even though Janice and Ray were maintaining their characters during the encounter. Their embodiment was enough to eventually convince the visitor to leave, but his decision to do so was grounded in a twenty-first-century understanding of power rather than an appreciation of the history of the sixteenth-century. With the patrons who decided to "kidnap" Anne Boleyn in order to save her, they were not intending to engage the Landsknechts for the purpose of gaining knowledge. Rather, they unwittingly stumbled upon the German guards as they created their own storyline in an intrasticious state.[16] In this case, the Landsknechts fulfilled their part of the story but were not pedagogical.

The German guards do present living history information to those who seek it out. When I spoke with several about which types of knowledge patrons seek, the responses were often regarding the questions of disbelief that visitors would ask. These included:

> Did you really sleep here?
> Did you come all the way from Germany?
> Is it hot in there? (Referring to the Landsknecht's armor.)
> Is that a real sword? Can I stab somebody with it?
> Why do you have a pouch between your legs? [field notes].

One visitor even approached the German camp, and finding one of the Landsknechts asleep on the ground proceeded to kick him in the head. When he groaned, the response was simply: "I'm sorry. I didn't think you were real" (field notes). For the most part, these patrons were obviously unwilling to participate in even the suspension of disbelief and sought instead to gain knowledge while gazing into the intrastice rather than entering it.

Because the Landsknechts were simultaneously ubiquitous and scenographic, despite their deep embodiment of the historical pedagogy they sought to impart, they did not draw the audience into the intrastice with them. Even as the German guards functioned for the members of the cast playing the royalty and nobility much as the men and women upon whom they model their portrayals did nearly 500 years earlier, they remain alone in the intrasticive and intrasticious states, while the spectators usually engage from the reality of twenty-first-century America rather than any immersive state of Tudor Oxfordshire.

The Free Lancers

The members of the Living History troupes actually perform sixteenth-century tasks, rather than pretend to do so. Because these performers are actually completing the duties people would have undertaken nearly 500 years ago, they also assume the attendant risks those endeavors require. For St. George, risks are minimal and the interaction with the public is based largely upon an ability to impart knowledge through spoken word illustrated by tactile experience, while for the Landsknechts the dangers are based mostly upon patron behavior. Not so for The Free Lancers, a troupe of professional jousters who compete in many venues in North America. They impart embodied knowledge primarily without use of a verbal text, without a word being spoken, often communicating more than any scholarly article on jousting. Watching these (early) modern men of steel as they charge towards each other in unchoreographed, full combat tilts illustrates to the spectators the ferocity, courage, and chivalry of a time gone by with a greater alacrity than any dialogue could muster. Everyone surrounding the jousters — the Royal Court, the joust cheerleaders, and the audience — performs a verbal text, while the riders themselves remain silent upon the field of battle, while continuing to convey significant information through their performance of embodied knowledge.

I worked with The Free Lancers in several different ways during the 2004 season at MDRF and experienced firsthand a small measure of the preparation needed to perform their wordless jousting text. During the performance day, as my character Elizabeth Seymour (Lady Ughtread), I was in the reviewing stand during at least one of the four daily jousts, miming the jousting rules for the audience and cheering on the knights. During the week, in between performances, I would practice with The Free Lancers, a part of The Cimmerian Combatives Company, a nearly twenty-five-year-old organization whose mission is to "fulfill the need for trained stunt combatants for theater, film and television productions."[17] Out of this group of more than 600 grew The Free Lancers, "created to provide a full measure of professional theater to jousts at Renaissance Festivals and special events across the country."[18] The troupe has performed at the Maryland Renaissance Festival since the mid–1990s and has also appeared at the now-defunct Ontario Renaissance Festival, the Florida Renaissance Festival, and the Tennessee Renaissance Festival. Roy and Kate Cox, the directors of The Free Lancers, offered certain cast members the opportunity to rehearse with the troupe and earn a chance to perform during a festival day not as jousters but rather as competitors in the squire games which precede the lance passes. I eagerly accepted the offer, thinking this was an excellent way for me to experience co-performer/witnessing. Though I knew Roy and Kate Cox and several of the jousters by name, I had never spent any significant time with them, and thus the offer provided me an opportunity to test boundaries of the co-performer/witness methodology that I was not experiencing while rehearsing scripted and improvisational works with the acting cast.

The week before the festival opened, I began my training with The Free Lancers and initiated a far deeper understanding of my intrasticiancy theory, my co-performer/witness methodology, and my understanding of the importance of embodied knowledge when performing an unscripted text of stage combat. Ripper Moore, a jouster who played the Earl of Cumberland, began my initiation with the group by teaching me how to groom and tack one of the horses, Titan, a huge — even by jousting horse standards — blonde

Jousters in action at the Maryland Renaissance Festival. Photographs by Katherine G. Cox.

Roy Cox, co-founder of The Free Lancers, raises his mount up to the excitement of the crowd gathered at the jousting arena at the Maryland Renaissance Festival. Photograph by Katherine G. Cox.

Belgian. (Titan died suddenly and unexpectedly during the 2007 MDRF season.) I began to have a greater understanding of the meaning of "embodied knowledge" as I tried and failed at even the simplest of tasks. I had to remember which brush came first; I was often wrong. I was careful to comb the mane in the appropriate direction, after having combed it the wrong way several times. I scrubbed and combed and re-scrubbed and re-combed and re-re-scrubbed and re-re-combed Titan's belly. The Coxes and Moore had emphasized above all else that no dirt be left on the horse's underside. It was not until I actually began to tack the horse that I understood why this was so important. Dirt left on Titan's belly could easily become trapped beneath the saddle strap, causing the horse extreme pain. In retrospect it seems quite obvious, but it was not until I actually performed the tacking ritual — embodied the knowledge being shared with me — that I truly grasped the significance of properly cleaning the horse. As for the tacking ritual itself, I worked with The Free Lancers for nearly ten weeks. On the final week, I almost completely saddled my horse without aid. Almost.

Once I had finished tacking Titan on my first night, Kate Cox began by teaching me the most basic of elements: how to mount the horse and how to sit on the horse, especially once it began moving. She taught me these important skills without allowing me to climb aboard a horse. She verbally explained the maneuvers to me as she effortlessly modeled them as we stood on the ground next to Titan's stall. I then mimed the mount, inaccurately. She physically corrected my posture, and I tried again. It must have been fifteen minutes before I could correctly simulate mounting the horse. Then she began teaching me how to sit and move when I was riding. It was a significantly longer period of time with a considerably greater number of corrections before she determined that I was capable of trying the pantomime on Titan. That I managed to mount him without falling off or incurring constant correction was a direct result of the embodied knowledge I had practiced. I was already beginning to have a far greater understanding of the nuances of the jousting troupe, even though I had watched them perform for nearly a decade.

As I sat atop Titan that first time, I was filled with a sense of pride that lasted only until the horse began to move. As Kate Cox called out directions to me from the side of the jousting field, I suddenly began to move in time with the horse. "It's the motion of love, Tony," she would call. "You have to move that pelvis" (field notes). As I felt the horse moving beneath me, I incorporated the pantomimed education into the reality I was now experiencing to create an embodied knowledge. All of this work was necessary for me merely to be able to ride the horse with confidence, grace, and poise, which led to a new understanding of the importance of embodied knowledge. It was only after I had achieved the ability to ride without constantly correcting myself or being corrected that I understood what Kate Cox had been trying to teach me. The definition of embodied knowledge became for me *the ability to accurately perform an historical act repetitively without conscious thought of the processes the undertaking requires*. Only when that basic knowledge was embodied could I move on to learning the games, which included spearing a block of wood and riding at a ring with sword. When, on my first pass with the sword, I skewered a ring, it was only because the repetitive act of riding down the list at full speed (as well as the handling of a sword) had become embodied in me through practice of the historical knowledge of sixteenth-century England.

For the jousters, the lance passes require an even deeper embodied knowledge. The Free Lancers employ seven different styles of jousting, requiring different equipment, targets, and techniques. As their horses are charging at speeds near twenty-five miles per hour, there is little time to think; their performances are a result of years of practice that culminate in a level of embodied knowledge that makes it possible for them to simultaneously control the horse, the lance, and their bodies. These unchoreographed lance passes present very real consequences for the participating jousters, as evidenced by the Free Lancers 2004 T-shirt motto: "INJURIES IN JOUSTING ARE EXTREMELY RARE (Bumps, bruises, cuts, contusions, strains, sprains, and minor breaks do not count as injuries.)" These injuries are genuine and reminders of the reality of twenty-first century America that exists when the helms and armor are removed and the knights return to their given names. Yet they carry with them the historical record of the sixteenth-century experience that comes with embodied knowledge. Performance scholar Freddie Rokem informs an understanding of how living history performers can occupy a space deeply immersed within the intrastice between the historical knowledge of sixteenth-century England and the reality of twenty-first century America. According to Rokem,

> The energies of acting are the theatrical mode of telling the present-day spectators about these historical or revolutionary energies.... And the energies of acting are the aesthetic embodiment of the revolutionary energies, making it possible for the spectators to "read" the energies on the stage metaphorically, as a kind of displacement or transposition of that historical past.... By showing these energies on the stage, which are cultural constructions, just like class, race, or gender, the actor becomes a hyper-historian. In presenting or demonstrating the event, this hyper-historian becomes painfully "present" at the event itself, carry the mimetic force of the theatrical event as it is presented on the stage.[19]

The Free Lancers harness the energies of acting and become hyper-historians, and in doing so they enter the intrasticious state. This immersion into the intrastice is akin to Rokem's contention that the hyper-historian becomes "painfully 'present' at the event itself." It is only possible for the jousters to experience this state because the mixture of historical energies (sixteenth-century knowledge) and contemporary energies (twenty-first-century acting) combine to create the embodied knowledge they carry with them into the lists for each and every lance pass.

On a sweltering September afternoon the heat is nearly unbearable for the assembled audience members clad only in tank tops and shorts, slathered (if they are smart) in suntan lotion, and wearing sunglasses to shield their eyes from the harsh rays of the sun as they gaze toward the enclosed oval of sand known as The Joust Field. The lists have been prepared and squires hold brightly colored lances up at each end of the field. The armored knights enter the list wearing full plate weighing nearly 100 pounds, their faces completely concealed by their helmets and visors, a colored plume the only distinguishing characteristic for each. As the squires call out to the knights the information they need to proceed with the lance pass — "he has received his lance" and "he is coming about"— the words are echoed from the reviewing stand above as the King, Queen, and assembled nobles look on. When they are ready, or sometimes even after they have begun galloping down the list if the horses are frisky and ready to go, one of the nobles gives the verbal command: "Charge on!"

The knights hurtle down the narrow space between the ropes, passing left shoulder to left shoulder, lances in their right hands crossed over the horses' necks, as they prepare to strike each other upon the gridded grand guarde and buff each has donned in addition to his normal armor. Known as the *Realgestech* style, this is the fiercest fashion in which the knights joust. Audience members on either side of the field are led in cheer by performers, rising to a crescendo as the horses near each other. The nobles in the reviewing stand add their own exhortations of "Put him in the dirt!" and "Unhorse him, Sir!" In a solitary moment of climax, the lances of both jousters find their marks, as the knights strike each other with sound hits that cause both lances to shatter. The noise from the collision of wood against steel is sharp and piercing. One knight teeters precariously in his saddle, but hangs on, and both knights are awarded five points. The crowds on both sides cheer wildly, even as pieces of broken lance soar through the air. As the knights slow their horses toward the end of the list, they prepare to engage again in the same ritual for there are more lance passes still to come (field notes).

While the knights are engaging in their battle, the members of the Royal Court, standing on the reviewing platform above, wager on the outcome. In this action the difference crystallizes between the acting in the review stand and the living history performance on the sandy jousting field. The Marchioness of Exeter (played by Diane Wilshere) and Lady Ughtread (my character) have bet a shilling on the outcome of the next lance pass; who-ever's knight earns more points wins the wager. As the knights again charge toward one another, we loudly cheer for our respective favorite. As the jousters hit each other's buffs soundly, both knights recoil as their lances shatter, one below the pennant (three points) and one above (five points). There is a brief moment of uncertainty as to whether one or both knights will stay on their mounts, but in the end they right themselves and return to the end of the lists. For these knights and the men portraying them, Cox and Moore, the consequences of the lance pass are very real. Either one could have easily become unhorsed following the resounding hits, causing him to fall from the horse in full plate armor onto the hard ground below, possibly sustaining seri-ous injury. For the Marchioness and myself— who cheered, then gasped, then cheered again — there is no consequence. We were not actually placing a wager. The bet was an improvisational piece of theatre. As we chatter to each other about the lance pass, and I congratulate her on her chosen knight's victory, no money changes hands. I experience no real loss; indeed there was never any possibility that I would. For all our talk on the reviewing stand and the-atrical framing of the event for the audience, we risked nothing. On the con-trary, in their silence below, the jousters risked all.

The audience at the jousts rarely, if ever, enters the intrasticious state. They may simply watch, allowing the willing suspension of disbelief to cre-ate an atmosphere in which they watch the jousters as if they are viewing a play or a movie. The musical group Queen's "We Will Rock You" and "We Are the Champions" from the soundtrack of the immensely popular film, *A Knight's Tale*, may even be playing in their minds. The spectators may applaud at the appropriate times, but they have not gone beyond the intrasticial state. The patrons gain knowledge of a sixteenth-century chivalric re-enactment of what had been used as combat training prior to the Tudor era. This knowl-edge is initially transmitted through the spoken text of the nobles, who explain the jousting style, equipment, and scoring procedures. However, the visceral way of knowing comes when the sights and sounds of the lance passes trans-mit information through sensory perception on behalf of the audience mem-bers. Audience members applaud for successful hits and gasp if a knight teeters on his saddle. The initial outbreak of overwhelming applause that accompa-nies an unhorsing is often followed by an eerie silence as the audience waits to see if the knight will recover. Unlike a play which may cause similar reac-tions, these events are unplanned, and at that moment the audience knows that the knights are literally locked in combat.

Some patrons are even resistant to learning from the embodied knowl-edge that the jousters perform. Though many patrons indicate on comment cards that the joust is one of their favorite shows, few actually write detailed notes about it. One of the most interesting comment cards I examined during the 2004 season came from a patron who was not only unwilling to participate in the suspension of disbelief, he was unable to accept that at least the combative aspect of what he had seen was real. The comment card, from a 19 to 30-year-old male who was visiting the festival for the first time, read: "I believe the joust would be better with more of a true recreation of the original. (Real lances and armor)" (field notes). I pondered this statement for a long time. The patron did not leave contact information, so no one at the festival could follow up on his comment. The office staff discussed the comment at length, trying to establish what he meant since the jousters at the MDRF wear real armor and use real lances. I initially hypothesized that he had seen too many movies, played too many video games, or participated in some other aspects of popular culture which depict the knight's lance as a long *metal* weapon.

As time passed, however, another conclusion came into focus. On the surface it would seem that living history performances such as the joust would be most likely to place patrons into the intrasticious state, since the actors would avoid anachronisms while presenting in an embodied manner detailed information based upon research and practice. The jousters perform their tilts for honor and glory and employ their embodied knowledge of the chivalric code and its performance for both educational and entertainment purposes. The spectators watch a compelling piece of historical theatre in which they participate by clapping, cheering, and sometimes jeering, even as they are absorbing the information The Free Lancers impart. Despite the quality of the performance, the audience is rarely drawn into an intrasticious state in which a ritual transformation can occur. Embedded in the reception aspect of the pedagogical process, even though the jousters are performing embodied knowledge, is the awareness that the audience needs to garner the imparted information, thus illustrating the chasm between the reality of twenty-first century America and the historical knowledge of sixteenth-century England. The educational nature of the jousters, despite their verbal silence, is therefore so effective as a pedagogical tool that despite its entertainment value, it distances the audience rather than brings it closer to the knights. The spectator's frame of the joust as not real — reflected by the comment card referenced above and perhaps a reflection of modern exposure to film — prevents them from any real depth of immersion in the intrastice.

Conclusion

The way that patrons frame living history distinctively activates the level of intrasticiancy they can achieve. In the case of St. George and the Landsknechts, the patrons have framed the performers as historians, people from whom they can learn. Because of the very nature of this framing, a pedagogical wall exists, and the performers are highly unlikely to be able to guide the patrons into the intrastice, even though they themselves may be deeply immersed — as Wujek commented, "in the zone" — in participation in the intrastice. There may be times when the "time warp" or blur happens for the performers, but it does not happen for the patrons. On the other end of the spectrum, perhaps explained best by the commentary that the knights should try "real" jousting, when that is exactly what they do, the patrons frame the lance passes as nothing more than another entertainment, a diversion for their viewing pleasure. Though they may be learning about jousting, they do not realize it. Therefore, they do not have the pedagogical wall which keeps them from moving toward the intrasticive or intrasticious states. Rather, it is that they see the knights much as popular culture, perhaps even hearing in their heads the Queen music that so dominated the soundscape of *A Knight's Tale* that they do not rely on the information. It is more as if they are at a three dimensional movie. While people will often take as real what they see in movies and argue history based upon that information, when confronted with the real life equivalent of the screen presentation, it is easier to accept the theatrical convention of the "willing suspension of disbelief" over any attempt to become an active participant in its creation.

5

Historical Elaboration: A Royal Day in Revel Grove

History and Elaboration

"Court, we are away!" booms a resonant masculine voice. With that command, the sixteen members of the Royal Court and their attendant Landsknecht guards and camp followers make their entrance into the village of Revel Grove to begin yet another festival day. Nine women and seven men swirl through the village on a warm autumn morning, their colorful costumes of sky blue and tree bark brown, moss green and fallen leaf gold reflecting the natural surroundings in which they walk. At the head of the procession are the king and queen, Henry VIII and Anne Boleyn, portrayed by Fred Nelson and Mary Ann Jung. They, along with the rest of the court, greet the entering visitors to the village with shouts of "Well met!" and "God ye good den!" among others. Occasionally one of the patrons will respond with a "Well met!" of his or her own, and sometimes even with a more ingenious reply. Shouts of "God save the King" and "God bless the Queen" ring from courtiers and patrons alike. With a flourish the court interrupts a village dance, the King "surprising" the mayor and deputy. After a brief, perfunctory exchange, Queen Anne Boleyn calls for a dance to celebrate the opening of the Harvest Celebration.

Anne Boleyn, her raven hair flowing freely down her back in direct contrast to the prevailing style of the day that hid all hair behind the ears under flowing veils, moves lightly. Onlookers are unable to see her feet under the blood red gown she wears, so she looks to be dancing on air. She seems sprightly and unconcerned as the dance concludes, and she wishes all well for the day. The court then proceeds down the path toward a small shaded hollow. Under the cover of the trees — resplendent in their own autumnal

121

colors — the court members situate themselves in an arc at a crossroads of the village, where everyone who has entered the gates will pass by. The court assembles for a photo opportunity, and many of the passing patrons stop by — some with the encouragement of court members, some all on their own — for the privilege of taking the picture of, or having their pictures taken with, their royal majesties. Thus begins the day for the actors in Revel Grove who are portraying historical characters taken from the pages of Tudor life.

Continuing to examine the multiple states of intrasticiancy present in a carnivalesque setting, this chapter focuses upon the performances of the storylines at the 2004 MDRF, which the festival billed on the front of the program as "The Year of the 3 Queens." The year portrayed was 1536, a time in English history when three different women lay claim to the crown of England, the title of queen, and the love of Henry VIII. As Marvin Carlson writes, "Among all literary forms it is the drama preeminently that has always been centrally concerned not simply with the telling of stories but with the retelling of stories already known to its public. This process naturally involves but goes far beyond the recycling of references, tropes, even structural elements and patterns that intertextuality considers."[1] The MDRF attempted to do exactly as Carlson proposes by elaborating upon the general common knowledge of Henry VIII's story. Condensing the stories of three queens into one nine-hour day certainly requires willing suspension of disbelief, but perhaps much less than one would presume. All of the events portrayed in the festival's storyline for the queens actually took place within five months. By the time certain areas of England received the news of the demise of Henry's first wife, another wife had fallen from grace. By the end of the festival day, one who had laid claim to the throne has died of a broken heart, another has been beheaded for treason, and a third has become betrothed to Henry VIII. Despite their different fates, the stories of all three of these women, and the courtiers in their respective camps, facilitated different states of intrasticiancy among the patrons at the festival.

Several questions are paramount to analyzing the difference states of intrasticiancy. First, do the stage shows tend toward intrasticial because they are scripted, more theatrical in nature, and separated from the audience by the boundary of stage versus house? Do the street scenes tend to be intrasticive because of their improvisational, conversational, and intimate qualities? Can an audience member take an actor's intrasticial or an intrasticive performance and, through his or her own needs, transform it into an intrasticious act? In this chapter, through examination of the various stage and street performances of the royal court and their reception by members of the audience, I hope to answer these questions and thus illustrate the differences in the three states of intrasticiancy, while simultaneously demonstrating how the actors participate in all of them depending upon the way the patron frames the interaction.

The performers' dramatizations of historical characters — and in some cases events — constitute what I have termed historical elaboration. This is *the process by which a theatrical practitioner takes previously accepted notions of truth and individually extrapolates from them an extended reality through the playwright's, director's or actor's depiction and/or portrayal of (a) non-fictional character(s) in an interactive performance venue.* The playwright creates a scripted form of historical drama based upon the broadened truth, but always with the knowledge that the interactive nature of the venue can cause changes to the written text at any time. The director and, most often, the actors expand upon reality through their improvisational choices.

The historical elaboration performances are first-person interpretation with an additional theatrical flair. Stephen Eddy Snow has chronicled the denigration of first-person interpretation in his work on Plimoth Plantation, so I will not reiterate it here. However, there are advantages to this type of work, as Snow writes: "The first person role-playing performance at Plimoth ... need not be looked upon as a sham, a fake, a fraud. It can just as well be viewed as a game, a play of illusion, an artistic means of presenting bona fide historical facts."[2] This acting both illuminates and elaborates upon historical information. Actors at the MDRF may choose to present an improvisation with another actor-character. These solo performances or small improvisational playlets — called "bits" by the members of MDRF — are truly at the heart of historical elaboration. These are similar to what Snow describes as an Improvised Scene at Plimoth Plantation. "'The Improvised Scene' may erupt anywhere. The spectators spontaneously gather to watch it."[3] During these scenes or bits the patrons often realize the opportunity to interact with the performers, to greater and lesser degrees.

While these bits often impart historical knowledge, sometimes they are improvisations designed to draw the patrons into the general "world" of Revel Grove. These bits are also a type of historical elaboration, though they rely heavily upon the character's rank and reason for being in Revel Grove more so than any particular historical event. For example, whenever Jane Parker (Lady Rochford) and George Boleyn, her husband and the queen's brother, would meet in the street, sparks were sure to fly as they snapped at each other about their loveless marriage (field notes). Nonetheless, these improvised scenes still belong under this category that differs from living history because historical elaboration neither attempts to portray a particular skill set nor takes on the attendant risks of living history. Rather, in historical elaboration actors place the emphasis on endeavoring to inform through a more encompassing approach to history. Historical elaboration provides an overarching view of the period being portrayed, as opposed to living history (which I examined in the previous chapter), which imparts a detailed depiction of a specific skill, craft, or art.

The Photo Opportunity

The photo opportunity in the morning is one of the few times during the day that all the members of the court will be in the same place at the same time standing (relatively) still. The setting is a shaded glade close enough to hear the strains of the pipe organ floating across the grounds and smell various delectable scents wafting from the nearby food vendors. Before the courtiers line up, each set of two approaches their majesties — at this time of the day King Henry VIII and Queen Anne Boleyn — and offers deference in the form of a bow or curtsy. Immediately audience members are aware that they have entered a frame of intrasticiancy as the contrast between the twenty-first century and the sixteenth century is palpable. In the twenty-first century ideal — if certainly not reality — of equality, the bowing and scraping that courtiers do to offer deference is anathema. Randy Dalmas, who portrayed Anne Boleyn's uncle, the Duke of Norfolk, explains: "I show the King proper deference, and expect it out of others, including patrons to some degree. And most do show the King and Queen respect, and to many people, these characters are the closest thing to royalty they will ever see, so some get quite a thrill out of meeting them" (field notes). These patrons are working with the intrasticive frame as they have begun to play at believing and may have an actual visceral reaction to meeting "royalty."

As patrons greet their majesties, they are often passed down the line to meet all the courtiers, who are now usually arranged by level of stately prominence, courtly importance, and/or noble rank. Courtiers are arrayed most often by birthright, representing a society in which social mobility was just beginning to become possible. The visitors to the village are often endowed by the courtier presenting them to the village as Lady and/or Sir So-and-so. As theatre anthropologist Victor Turner wrote,

> I have argued that initiatory passage rites tend to "put people down" while some seasonal rites tend to "set people up," i.e., initiations humble people before permanently elevating them, while some seasonal rites (whose residues are carnivals and festivals) elevate those of low status transiently before returning them to their permanent humbleness.[4]

While they are in the village, performers endow patrons with title and privilege, including Lady, Sir, Lord, Master, and Mistress. Nonetheless, these patrons have a quick lesson both in Tudor politics and ethnographic performance as the court members teach them how to properly show their own reverence to their majesties in the form of the bow (for males) and curtsy (for females).

Many patrons are willing to play along with the actors when they instruct them in these activities because the visitors have decided to immerse themselves more deeply within the intrastice. Snow writes of Plimoth Plantation, "most of the audience is willing to suspend disbelief and accept the symbolic time — 1627 — even though their digital wristwatches measure the minutes of their participation in the performance."[5] However, at the MDRF, in the year 1536, many participate in more than the suspension of disbelief, which requires only the thought process. When the patrons begin to actually bow and curtsy, rather than merely observe others doing so, they are playing at belief and entering the intrasticive state. Some performers are adept at facilitating the transition between immersive states and believe it is part of their job to do so. Lisa Ricciardi-Thompson, who portrayed Margaret Wyatt (Lady Lee) at the 2004 MDRF, stated:

> There are some that have no idea what they've walked into. They expect Busch Gardens or some similar venue where any characters they may encounter have five foot heads and clown shoes. I think these are the people we want to encourage to play, to expose them to something new and different from their usual entertainment. I find these people are the most fun to play with [field notes].

It is the actor's responsibility to move the patrons from intrasticial to intrasticive, from the willing suspension of disbelief to playing at belief.

These bows and curtsies are marked as period conventions. Men do not simply bow at the waist and women do not grab their skirts and make a quick up-and-down motion. Rather, the men take one step back on a bent leg, remove the caps from their heads (or pantomime doing so if they are not wearing caps), and sweep the (imaginary) hat in front of their outturned calf. The courtier instructing the men in how to make this bow will often also give additional tidbits of information. "Ladies love to look at our calves; thou shouldst make a good show of it," or "Thou shouldst keep the inside of thine hat to thyself; their Majesties hath no desire to see thine vermin." The women are likewise instructed that "grabbing one's skirt is gauche" and "remember to keep thine back perfectly straight; His/Her Majesty doth expect thine good posture" (field notes). These imitations of sixteenth-century manners and the accompanying pithy remarks are another example of historical elaboration.

The montage of courtiers at this morning gathering, during which patrons are actively encouraged to meet their Majesties, presents one of the most curious of temporal-spatial intrastices. For not only are the visitors allowed to meet the court, many of them also want to either take pictures of their Majesties or have their pictures taken with them, hence the cast-coined name for this event as "the photo-op." As Snow writes, "Yet the interpreters must keep up their 'front.' What are actor/historians to do, for instance, when a twelve-year-old boy presents them with a Polaroid snapshot he has just taken? The performers must learn to maintain a kind of split consciousness akin to Brecht's *Verfremdungseffekt*."[6] For the actors at the MDRF, this split consciousness occurs within the intrastice as the performer maintains an awareness of both the reality of twenty-first century America and the historical knowledge of sixteenth-century England while simultaneously immersing himself or herself within the pretext of Tudor Oxfordshire in a manner that is convincing enough to sway the patrons to their own entrance into a state of intrasticiancy. This duality is at the crux of why I consider the festival to be an environment exemplary of several different immersive states within the intrastice. People are not truly time traveling. Neither performer nor patron really exists in the sixteenth century. The twenty-first century is always present. However, maintaining the illusion — whether through the willing suspension of disbelief, playing at belief, or active creation of belief — places actor and visitor alike into the intrastice that is both here and there, both now and then, in the pretext of Tudor Oxfordshire. For the MDRF actor it is even more difficult to walk the line between the contemporary moment and the historical past when the patron asks the *performer* to *take* the picture. Sometimes members of the cast will ignore the entrance of the twenty-first century implement into the sixteenth-century world they are trying to create. However, just as often one will make a comment upon the camera: "Zwounds. Indeed must be one of those Flemish painters. I do hear they createst the tiniest pictures thou didst e'er see" (field notes). In this case the performer has taken historical knowledge of the Flemish talent for miniature portraits and elaborated upon it to mask the twenty-first-century intrusion of the camera. Other cast members attribute the camera to "that wonderful Italian inventor, da Vinci" (field notes). In either case, they are using their knowledge of the history of the period and elaborating upon it.

Likewise, when receiving photographs that patrons have taken, cast members will almost certainly refer to them not as pictures, but as paintings. For example, Anne Boleyn told a visitor who gave her a picture, "A lovely *portrait* indeed M'Lord. Thou didst capture Our likenesses full well. Thou art truly a fine painter" (field notes). Thus, the actor maintains character while not offending the patron. Indeed, the performer in this case drew the patron closer to the intrasticive state by conveying a title upon him (M'Lord), endowing him with an occupation (painter), and praising him for his skill at his craft (truly a fine painter). The choice was then up to the patron to decide whether to withdraw to the intrasticial state of willing suspension of disbelief with a hurried "thank you" and a quick exit, or to continue to play in the intrasticive by further engaging in conversation with the cast member. This particular patron spoke with the queen at length, thus placing him in the intrasticive state.

This choice of how to situate the activity is what Erving Goffman terms "keying the frame." A frame already exists in which the patron and the performer are engaged in an interaction, in this case the exchange of a photograph/portrait. The patron now can rekey the frame, thereby creating an event for which, in Goffman's words, "a systematic transformation is involved across materials already meaningful in accordance with a schema of interpretation."[7] Within the exchange of the photograph, Goffman's "already meaningful" materials, if the patron takes the opportunity and uses it to create a character — the M'Lord Painter bestowed upon him — then he is rekeying the frame. According to Goffman, "Participants in the activity are meant to know and to openly acknowledge that a systematic alteration is involved, one that will radically reconstitute what it is for them that is going on."[8] The actual activity does not change: a photo was exchanged. However, in the first frame, the patron participant was merely handing an actor a photo. If the patron rekeys the frame, instead he is now handing the courtier a portrait, and has thus transitioned from the intrasticial state to the intrasticive.

Sometimes patrons approach the courtiers at the photo-op already having made up their minds to play in the intrasticive state. One couple, patrons dressed in appropriate Tudor courtly attire, approached the King and Queen and offered their reverence. The woman then presented each of their Majesties with significant gifts. She had also prepared sachets for each of the ladies in the court, small golden bags with sweet smelling spices in them, tied at the top by a golden ribbon. She greeted each courtier by name and bowed to each of us as she welcomed us to Revel Grove and wished us all an enjoyable day. When a courtier would respond to her, she answered in kind, with a strong effort at period language. She was obviously there not just to witness playing, but rather to play too. (See Chapter 6 for more on the patron playing this character, whom she called the Queen of France.)

Amidst the pastoral setting, red, amber, and olive-colored leaves shaded the courtiers, attired in similar colors, from the hot autumn sun. A variety of visitors pass through the shaded hollow, some like the Sachet Lady dressed in courtly garb, some clad as peasants, others in jeans and t-shirts. The intrusion of the distinct modern concept of time comes swiftly as the show's stage manager, Jen Silber, motions to their Majesties that it is time to proceed to the first formal stage show of the day. With a hearty, "Alas our time here does grow short and our duties call us away" from the king, the cast members hurriedly depart — two by two, males to the left of the females whom they escort — toward the nearby Market Stage for the official courtly welcome, *The Royal Arrival.*

In this scene from *The Royal Arrival*, Queen Anne Boleyn (Mary Ann Jung at the far left) attempts to keep up a happy demeanor as Henry VIII (Fred Nelson at center) speaks; Mistress Jane Seymour (Brittney Sweeney, second from right) pays close attention to His Majesty while her sister, Lady Elizabeth Ughtread (played by the author) laughs in merriment at His Majesty's words. Photograph by Carrie J. Cole.

"The Royal Arrival"

A loud fanfare announces the entrance of the royal court for the first storyline play of the day. This scripted and staged work is akin to what Snow has termed "The Planned Scene" at Plimoth Plantation. "The last principal method of organizing time and space in this living history performance is 'the planned scene.' In this type, the visitors sit or stand just as if they were at a play. They are, in these instances, truly 'spectators': 'ones who look or watch.'"⁹ In Revel Grove, these Planned Scenes can be performed on a number of actual stages, all of which have seating available for the audience. At the MDRF these scenes are formally called in-house stage shows, and the cast most often refers to them as simply stage shows. In 2004, the in-house stage shows were specifically focused upon the Royal Court storyline of the three queens.

The Royal Arrival was produced on the Market Stage in 2004. Usually the court enters through the front gate and has the formal entry as part of the opening gate ceremony with the villagers, so it was unusual to have a full script and proper stage for the arrival. The courtiers, walking in pairs, stride under a set of green, yellow-gold, and white banners (Henry's livery colors) held aloft in the breeze by members of the Household of Hengrave Hall, the living history component of the festival. The court is greeted by Sir Thomas and Lady Kytson, master and mistress of Hengrave Hall, who are considered the ranking nobility in Revel Grove. No sooner have the courtiers assembled and been greeted than the fighting between their majesties begins. The script for the show, written by the festival's artistic director, Carolyn Spedden, illustrates the growing tension between the current monarchs, Henry VIII and Anne Boleyn. As the day's events are read aloud, the king, who has been flirting with Jane Seymour throughout, responds to a request to attend a "sheep shearing contest" with, "Send the queen. Lord knows she's been fleecing me for years."[10] Through their interchange, Spedden has explicated the relationship between Henry VIII and Anne Boleyn, using the historical elaboration method. Henry and Anne's fights were legendary, and though the exact words Jung as Anne and Nelson as Henry spoke at the MDRF were not taken directly from any historical record, they certainly reflected the attitudes, emotions, and natures of the two monarchs.

In Spedden's play, following the barbed exchange between Henry and Anne, the queen confronts Jane Seymour about her "distracting" behavior. During the reading of the day's events, Jane — played by Brittney K. Sweeney — was alternately flirting with the King and showing off a necklace she wore to the various court members assembled, myself included. When Anne challenges Jane, she questions her about what is around her neck. "I recognize this," the queen says. "'Tis from the King!"[11] With that realization, Anne rips the locket from around Jane's neck. This exchange is also an example of historical elaboration, taking a well-known event from Anne and Jane's battle for Henry, recreating it on the stage, and completing the scene with invented dialogue. Jung reflects on the scene: "I really liked the morning script immediately because it introduced the conflict with both humor (King and Queen screaming) and the actual event of Anne ripping the locket off Jane's neck. Authentic and fun, if worrisome that I'd hurt Brittney" (field notes). Jung's fears of hurting the actor playing her character's successor were well-founded as art imitated life one day when the ribbon refused to break away from Sweeney's neck, and she was actually injured, though almost certainly not as severely as Jane had been on that day nearly 500 years earlier.

Following the blow-up between the queen and Jane Seymour, Thomas Cromwell — played by Stephen Kirkpatrick — announces to all that the Dowager Princess of Wales is on her death bed. The Dowager Princess is the former queen, Katherine of Aragon. Each courtier was allowed to choose how he or she would react to the news based upon his or her relationship to the former (or some would say current) queen. Michael Worton and Judith Still write, "Imitation is thus not repetition, but the completion of an act of interpretation."[12] Each actor is not merely completing an act of repeating a gesture, but rather interpreting what his or her character would have done based upon the historical facts available. The Marchioness of Exeter (played by veteran festival performer Diane Wilshere) was Katherine's staunchest supporter still at court, and she reacted with visible distress, while many members of the court crossed themselves. George Boleyn (played by J. Owen Dickson) reacted with glee and went to greet his sister, Anne, to exchange a hug and good wishes. The ability for the actors to choose their characters' reactions based upon their research into the historical personage each portrays is another example of historical elaboration. While some spectators are unaware of the names of all the courtiers involved in the intrigue between Henry and his wives, a good number are sufficiently well-versed in Tudor history to know at least the major players. Cast members are trained to introduce themselves whenever they speak to patrons in the streets of Revel Grove, so often audience members at the stage shows will have met at least one and often several of the characters now performing in the plays. The personal interaction visitors have with the performers on the streets of Revel Grove can lead to a deeper immersion into the intrastice for the patron, who rather than merely suspending disbelief while watching from the viewing area, may actually play at believing as a member of the village witnessing the actions of the court.

"Katherine's Story"

Following his exit from the Market Stage, King Henry processed through the village with Jane Seymour. Because his next in-house stage show began shortly after *Royal Arrival* ended, Fred Nelson had to make a fairly quick exit from the streets of Revel Grove as he prepared to begin the first of what one patron termed "The Royal Miniseries." This in-house stage show, written by Spedden along with the other two queen scripts, was entitled *Katherine's Story*. The play attempted to explain what had happened to Katherine of Aragon since she was last seen in Revel Grove. The festival had been gearing up for a year of major conflict between Katherine and Henry when the actor (Bill Huttel) who had portrayed the Tudor monarch for eleven years died unexpectedly of a heart attack shortly after the end of the 2001 season. Joy Evans, who had been playing Katherine for five seasons from 1997 through 2001, began a new role the next year, the first season after Huttel's death. Though in 2001 the festival portrayed a day in 1529, when Henry and Katherine were still living together as king and queen, in 2002 the faire portrayed 1533, and the storyline focused on Anne Boleyn's coronation. The princess of Aragon's disappearance was never fully explained, so *Katherine's Story* filled in the gaps.

For Evans, the play was a wonderful opportunity to finish the storyline she had pursued for five years. "I felt very incomplete after Bill's passing and the fact that we did not get to complete the storyline. It was a great pleasure to do just that in the dramatic piece Carolyn created" [field notes]. Despite being absent from the storyline for the preceding two years, Evans's Katherine is immediately recognizable on stage, not just because the festival costumer chose to put her in the gown she had previously worn, but also because she had created a persona of Katherine that was endearing to regular patrons.

Katherine's Story was written in a manner similar to the modern play *Love Letters*, as both the King and Queen individually told their sides of the story, with a courtier/narrator — played by Evans's real-life husband Glenn — moderating. The story was compelling, often using historical documents as the text. With each passing letter sent between the two, the story of love, honor, duty, and betrayal became clearer. As Henry read one of Katherine's letters, and she circled about him while he was unaware, the tension mounted. When Joy Evans — clad in black and burnt red in striking contrast to the pale blue, white, and royal blue of Henry's schaub and doublet — spoke the words in Katherine's last letter to Henry, there were often open sobs from the audience. Her voice full of resolve, love, and fear, she spoke:

My Lord and Dear Husband,

> I commend me unto you. The hour of my death draws fast on, and in my case being such, the tender love I owe you forces me with a few words to put you in remembrance of the health and safeguard of your soul which you ought to prefer before any consideration of the world or the flesh whatsoever, for which you have cast me into many miseries and yourself into many cares. From my heart I do pardon you all, nay I do wish and dearly pray God that He will also pardon you. For the rest I commend unto you Mary our daughter. I beseech you now to be a good father as far as I have heretofore desired. Last I vow that mine eyes desire you above all things.

Katherine, the Queen[13]

Spedden used historical elaboration when she chose to use Katherine's actual words to Henry, rather than writing something new. Spedden relied on her research into Henry and Katherine to provide the text for much of the play. In Katherine's final speech, Spedden charged Evans with speaking the words that had previously been confined to the written page. According to Evans, "Speaking Katherine's actual words was very special. I had a great response from many patrons who approached me to tell me how moving the piece was for them as well" (field notes). Thus, Evans elaborated on the historical facts by adding voice and movement to the textual evidence, extrapolating to create an extended reality for the audience members watching the play.

The audience reactions to *Katherine's Story* were positive, but varied as to the levels of intrasticiancy they illustrated. Some commented on it as a play. "*Katherine's Story* was wonderfully written, directed, and acted. Bravo," wrote a female returning patron between the ages of 31–40 in the Royal Registry, the comment box for the festival. "Awesome!!! Especially impressed with *Katherine's Story*. Great Theatre," commented a returning male patron between 41–50, also in the Royal Registry. These two comments on *Katherine's Story* exemplify the intrasticial quality, as they respond to the show as a piece of theatre. For other patrons, it was more than a play. Joy Evans comments, "This year's response was wonderful — someone even cried out 'Long Live Queen Katherine' as I entered the stage one day! It was very positive and gratifying to be rewarded for my portrayal" (field notes). While playing Katherine is work for Evans as she creates the willing suspension of disbelief, for this patron her cry was a ritual act of respect for her queen, an active creation of belief, an intrasticious moment illustrated through an unsolicited and heartfelt conveyance of sympathy and empathy.

Evans also received commentary on her portrayal of Katherine in the streets, even though she played Katherine only on stage in 2004. Following *Katherine's Story*, Evans would change costumes because she played a completely different role in the streets. This character — Gertie Gizzard, Kingess of Gizzardonia — could *never* be mistaken for the stately Katherine. Aside from the completely different costume, Evans's accent and mannerisms as the inelegant, nouveau-riche Gizzard were quite dissimilar from the sophisticated, proper princess of Aragon. Evans commented on how patrons negotiated the dual roles she played: "Though I was not on the street as Queen Katherine — many approached me as Gertie and talked about that other woman who looks like me; they were wonderfully complimentary" (field notes). Note that the patrons do not want to break character, and so they do not want to tell "Joy" that SHE was wonderful as Katherine, but rather the visitors tell "Gertie" that they saw Katherine, and she was spectacular. It is an interesting way of entering the intrasticive state of playing at belief as the patrons attempt to navigate the dual worlds of stage and street as well as sixteenth-century England (Katherine and Gertie) and twenty-first century America (Joy).

Visitors to the village have the power to decide in which frame of intrasticiancy to participate (intrasticial, intrasticive, or intrasticious), and they can move between these frames or change the frames if needed. A patron can rekey the frame, as a story Evans tells of a patron who visits the faire almost daily illuminates: "One middle-aged woman I met years ago has become a devoted fan. I happened on her, discovered it was her birthday and created some handsome escorts for her and fun things to do. She tells me now how special it made her feel, what a difference it made in her happiness. We now know her to be a lovely person — she also dresses daily" (field notes). When Evans speaks of the woman dressing daily, she refers to the patron's decision to join the festival realm by purchasing a costume and wearing it to Revel Grove each day. Before she became directly involved with Evans, when she merely watched from afar as with a traditional play on a stage, this patron would wear regular twentieth-century street clothes. After moving to playing at belief during the scenario Evans created for her, the woman then chose to actively create belief, partially by joining the realm of Revel Grove in physical appearance of sixteenth-century garb. This is a rite of passage, an intrasticious moment where someone comes out truly changed because it has been framed as an important life ritual. Joy Evans as Queen Katherine, while facilitating what she expected to be an intrasticive state playing at belief, created a frame that this woman keyed as intrasticious in nature.

That the patron now comes in costume every day is part of the illustration of her movement from one state to the other. As Goffman wrote, "Thus, the systematic transformation that a particular keying introduces may alter only slightly the activity thus transformed, but it utterly changes what it is a participant would say was going on."[14] Evans was creating a play environment for the patron, but the woman took it instead as a deeply meaningful and life altering experience. As Queen Katherine, Evans had the ability to make arrangements that other characters might not have, and some patrons take the capacity of the character and view it as real power. Evans comments:

> Some patrons very much want to believe you are who you say you are. There are those who take it all more seriously than we think is expected. It is literally a "part of their lives," and they not only look forward to coming but build their lives around it to some degree. Many would whisper in my ear or pull me aside during the end of my Katherine reign to let me know what Henry was up to, warn me of my enemies, to say I would forever be their Queen, to wish me (Katherine) well [field notes].

When those patrons conversed with Evans as Katherine, they spoke as if what they said truly mattered in her life. It was more than playful banter; they were real warnings to her of Henry's treachery, despite that Joy Evans as an actor would obviously know what the character of Henry was planning for her character of Katherine. For these patrons, it is ritual and compulsory not only to attend the festival, but also to communicate their greater knowledge. In these instances, the patrons create the situation of belief in which they *need* to tell her of what is happening, as if she has no knowledge. For these patrons, this is the intrasticious state in action, while for Evans, she is keenly aware of their deep immersion at that particular point.

The Queen's Knighting Ceremony

Some patrons DO believe characters are who actors say they are, although most often these are the children attending festival. By looking through their eyes the different states of intrasticiancy can come into focus. For children, the intrasticious state is not so much an active creation of belief as it is actual belief. Perhaps when adults function in the intrasticious state, they are mirroring memories of youth when belief came much more readily. That belief is never so much in evidence as at the Queen's *Knighting Ceremony*. After being taught how to bow and curtsy and instructed to think of one good deed they had done for another person, the children would process up to her majesty to be knighted. As they kneeled on one knee (or sometimes two), Anne Boleyn would touch each of their shoulders and the top of their heads as she pronounced, "In the name of St. Michael, and of St. George, and of the Holy Trinity, I, Anne of England, knight thee _____. Stand and be recognized" (field notes). Often during this speech the children would be slightly fidgety, sometimes fearful of the sword coming down on their shoulders and their heads. But there were other times when they were truly taken by the process.

One particular case stands out as an illustration. I quote here directly from the field notes I wrote the day following the event.

> I had a moment yesterday that reminded me why we all do this every year despite uncertainties of weather, drunken patrons, and work place politics. I was at the *Knighting Ceremony* with Mary Ann, and this trio of sisters came up. The two older girls, about six and eight I would judge, flanked the youngest, who could not have been more than three. Through the entire process of the knighting, this youngest child kept her eyes steadily fixed upon Mary Ann's face. She looked not at either of her siblings, nor at the sword that came down on each shoulder and on her head. Her eyes, wide with wonder, were constantly upon the queen, her ears intent on every word Mary Ann spoke. When Mary Ann told her finally that she was a "real knight of this kingdom" and bent down to help the little girl to her feet, the youngster's face — which had been solemn and intent — lit up with a bright smile. This is our play. This is our work. For this little girl, it was about a reality that required no conception of [intrasticiancy]. For her, it was as real as any tangible piece of evidence could make it. The knighting certificate with her name on it may be the only memory [of this] she has in years to come, but for one moment, one hour, one day, she was a true knight, a young dame, and she believed it as much as she believed her own name [field notes].

It would be easy to dismiss this moment as that of a young child, one who did not have an understanding of the difference between reality and fantasy, but there is much that can be learned from it, as with the children (and adults) who clap to save Tinker Bell in productions of J.M. Barrie's *Peter Pan*. As Tracy C. Davis writes, "No doubt some of the applauding spectators *did* believe in fairies and were affirming their belief."[15] There can be a fine line between actual belief and creating belief, and sometimes adults can enter that same state, that intrasticious place, as did one gentleman who filled out the Royal Registry following his visit to Revel Grove. He entered his sex as male, his age as 61+, and noted that he was a returning patron. His only written comment was succinct and poignant as it illustrated the intrasticious state he had achieved: "I kissed her royal hand — never will forget it" (field notes). Just as with the young child at the *Knighting Ceremony*, at the interaction and even as he wrote the comment card, he accepted the royalty of the queen.

Anne in the Streets

Following the (*Knighting Ceremony*), I had the privilege of escorting an unknowing Anne Boleyn, who wore a blood red dress that could be taken as a foreshadowing of her imminent demise, to her arrest. During this brief time on the streets of Revel Grove, Mary Ann Jung made the most of her last moments as queen, inviting patrons to the grand "Robin Hood Pageant" that would turn, unbeknownst to her, into her betrayal and arrest. "His Majesty is to play Robin Hood, and I shall be Maid Marian, and all our quarrels will be forgotten," Jung would say to patrons (field notes). She would playfully chastise those who did not bow or curtsy, look questioningly at those who would inevitably warn her to "not lose her head," and show her own respect to the elderly patrons who graced the streets of the festival. When we would come upon patrons wearing Boston Red Sox caps, and there were a fair number of them in the fall of 2004, I would comment, "Look Your Majesty. This goodly gentle doth prominently display the Boleyn 'B' upon his chapeau. He indeed must be a most close relative to You." The Red Sox "B" logo is amazingly similar in design to the infamous Boleyn "B" which is viewable in several pieces of portraiture of Anne Boleyn from the sixteenth century. Jung would most often reply to my commentary by saying, "Indeed! Oh, cuz, 'tis been far too long. 'Tis wondrous indeed to see thee again." She would usually accompany these lines with a kiss to each cheek of her newly-found cousin. In the afternoon, after Anne Boleyn's demise, I would often warn patrons wearing the Red Sox caps of so openly displaying their loyalty to the former queen, and I would turn their hats inside out.

Never once did I see a patron not willing to play along with the endowment Anne Boleyn bestowed, perhaps because the MDRF environment engenders a level of playfulness — both among performers and between performers

The fair maids and merry men at the Robin Hood Pageant during Queen Anne's Arrest. The queen is confident that a pageant will be just the thing to rekindle her love with King Henry. From left, Sonia Motlagh (kneeling) as Lady Jane Parker, Viscountess Rochford; the author (standing) as Lady Elizabeth Ughtread; Mary Ann Jung (seated) as Queen Anne Boleyn; Diane Wilshere (standing) as the Marchioness of Exeter; Laura Lynn Gansler-Was (kneeling) as Lady Mabel Fitzwilliam; the late Karen Cannon as Lady Elizabeth Boleyn; Michael Winchester, Jr. (standing) as Sir Francis Weston; Jeffrey Bryant (sitting) as Master William Brereton; and J. Adam Wyatt (standing) as Master Mark Smeaton. Weston, Brereton, and Smeaton all went to their deaths along with Anne Boleyn and her brother, George. Photograph by Carrie J. Cole.

and patrons — not always found in other theatrical venues. Performer Randy Dalmas explains why this intrastivice level is so readily achieved at festival:

> Since a large percentage of our work is also improvisational, a sense of playfulness is almost a requirement between the performers, patrons, and to a certain degree, the craftspeople and workers around the festival. I also believe that in any creative environment, a sense of play is necessary to foster the risks needed to be taken to be creative. The sense of play is common in theatre, especially in the trust relationship created between performers. When successful, the relationship is evident and extends to the audience, when either directly or indirectly they are allowed to participate in the relationship between the actors. The most successful performers have mastered the ability to display that playfulness [field notes].

The interactive nature of the type of theatre provided in the streets at the MDRF offers a greater opportunity for audience members to actively participate, and therefore to achieve a greater level of playfulness. This, in turn, leads to a movement from the intrastical stage to the intrasticive, as patrons react to the actors' own willingness to engage in the interactive improvisation. This brief time in the streets with Jung and me before the stage show in which she was accused and arrested offered a few moments of lighthearted drama and playfulness before the heavily dramatic deep play that would soon follow.

"Queen Anne's Arrest"

As I mentioned earlier, the *Arrest* began as a "Robin Hood Pageant," and it was produced on the largest of the festival's stages, The Globe. However, initial scenes between Thomas Cromwell, Thomas Howard (the Duke of Norfolk), and Jane Parker (Lady Rochford) indicated that the play would eventually take an extreme turn. Following the narration of the Robin Hood tale by Anne Boleyn's aunt — Elizabeth Boleyn, played by the late Karen Cannon — the story unfolded with the "Dance of the Woodland Fairies," the entrance of the "Merry Men," and the unveiling of the "Fair Maids of the Forest." All of this was followed by the most hilarious and anachronistic moments of the show, if not the entire faire. Lisa Ricciardi-Thompson, as Margaret Wyatt (Lady Lee), performed the "Dance of the Stag." Following an elaborate set-up, she eventually would break into song and dance, improvising each day something different, but usually along the lines of "I'm too sexy for my moo" or "Who let the stag out?" These contemporary American popular culture references inserted into a show designed to illustrate a historical moment only serve to further the temporal-spatial intrastice. Audiences could laugh at the anachronisms, but then only a few minutes later were drawn back into the sixteenth century as Anne Boleyn and four male members of the court were accused of treason and adultery.

Spedden again used historical elaboration to bring about the climax of the play. Instead of performing a "Robin Hood Pageant," the Duke of Norfolk instructed Anne and her accused lovers to play a masque of the King's own writing, entitled *The Tragedy of Anne*. Spedden began with an historical fact. Henry did write a masque called *The Tragedy of Anne*, and he did give it to the Bishop of Carlisle, as the Duke of Norfolk says in the play. However, in reality, the masque does not survive, so we do not know the text. Spedden created the words for the masque, telling the story of a noble knight and his unfaithful wife, an allegorical reference to Henry's allegation of adultery against Anne. While the accused played out the story in pantomime as

George Boleyn narrated on the main stage of The Globe, above on the balcony various court members provided testimony against Anne, sometimes willingly and with glee (as with the Marchioness of Exeter), and at other times only through trickery and with great hesitancy (as with Lady Lee and Lady Fitzwilliam). The pantomime culminated and the men were led off stage by guards, leaving Anne Boleyn alone to face the Duke of Norfolk's accusations. Following Norfolk's command to remove her, fighting against two guards, and leaving the stage and moving into the audience, Jung performed the emotionally-charged final speech of the show.

Jung, who has a B.A. from the University of Maryland–College Park in British History with an emphasis in the Tudor Era, states that she "liked that it used her actual words and again made Anne sympathetic and clearly innocent of the charges." She continues that she initially hated the "silly blocking of ladies dance" but then realized that "it provided stark contrast to the ending and therefore gave [the] arrest more punch and surprise" (field notes). Jung delivered the final speech, which Spedden wrote using Anne's own words from her trial, with a mixture of heavy emotion and determination that characterized the queen's life. Jung said that she felt a strong need to do her justice and was much moved when saying the lines and was thrilled that people actually cried or were themselves touched. She states that it "felt almost sacred and therefore if any drunk interrupted or laughed [it] made me and other actors angry" (field notes). The laughter seemed an inappropriate response, especially when both performers and patrons had entered into a deep level of immersion, perhaps even the intrasticious state.

Many in the audience did cry, including (as one performer reported to me) a very large "Scot" who repeated over and over, "But she's innocent." It is an important aspect of Goffman's frame analysis that members of a frame do not have to actively participate in the event that the frame concerns in order to be elements of that frame. He writes, "the primary perspectives, natural and social, available to members of a society such as ours, affect more than merely the participants in an activity; bystanders who merely look are deeply involved, too."[16] This patron and many others who merely watched the performance were drawn in. I argue that unlike a traditional theatre piece, there is a greater level of connectivity; though a particular show may be occurring on stage, many of the patrons have had close interactions with the performers on the streets. For example, the Marchioness of Exeter often spoke derisively of Anne Boleyn during her interactions with patrons in the street. Her vitriolic proclamations against Anne on the stage during *Queen Anne's Arrest* were foreshadowed not just by the performances she gave during the morning before the show, but also by interactions during the 2002 and 2003 seasons during which she actively voiced her displeasure with the queen.

Procession

Following the arrest, guards conducted Anne Boleyn and the four courtiers also accused of treason on a solemn march through the streets of Revel Grove, amidst performers and patrons of all ilk. Often others would join in or follow the procession. These processions are similar to those at Plimoth Plantation, as explained by Snow: "Processions can either be 'improvised' or 'planned.' Usually they move to a fixed goal."[17] Though at the festival, improvised processions do occur, this particular procession was obviously a planned event. This is also one of the closest moments to carnival, as members of the cast and patrons at times were visually and vocally indistinguishable from each other as costumed visitors to the village would join in the walk or cry out from along the path. One patron, a young man costumed as a peasant, would follow the procession daily, crying out, "God save the Queen. She didn't do it" (field notes). For patrons looking on who were not familiar with the festival, there would be no way of knowing that this peasant was not a part of the show. Dressed in appropriate attire, he seemed very knowledgeable about the situation, while simultaneously appearing to have a heartfelt care for Anne Boleyn, which was the effect Jung and the other accused were trying to create: "We all really wanted them for one minute to feel how awful it must have been. I tried hard to really look through eyes which knew they'd never see any of this again — the beauty or the sorrow" (field notes). This young man followed the procession rain or shine, appeared genuinely touched by the proceedings, and several times actually attempted to interfere with the forward progress of Anne and the accused to their "deaths." I believe he had entered into an intrasticious state and was more than just playing along as it became ritual for him to attend the procession every day.

Some patrons had the opposite reaction to Anne Boleyn, but it was no less visceral, which can sometimes cause a tension when moving from one state of intrasticiancy to another. Laura Lynn Gantzler-Was, who played Anne Boleyn's lady-in-waiting Mabel DeClifford (Lady Fitzwilliam), explains: "For the patron, they need to accept that while it's entertainment, with characters much like a play, it's also interactive and the entertainment 'effect' is nulled if it is ... taken too seriously, such as people who spit on or throw things at 'Anne Boleyn'" (field notes). While the entertainment effect may be nullified if people take it too seriously, this is the precise moment where the movement from intrasticive to intrasticious happens. This is the time when the patron is engaging in an event that has a profound effect upon him or her, and what they desire to gain from it is not entertainment, but rather a form of ritual catharsis.

At the end of the procession, Anne Boleyn made a final speech, which drew upon the energy from the show, the procession, and historical fact. The power of Jung's final speech during the stage show carried out into the procession through the streets. As they marched through the village, she and several fellow actors recited quotes from the historical record of the trials of Anne Boleyn and the others accused with her. Without a crown or hood to cover her hair, the trademark long dark locks of Anne Boleyn were evident to all observing the macabre parade. According to theatre historian Freddie Rokem,

> The actor as witness and hyper-historian is not only dependent on a specific knowledge about the historical past, the "real," that he or she brings to the spectators. The way in which the witness appears on the stage and communicates with the spectators — the aesthetic dimension of his or her appearance — is also of central importance for the creation of a theatrical discourse performing history.[18]

Rokem's explication of the actor as performing historian helps to explain how Jung could draw on both knowledge of sixteenth-century English history and twenty-first-century performance to create the impact she desired. According to Jung, "Being knowledgeable about the details of her last days was therefore a blessing and a curse. An actress without that info wouldn't question or care, but as a historian I very much do" (field notes). Because of her educational background and theatrical experience, Jung was able to create an aesthetic dimension out of historical information, but it was not without difficulty.

Spedden left the final speech Anne would give to Jung, who was long experienced with the character and her history. According to Jung:

> I was directed to make it up, by which they knew I'd select other excerpts of her actual words. I chose to keep it brief and to use her last words from Tower Green since the stage speech was from her trial. I made a distinctly modern choice to not say her glowing praise of Henry and to change it instead to a plea for baby Elizabeth, which I made up. Since she could not have risked such a plea it was my gift to Anne's memory and had great effect on people watching. Anne did not cry when she spoke her final words, but I usually found myself unable not to! [field notes].

Jung's choice to change the glowing praise of Henry into a plea for Elizabeth as a tribute to the woman she had portrayed for many years is a clear case of historical elaboration. She began with common knowledge, and then she extrapolated from it, creating an even more moving theatrical moment. Many of the patrons with whom I spoke specifically mentioned the plea for baby Elizabeth as what they remembered most from that final speech (field notes). The historical elaboration became the most memorable moment of the performance for many of the spectators, and their willingness to play at the belief that the plea for Elizabeth would have been one of Anne Boleyn's final requests illustrates their immersion in the intrasticive state.

Between Two Queens

After Anne Boleyn had been arrested, but before Jane Seymour had made her ascension to royalty, I had a few hours without a stage show in which I could engage in street bits. I spent a significant amount of this time during the run of the festival with fellow performer and court member Sonia Motlagh, who portrayed the Viscountess of Rochford, George Boleyn's wife, who had accused him of adultery with his sister, the queen. Almost immediately following *Queen Anne's Arrest*, Motlagh's character proclaimed herself a widow, and a not very unhappy one at that. My character was also a widow, and often we would walk side-by-side commenting quite loudly about the advantages (her view) and disadvantages (my view) of being unmarried. The Viscountess would try to convince me that without a husband I had more freedom to do as I pleased, especially since my sister was sure to be the next queen of England. I, on the other hand, attempted to explain to the Viscountess that I wanted to serve King and country the best I could, by being a good wife and mother. Often we would stop at groups of patrons and explain both of our points of view and ask their opinions. Nearly every time we approached patrons who were in twenty-first century clothing, they agreed with the Viscountess. Only when speaking with visitors who had begun to more deeply enter the intrastice and embrace sixteenth-century values, did I usually find some sympathetic support.

One of the activities in which Motlagh and I frequently engaged during our walks around the village, sometimes accompanied by Master Cromwell (portrayed by Stephen Kirkpatrick), was shopping for a betrothal present for my sister, Jane. This is one of the few times that as a cast member, I had a solid reason for and ability to interact with our vendors, who provide so much of the ambience at the festival. We would go from shop to shop looking for the perfect betrothal gift. As we left each vendor, I would declare loudly that I had indeed found "the perfect gift, one fit for a queen, my sister" (field notes). If anyone showed interest, I would explain exactly what I had found in that particular shop. Sometimes it was a lovely piece of jewelry; others it was a matching set of crystal glasses. Embroidery, tapestries, fine gowns, a new matrimonial bed, and a lovely jeweled eating dagger were among other items I "found" for gifts. Sometimes the merchants would go along with my game and make suggestions, most often inappropriate, but which the audience found amusing. For example, one merchant suggested that my sister could use a leather flogger to keep her new husband in line. Another suggested a sword to defend herself from the king. Of course, I brushed aside these suggestions as mere jests because "my sister and the king would be married for eternity" (field notes). This usually elicited a laugh, but rarely did

anyone try to actually "prove" me wrong. These merchants thus were participating in the intrastice and immersing themselves by not allowing their
twenty-first-century knowledge to ruin the sixteenth-century experience for
those who were either not aware of how my sister eventually met her demise
or who had decided also to immerse themselves so deeply in the intrastice
that they completely ignored their own comprehension of the actuality of the
situation.

During these many walks, we would often venture back toward the front
of the village where Master Thomas Tallis (portrayed by Gary Schwartz) had
set up his virginal. The lilt of the music from the small piano precursor would
waft on the breeze as we approached the crimson-velvet clad musician. In history, Tallis was a composer of renown, most famous for the Tallis Canon
which bears his name. He was also a man of incredible diplomacy, having
served through the reigns of Henry VIII and all three of his children. He composed both secular and religious music, and much of his work has survived
to the present day. Schwarz began taking Tallis's style and creating his own
works using the composer's repertoire as a model. By 2004, Schwarz was at
work on his third compilation of Tallisesque music, and he named each piece
for the character or characters who inspired it. He had previously written a
piece entitled, "The Household of Hengrave Hall/The Duchess of Norfolk,"
for which an earlier character I had portrayed was the inspiration. When the
Viscountess and I approached one day, he told us that he was composing a
song in our honor, a song for the merry widows. The light lively composition that Schwarz played that day was a perfect example of the intrastice in
action. Using his knowledge of the sixteenth-century historical record of
Tallis's compositions and an instrument appropriate to that period, in the
pretext that was Revel Grove, Schwartz composed a beautiful song that
could just as easily been one of the actual Tallis's musical scores. I was so enrap-
tured with the music he had composed for us that I began to dance a little
and completely lost track of time. I nearly missed my "robbing" that day,
and I had to cut through the backstage area to make it to the tavern on
time.

"Jane's Betrothal"

Meanwhile, Anne Boleyn and her accused lovers had barely left the streets
when Henry began planning his betrothal to Jane Seymour. For some this
quick change might have seemed a bit abrupt, even for Henry VIII. However, it is recorded that Henry waited in a boat on the Thames for the cannon from the Tower of London which signaled Anne's death, then immediately
proceeded to the Seymour residence. The very next day, he and Jane were

betrothed, and they were married ten days after that. The MDRF condensed the timeline of the betrothal by only a few hours.

Jane's Betrothal, like *The Royal Arrival, Queen Anne's Arrest,* and *Katherine's Story,* was another in-house stage show. It began with the ladies of the court fussing over the planning of the festivities. At one point, four court ladies — the Marchioness of Exeter, Lady Mabel Fitzwilliam, Lady Anne Stanhope Seymour, and Lady Elizabeth Seymour Ughtread — all gathered around Jane, trying to straighten her dress and make her presentable. The fussing was interrupted by a loud boom from offstage, which signaled the cannon from the tower. Of the planned scene at Plimoth Plantation, which is akin to the storyline play at the MDRF, Snow writes, "A preplanned scenario and rehearsal time are the major defining characteristics of this final category of

King Henry addresses the audience following his betrothal to Jane Seymour as members of the court look on. From left, Diane Wilshere as Lady Gertrude Courtenay, Marchioness of Exeter; Brittney Sweeney as Mistress Jane Seymour; Laura Lynn Gansler-Was as Lady Mabel Fitzwilliam; Fred Nelson as King Henry VIII; the author as Lady Elizabeth Ughtread; Stephen Kirkpatrick as Thomas Cromwell, newly-appointed Baron of Oakham; and Christopher Ellison as Sir Edward Seymour, Viscount Beauchamp. Photograph by Carrie J. Cole.

performance organization, along with the fact that interpreters do not expect on these occasions to interact with the visitors."[19] Although we may expect not to interact, and not to have visitors interact, that is not always the case. The four women on stage reacted to the cannon with varying degrees of sympathy towards the sound which signaled Anne Boleyn's final demise. The audience also had varied reactions to the cannon. Most often they gasped at the loud and unexpected sound, but then returned their attention to the court ladies on stage.

If the audience is in an intrasticial state, the interaction is often kept to a minimum, usually with the audience participating by clapping or laughing, and in this case gasping. However, if the patrons have entered into the intrasticive arena, interaction can and most likely will happen. For example, once, while all the women were fussing over Jane just before the cannon exploded, a woman in the audience shouted, "Long live Queen Anne!" (field notes). The cannon shot followed on the heels of the woman's cry. Melissa McGinley, who played Anne Stanhope, had to deliver the first line following the cannon shot. That day it came out differently, as she reacted to the patron's interaction. Her line, "Well, it is over. Anne Boleyn is dead," was normally delivered softly, but with a distinct detachedness, a factual commentary. On the day of the interruption, McGinley delivered the line in a tone much more sympathetic to Anne. She said she felt she had to "soften the blow" (field notes). The patron's apparent immersion into at least the intrasticive, and quite possibly the intrasticious, state occasioned an adjustment from the performer. McGinley reacted within the intrastice as well, her character holding the responsibility for the patron's safety within the intrasticial moment. Thus, she spoke with a level of compassion directed simultaneously to the deceased Anne and the patron who supported her.

Jane's Betrothal provided further opportunity for audience interaction, both solicited and not. When the King finally arrives for the betrothal ceremony, Edward Seymour — played by Christopher Ellison — would approach the stage first and announce, "All rise in right honorable deference to His most royal Majesty, King Henry VIII." Rarely did a patron not rise in response to this request, standing as Henry approached the court members on stage who bowed or curtsied. The King would eventually tell the patrons to be seated and the court to rise. This solicited patron interaction is suggestive of an intrasticive state, as they played along at the behest of a character.

However, as the ceremony proceeded, after Henry and Jane were officially betrothed, and were engaged in their kiss, the audience would applaud without solicitation, taking their twenty-first century knowledge of marriage ritual and placing it into the sixteenth century context. Turner writes how the relationship between mundane life and cultural performances is "reciprocal and reflexive — in the sense that the performance is often a critique, direct or veiled, of the social life it grows out of, an evaluation (with lively possibilities of rejection) of the way society handles history."[20] The audience participated in applauding the king's betrothal to Jane, and in doing so condoned his historically known and perhaps less than honorable actions towards both Katherine of Aragon and Anne Boleyn. This critique of social life may be an understanding that the end justified the means.

The End of the Day: "Pub Sing"

Accompanied by a trumpet fanfare and cries of "God save the King" and "God Bless the Queen," the royal court arrives at the White Hart Tavern to conclude the festival day at the nightly *Pub Sing*. Their newly-betrothed Majesties enter halfway through this show, after officiating at the final joust. They are given a place of honor as Jack Rackham and the Pyrates Royale host the final stage show of the evening, and the court and villagers gather around as their workday draws to a close. After a final song, which is always more romantic and sweet and less bawdy and raucous than many of the others sung during the show, the King and Queen bid farewell to the citizens of Revel Grove and encourage them to follow the court to the front gates. As the autumn days grow shorter in Revel Grove, darkness descends on the final weekends well before the *Pub Sing* has concluded. The Landsknechts carry torches as they escort the Royal Court to the front gates of the village. These torches are reminiscent of carnival settings of ages past. "The Roman carnival ends with the Fire Festival, or *moccoli*, which in Italian means 'candle stumps.' This is a grandiose pageant of fire along the Corso and the adjacent streets. Each participant in the parade carries a lighted candle."[21] Many patrons bring their own lanterns and follow along in the procession, bringing a close to the carnival, at least for that day.

The final procession is another in a long line of historical elaborations performed throughout the day at the MDRF. These moments provide an opportunity for visitors to participate in all three levels of intrasticiancy, each of which is distinct from the others. Moreover, there is a different goal for patrons participating in each of the categories of intrasticiancy. For those who frame the festival as intrasticial, the goal is to watch and be entertained without needing to actively participate. For those who seek the intrasticive it is the possibilities presented for play in the temporal-spatial intrastice, while for those who want the deepest immersion — into the intrasticious state — the goal is to succeed in having a ritualistic experience and to walk out through the gates a changed person. Some enter and leave with the same expectations. Others find that they change once they have entered the intrastice, primarily through the interaction the visitors have with the characters who engage in the historical elaboration. The intrastiancy is achieved in several different ways and for many different reasons, but that it is manifest at MDRF is not in question.

This co-existence and temporal-spatial intrastice is achieved through what Ricciardi-Thompson terms a "unique look at history that is both fun and educational." She also provides an interesting possibility as to why the temporal-spatial intrastice is possible. "Life is life no matter what century you live in. The same trials and tribulations exist now. We all seek spiritual, economical, and social fulfillment" (field notes). The MDRF provides opportunities for all three, and the choice of the patrons and performers in regard to the states of intrasticiancy in which they participate perhaps is an indicator as to whether the fulfillment each most seeks is spiritual, economical, or social. Because of the close proximity in which patrons interact with performers in Revel Grove, the level of intrastiancy can be the same whether during a stage or street performance. The natural boundary between stage and house are far less evident in the milieu of the Renaissance festival. However, the ability for the actor to improvise and lead the patron from one state to another is much greater when on the streets of the village, as illustrated by the stories of patrons following characters throughout Revel Grove. Audience members make choices and frame the different playlets and in-house shows according to their own desires, thus transitioning what might often be an intrasticial performance for an actor into an intrasticious moment of reception for the patron. In the next chapter, I examine in depth patron immersion into the intrastice as visitors experience the sensescape, interact with the performers, and create meaning amongst themselves.

6

Performers, Patrons, and Playtrons: Interactions and Interfaces in the Intrastice

Offering over one hundred unique artisans, nearly fifty food booths, five taverns, and seven stages, populated by hundreds of actors, re-enactors, and musicians, Revel Grove provides entertainment enjoyable to a wide variety of patrons. Some spectators who visit the MDRF never enter any level of intrasticiancy. Some visitors think that the village is simply a huge outdoor craft show and delight in having all of their Christmas shopping completed well before Halloween. Others visit because MDRF provides the opportunity to swill alcohol without ever questioning or caring why some of the people are dressed in sixteenth-century attire. Additional patrons envision the festival locale as a vast playground for their children, and the cast as nothing more than free babysitters. Nonetheless, alongside these patrons, a significant number of visitors who pay to enter the gates of Revel Grove appear to fit into one of the states of intrasticiancy at some point during their stay.

In this chapter, I will concentrate on the patrons who experience some form of intrasticiancy and examine how they exemplify the intrastcial, intrasticive, and/or intrasticious state(s). In order to accomplish this task, I analyze the manner in which performer-patron interactions and patron-patron relationships influence and in turn are influenced by the state of intrasticiancy in which visitors participate. These are the moments when an interface occurs within the temporal-spatial intrastice which exists as visitors experience a pretense of sixteenth-century Tudor Oxfordshire formed by the melding of the reality of twenty-first-century America and the historical record of sixteenth-century England. I define the interface as *a condition which sanctions mean-*

147

ingful communication between any combination of at least two systems, objects, and/or individuals in a theatrical event. Each person's particular knowledge and method of creating meaning is part of this interface. Audiences at the festival use their prior experiences, in the words of sociologist Erving Goffman, "to frame" their faire encounters and thus participate differently in the states of intrasticiancy.

In all three intrasticiant states there are interfaces between performers and patrons. Unlike the stage performances in which some separation exists between audience and actor, a vast majority of the daily activity at the MDRF takes place "in the streets," with patrons and performers in extremely close proximity. Within this intimate interactive space a performer most clearly recognizes a patron's place within the temporal-spatial intrastice. Performers must first assess the patron's level of immersion in intrasticiancy before proceeding with the encounter:

1. Some patrons do not want to play; they are not in a state of intrasticiancy.
2. Some patrons are willing to suspend disbelief, but do not want to play in any active way.
3. Some patrons want to attempt basic play and will engage briefly if an actor approaches.
4. Some patrons want to play and will approach the actors in character or will engage enthusiastically when approached, respond, and continue the action.

The interface between performer and patron begins with the assessment the performer must make regarding the patron's state of intrasticiancy. This first interface thus occurs before the performer actually engages the patron and can clearly be separated from the actual interaction. Meaningful communication has already occurred, leading the performer to a decision regarding whether and how to approach a patron. During the communication that follows, many more interfaces may occur, depending upon the direction the bit — a piece of interactive improvisational street theatre — takes. Also, the performer must always be aware that the patron may switch frames at any moment during the interaction.

As sociologist Gary Alan Fine has written, "Frames have different levels of stability. By that I mean that some frames oscillate rapidly — up-keying or down-keying frequently — while other frames are comparatively stable. The actor must remain in the part of his character continuously while onstage."[1] At the MDRF, the actor on the street must also remain in character. On the other hand, patrons may switch frames at will, and unlike actors on the stage, actors in the street may be interacting with them at the exact moment a patron moves from the intrasticial to the intrasticive state. As the patron switches frames, a new interface forms, forcing the actor to reassess the situation and then continue or conclude the bit in an appropriate manner. I add here the qualification that the actor, too, may be in a state of intrasticiancy. As the actor and patron interact, the patron may switch states and completely drop out of the conversation; the actor may also switch states of intrasticiancy, but cannot leave the character or the conversation behind at will because there is a necessity for closure. This conclusion may simply be a matter of theatrical aesthetics, such as providing an appropriate dénouement to the encounter. Many actors at the MDRF have both signature greetings and farewells they use to indicate the beginnings and endings of street performances. However, the need for closure may have a greater significance than its mere aesthetic value. If the patron is in an intrasticious state, the culmination must also include the actor's ability to finish the interactive improvisation while keeping the patron physically and emotionally comfortable. The aesthetic, emotional, and physical needs that an actor must consider before concluding a bit are all interfaces between performer and patron within the setting provided by the contemporary American Renaissance festival.

For many patrons, the opportunity to merely attend the stage shows and acts is enough, and this places them firmly within the intrasticial state. These visitors never attempt to leave twenty-first-century America, as they simply suspend disbelief to witness the mere portrayal of sixteenth-century England. The interface occurs on the surface level as the patron glances upon the pre-text of sixteenth-century England from a firm footing in twenty-first-century America. In theatrical terms, the patron easily progresses from actual disbelief to suspension of disbelief and back again. Writing about the audience intervention in J.M. Barrie's *Peter Pan*, theatre scholar Tracy C. Davis explains that the patrons at the theatre made different choices regarding their reactions to Tinkerbell's impending doom. In explaining the concept of dramatic license, Davis also illustrates that audience behavior varies based upon how certain patrons frame the event. According to Davis, "Audiences could retain disbelief but they could also recognize and choose the time and place for both belief and disbelief."[2] Davis's research is germane to this study when considering the ability of the spectators to "recognize and choose the time and place" during which they would either believe or not. Davis's concept informs an understanding of the intrastice I describe, as patrons at festival choose — at least initially — their level of immersion.

I add the caveat of "initially" to account for two different possibilities in which conscious choice may cease to exist for a period of time. First, there are occasions when slippage occurs between the intrasticial and intrasticive states or between the intrasticive and intrasticious states due to an unexpected increase in a patron's level of involvement in a particular situation. Second, there are times when a patron who has entered into an intrasticious state may experience an unexpected ritual transformation. Therefore, while Davis's assertion that audience members have choice between different frames illustrates some levels of intrasticiancy, the occurrences within the intrastice also allow for times when there is a cessation in the spectator's conscious framing of the theatrical event. For example, though patrons initially may come to the festival viewing it as a mere entertainment, sometimes they leave feeling a sense of transformation, of having found a "home," as many have described it to me (field notes). As Goffman states, frames can be rekeyed, and in some cases that change is not controlled by the person experiencing the rekeying. Some patrons may not exert their will with regard to changing frames, while some may be unaware that the frame has shifted, and still others may be caught up within a ritualistic alteration and temporarily lack the agency to control the frame.

On the surface, visitors may frame the festival much like any other theatrical event that employs history as a basis for its existence and narrative. For those spectators who wish to participate on the intrasticial level, this creates an atmosphere that is a cross between Plimoth Plantation or Colonial Williamsburg and Disney World. The MDRF becomes a place where history exists for recreation with little regard for pedagogy, with the exception of the living history aspects of the festival discussed in Chapter 4. Patrons who wish to experience the intrasticial state participate in many diverse activities not unique to festivals. As Stephen Eddy Snow writes about the visitors to Plimoth Plantation,

> Some people do, undoubtedly, enter the gates of the Pilgrim Village for the same reason that they walk into a bar or a movie theatre or, for that matter, take drugs. They want to escape the pain of a centreless existence. For this type of tourist, the plantation is a kind of amusement park and conforms to this individual's regular pattern of amusements and diversions.[3]

Snow sets up an interesting contrast in this quote, likening going to Plimoth both as a mere amusement and as an escape from a centreless existence. I maintain that this difference occurs because of a patron's level of immersion into the intrastice; amusement exists in the intrasticial or intrasticive levels, while escape occurs in the intrasticious state.

There is something deeper occurring when the theatrical event provides an escape from ordinary life. In the intrastice at the MDRF, this would indicate a desire to flee from the realities of twenty-first century America to find solace in sixteenth-century England. And that is more than mere diversion. For some patrons who seek a different realm than the reality twenty-first-century America provides, merely watching shows is not enough; interaction with actors on the streets of Revel Grove is a key element to their festival day. Their enjoyment is predicated upon having interacted with cast members in a meaningful way, even if the context of the contact was humorous. These patrons are participating in the intrasticive state. Finally, for some patrons, their experience of the MDRF theatrical event is a ritual transformation that is only complete if they are actively participating in an intrasticious manner — through costume, speech dialect, and assumed personality — either with performers or each other.

Separating Performers from P(l)a(y)trons

The MDRF, like many Renaissance faires, features performances in the street amidst patrons who are wearing clothing indicative of the sixteenth century. While actors label these garments "costume," most festival patrons nationwide refer to their attire as "garb." Even casual visitors to the village may don bits of garb, from individually purchased pieces such as jester hats and flower garlands to entire costumes — rented or bought — representing different classes ranging from peasant to clergy to nobility. Visitors to the village also purchase food and drink, including turkey legs and mugs of ale. From the many vendors available, audience members also procure a wide range of merchandise that can include musical instruments, mugs, and jewelry. When patrons appropriate theatrical conventions such as dressing in costume and displaying purchases that fellow visitors could easily construe as props, what separates them from the performance cast at the MDRF? Goffman defines performance as an "arrangement which transforms an individual into a stage performer, the latter, in turn being an object that can be looked at in the round and at length without offense, and looked to for engaging behavior by persons in an 'audience' role."[4] Donning costumes and using props could be the "arrangement" that might change a visitor into a performer, if other patrons can then view that person without causing an affront. This part of the definition seems to qualify patrons as performers. However, Goffman's caveat that the individual must be able to be "looked to for engaging behavior" leads to an understanding of how performers and patrons at the festival differ. The members of the Company of the Rose are not only expected to entertain, they are paid well to do so. The cast members have also undergone a rigorous rehearsal program designed to prepare them for the interactive improvisational acting form that is characteristic of festival performances on the streets. While patrons certainly create their own personal performances in many ways, a distinct line separates the trained, professional actors from the inexpert, paying audience members at the MDRF.

Audience members dressed in twenty-first-century street clothes, often called mundane clothing or civvies, walk the streets of Revel Grove alongside other visitors who wear garb every day. The garb-wearing group is part of a different type of audience, referred to in many cases by both performers and visitors as a "playtron," though some shun the use of the term as derogatory (field notes). What is a playtron? The simple answer is a patron who plays. There is a deeper meaning, however, and a more complicated answer is needed to fully account for this particular audience member. Though different playtrons may display a wide variety of tendencies, they most often exhibit a set of traits in common that makes them identifiable to each other and to the staff at the MDRF. I define a playtron as *a visitor to a Renaissance festival who pays to enter the gates, wears garb that illustrates character or at least class and nationality, attempts language and accent appropriate to that garb, and interacts with performers, other audience members to whom he or she is known, or both*. The qualification regarding interacting with audience members "to whom he or she is known" is very important at MDRF. While playtrons are always welcome to interact with performers on the street and with their known group of friends, they should not approach other visitors to the village — in garb or not — with the intention of entertaining those patrons.

Simply greeting people with a "Good day, m'Lord," answering a question regarding the location of a stage, privies, etc., or executing a proper bow or curtsy are not attempts at entertaining patrons. These greetings, answers, and acts of deference are illustrations of common civility and the responsibilities that come along with the garb, accent, and knowledge of the festival's social framework. According to Goffman, social frameworks "provide background understanding for events that incorporate this will, aim, and controlling effort of an intelligence, a life agency."[5] These social frameworks for the patrons at MDRF become part and parcel of nineteen days of differentiated existence. People play their own games with their own rules, separate and apart from the official storyline of the MDRF. For example, one of these frameworks includes becoming part of either the International Wenches Guild or the International Brotherhood of Rogues Scoundrels and Cads [sic]. Neither of these guilds is a part of the official structure of the MDRF, but the playtrons who belong to these guilds are often in Revel Grove from opening until closing each of the nineteen days. However, many of the playtrons with whom I spoke stated an aversion to interacting with the cast (field notes). Thus, their framework exists alongside the MDRF storylines, often neither contributing to them nor interfering with them. While some patrons seek immersion within the primary frame, others re-key the frame. When playtrons rekey the frame, to others it is unnoticeable, but to them it significantly alters what is happening at the MDRF.

Conversely, some patrons attempt to become a part of a social framework that is not theirs. Neither patrons nor playtrons should approach visitors they do not know and attempt to entertain — i.e., sing, juggle, portray an historical character, and/or further his or her own personal "storyline" — thus endeavoring to become one of those which Goffman references as being "looked to for engaging behavior." Patrons venturing into this territory can become very problematic. First, all of the performers at the MDRF must audition for their positions in the Company of the Rose or the Company of St. George. This process requires performance of a monologue and an improvisation (Rose) or an interview (George). Second, the performers hired by the MDRF engage in an intensive and extensive rehearsal process which usually lasts for seven weeks. This rehearsal process includes both scripted stage shows and improvisational exercises along with language and history classes. Most of the rehearsals involve character development, which can be both challenging and rewarding, particularly when there is no playscript from which to work and actors use personal research and improvisational exercises to create their characters. Personal research for cast members at the MDRF may include reading books on historical characters, learning period tasks appropriate for a character, and memorizing poetry or other words from primary sources a historical figure has written. The management of the festival charges these cast members with representing and upholding the mission and artistic vision of the MDRF. If these performers are unable to do so, they are released from their contracts. The actors have a responsibility to follow the extensive rules the festival management has set out, especially those which relate to contact with any patron. Learning these rules is also part of the rehearsal process, and neither patrons nor playtrons have been trained in these particulars.

Though a playtron may learn some or even most of the rules, he or she would be under no obligation to actually follow them. Auditions are advertised every year, and most playtrons never attempt to become a member of the company, which would require adherence to the rules. Since performing becomes work, the patron would not be free to do as he or she wished throughout the day, would have to attend rehearsals for seven weeks during the summer, and would have to commit to a performance day that often begins with dressing at 9 A.M. and ends after 7 P.M., during which time the patron-turned-performer would be expected to follow all of the rules and regulations of the festival. This is no longer leisure time, and thus most playtrons never attempt to become members of the cast. Many may pass as performers at times, but festival staff rarely learn of these instances unless a cast member witnesses them or the playtron breaks one of the rules and another visitor complains to management. The playtrons have not been trained in the specific form of improvisation the festival employs to promote intrasticiancy, and they may easily fall into and out of their chosen roles, which festival performers refer to as "breaking character." Moreover, playtrons can break character without fear of personal repercussions since they are not employees. Yet those decisions can create a negative impact on other visitors who may witness a character break or experience an inappropriate action on the part of someone who is not actually a member of the cast. For these reasons, playtrons should not engage in any attempt to entertain those with whom they are not acquainted.

While in another theatrical setting this would seem obvious, i.e. if a person patronizes a "traditional" theatre, he or she is highly unlikely to mount the stage in the middle of a production of *Romeo and Juliet*. In any other profession such behavior would appear preposterous, i.e. a patron at a retail establishment or a restaurant would certainly not attempt to sell that company's product to another customer. Though a patron may make a recommendation, i.e., "these tights never run" or "the ribs are succulent," it is ridiculous to think that customer would then ring the hose up at the register or enter the kitchen to cook the meat. The festival equivalents are the difference between recommending a particular show — "go see Shakespeare's Skum" — and approaching a patron and saying, "I'm William Shakespeare." Nonetheless, this active attempt to participate as a performer though actually a patron occurs with greater frequency at the festival than in other venues.

Even if a patron is not personally attempting to represent himself or herself as a member of the acting company, others can initiate that impression. Before I became a member of the cast, there were some patrons who assumed I worked at the festival simply because of my knowledge of the venue. Though I did not attempt to actively perform, I did often give directions to privies, stages, and shops, and on more than one occasion other patrons would ask me if I worked at the MDRF. Beyond my personal experience, outside sources occasionally provide evidence of the playtron participation. For example, according to a 2 September 2004 article in the Fort Meade paper *Soundoff!*, Melanie Moore writes, "Kass McGann, a lady in waiting to the Queen of France by way of Easton, Pa., said she loves the Maryland Renaissance Festival. 'We got started because a friend of mine is playing the Queen of France this year. She asked us to come down and be one of her ladies-in-waiting,' said McGann." This is problematic for several reasons. First, while McGann's friend may in her own personal world be playing the Queen of France, she is not on cast at the MDRF, nor are any of her ladies in waiting. Either the reporter or McGann failed to make that important distinction, thus creating a false impression whereby anyone who read the article and then visited the faire could assume that the Queen of France was indeed a part of the acting ensemble. Second, the festival has no control over the woman "playing" the Queen of France since she is a patron and not a contracted performer. Therefore if she is performing in the streets, until someone affiliated with the festival witnesses it, the woman could be executing actions inappropriate to the festival's vision. Additionally, during some seasons, a member of the MDRF cast has portrayed a Queen of France. Such an instance in which there was a hired, professional actor portraying a character and a playtron who was performing the same role could lead to a great deal of confusion for visitors to the village. Finally, and most significant to this study, there are especially important issues when considering intrasticiancy. Persons untrained in the particular method of interactive improvisation that the festival employs would have a difficult time assessing a visitor's place in the intrastice and guiding the audience member through a performance appropriate to his or her level of immersion. Even many performers at the MDRF are known as "one-year-wonders" because they fail to return for a second season. While these actors are often quite skilled in the scripted stage shows, on the streets they are usually ineffective and often unhappy. With patrons who have not been trained in the skills interactive improvisation requires, the ability to guide visitors through the intrastice is even more difficult.

Nonetheless, playtrons do perform at festival in certain ways, and these performances fulfill personal needs and desires. In the case of the Queen of France, the playtron was Jane Stuart, a visitor to Revel Grove well-known to many festival performers. Stuart says she was careful to choose a character not appearing in Revel Grove as part of the cast ensemble in 2004 and chose an historical character because it provided "a chance to research a person more closely and try to act out a person" (field notes). She chose the Queen of France because she has French ancestors and speaks the language. Stuart, unlike many of the playtrons with whom I interacted, has a background in theatre. She interacted significantly with the members of the Royal Court, paying homage to the king and queen, giving them each a gift, and then presenting small hand-made tokens (sachets, also called sweetsacks, an oft-exchanged period gift) to each of the female courtiers. Why expend so much time, energy, and effort when she is a playtron? According to Stuart:

> I give gifts to the cast members because they "are the stage" of MDRF. Any faire I attend, I give the nobles a small token that is from the country I represent that day. I give them the respect any noble would/should expect. It also re-enforces who they are at faire and [that they] should be given way when approached. Somehow people now[a]days lack the manners people had in the "olden days." Guidance is needed sometimes [field notes].

Stuart's words illustrate an understanding of both the historical knowledge of sixteenth-century England and the reality of twenty-first-century America. She interacts within the intrastice in the pretext of sixteenth-century England when she reverences their majesties and presents the tokens to the courtiers. Her intrasticive time with the Royal Court allows her to play at belief because the cast members engage her at her level of immersion into the intrastice.

Nonetheless, a problem may occur when Stuart then progresses through Revel Grove and interacts with other patrons. Stuart explains:

> Some people at faire have a hard time understanding who the actors are and who are the folks just playing around. WE who play around give more histori-cal information out as to what is happening in the time period than the cast would. WE should also make the distinction that we are not paid actors, just people having fun dressing up [field notes].

Two issues arise when analyzing Stuart's comments. First, the question arises regarding what historical information they are imparting, to whom, and how. Second, and perhaps even more importantly, if Stuart and other playtrons like her are making a distinction to spectators that they are not "paid actors," then they are potentially interfering with other patrons' immersion in the intrastice by calling attention to the false nature of the characters on the street. Since playtrons are not trained in the interactive improvisation that is the MDRF's hallmark, they do not understand the way performers are taught to dispense information without exiting the intrastice and thereby maintaining the pre-text of sixteenth-century England rather than privileging the reality of twenty-first-century America.

Furthermore, the cast members at the MDRF understand that they play their characters not solely for themselves but for the pleasure of the patrons. For the actors, playing their assigned roles does not constitute recreation. Rather, it is the performer's labor and livelihood. In conventional theatre set-tings, this differentiation between audience and performer is clearer, as evi-denced by the following, transcribed directly from my field notes:

> People don't understand what it takes to work here. They think you can just call up in the middle of the season and get a job as a performer. Case in point: working in the office I took a phone call from a guy who wanted to perform. I explained that audition information would be available on the website in the spring of 2005 for next season. I explained that we had finished hiring in June and had been in rehearsal since the second week of July. I thanked him for his interest and told him to check the website for further details on auditions. Five minutes later he called back and spoke with our business manager. She had heard me speaking to him and asked me to take the call, thinking he wanted a position in food, etc. I went to get his address information to send him an application for workers (positions which would be filled throughout the faire as they became available). He told me again that he was interested in being a street performer, not working selling food. He told me he was a member of the SCA [Society for Creative Anachronism] and that he had a character already pre-pared, an Irish mercenary.
>
> I explained again that our street acts and performers had been contracted

since the spring and had spent seven weeks in rehearsal. I again told him that he was welcome to audition the following year. He then asked me if that meant that he could not come in costume. I explained that he was welcome to come in costume. He then asked what the difference was between coming in costume and speaking in accent and performing. I explained that coming in costume was fine as long as he was only chatting with his acquaintances. He wanted to know if he could wear a sword as part of his costume. I explained that weapons are not allowed at the MDRF except for contracted employees.[6] He told me that without his weapon he would not be able to get into his character as an Irish mercenary. After explaining once again that he could not bring a weapon through the gates and that if he tried security would send him back to his car to leave it there, he told me that without his weaponry he could not be the character he wished. I suggested that he either try without the weapon or choose another character. I then wished him well in whichever decision he made and hung up [field notes].

I do not know what particular choice this playtron made, but the situation is indicative of the differences between performers and playtrons. An actor playing an Irish mercenary would not need to rely on a prop in order to convey the character to a patron. Indeed, many of the performers at the festival are not allowed to carry weapons; those who do wear swords must have a special mark upon their performer's pass. These actors must display their passes to festival security on demand in order to prove their right to carry blades, even if the weapons are necessary for their characters, i.e. the characters are part of the *Human Chess Game* or *Arming the Household*, MDRF shows that rely heavily upon combat and combatants to entertain the audience. However, this playtron was not proposing to play a role for an audience. Like many others who attend in costume and create names and personas for themselves, this playtron wanted to play his chosen persona — an Irish mercenary — as an internal, self-contained, and self-generating act designed to fulfill his personal needs and desires, illustrated by his inability to "be able to get into his character" without the aid of his props.

At least Stuart and the Irish mercenary playtron both had a costume and a character with some sort of relationship to the Renaissance. Wench costumes, which are not historically accurate, are plentiful at the festival, and the display of the female bosom is nearly unavoidable. However, some patrons do not attempt to dress within the time period or setting, instead costuming more as if for carnival, in outlandish costumes with no recognition of the Renaissance. While some patrons may accidentally wear clothing from another period because they lack historical knowledge, in many cases it is a personal choice. A man clad only in a loin cloth and a Viking helmet or a woman wearing nothing except a chain mail bra and skirt are rare but not unknown occurrences within Revel Grove. In both instances, more than the costume is available for viewing. Describing Roman saturnalia, Mikhail Bakhtin writes,

> At the given signal the serious Roman citizen, who all year round feared to make a *faux pas*, immediately put aside his circumspection. Let us stress this complete liberation from the seriousness of life. In the atmosphere of carniva-lesque freedom and familiarity, impropriety also has its place.[7]

These patrons exist in a different time and place: in all likelihood, one that exists only in fantasy. Patrons who engage in these fantasies often find themselves immersed in an intrastice of their own creation and from which there is little chance of escape during the festival. These patrons are most likely to commit the improprieties of which Bakhtin writes.

The season following the one in which I did the bulk of this research, I returned to the festival again. I experienced a patron who committed the utmost of the improprieties that Bakhtin describes. I quote at length here from my field notes about this particular encounter because it serves to clearly illustrate the danger that occurs when a playtron crosses the line:

> All I wanted was a day off. I came back to perform on Labor Day Weekend of 2005, to reprise my role from last season, Elizabeth Seymour, Lady Ughtread, Queen Jane Seymour's meddling elder sister. I performed on Saturday and Sunday and thoroughly enjoyed myself. I was even a guest performer for *Cooking with the Kytsons*, the show I had co-created with Paula Peterka back in 2001 when I was playing the Duchess of Norfolk. Other than the cooking show, all of my time was spent doing what I enjoy most, playing in the streets with patrons. It was truly a joy not to have any other obligations than street performance where I could spend all of my time talking to and playing with the visitors to Revel Grove. I was able to spend time with my "sister-in-law" Anne Stanhope, the Viscountess (Melissa McGinley). I decided to take Labor Day Monday off from performing in order to actually see some shows I would otherwise not have the opportunity to watch.
>
> On Monday, I appeared not in the blue silk court gown I had borrowed from Paula, but rather in a pair of white shorts, an orange tank top, and a pair of white tennis shoes. I was so comfortable, and I spent most of the day touring the village and watching my friends and co-performers and enjoying the time with my colleague, Carrie Jane Cole. We were up near the wine garden, and Carrie had momentarily left my side, when a man dressed as a pirate approached me. He initiated a conversation with me, and at first I thought he was a patron with whom I had previous contact, but whose name and face I could not remember. Soon, however, I began to realize that he was not acting like a patron, but rather as a performer, as he began to engage me in a "bit." I looked over his costume for a performer's badge, thinking that perhaps he was a new member of the cast that I had not met. Nope. No badge. Then, his "bit" began to take a turn that confirmed what I already suspected: he was a rogue playtron out engaging people on his own.
>
> His "bit" with me became rather vulgar, beginning with a comment about

what my name should be. He had grabbed a hold of my hand, ostensibly to perform one of the simple hand kisses that are so often witnessed at the festival. However, he had not let go of my hand, and it took a certain amount of force for me to actually remove it from his grasp. By this time Carrie had returned to my side, and she noticed, almost immediately, that something was awfully wrong about the situation. The man continued on even longer with what I think he believed was a pirate/Renaissance version of a pick-up line. I continued to scan the crowd, searching for a member of security, for in addition to his inappropriate comments, I could smell the alcohol on his breath. I really didn't want to report him. I just wanted to enjoy my day off. I was still on the fence as to whether I should just let him go when he finally prepared to leave. But then, he made my mind up for me. As he turned away, commenting, "You have no idea who you're dealing with," Carrie and I looked at each other before I said, "Nay, Sir, you have no idea who you're dealing with."

And then, with his backside to me, he bowed, flipped up the pirate coat covering his tight-clad legs, and exposed the approximately twelve- to fourteen-inch dagger he had concealed under his coat. Since weapons are not allowed onsite unless you are a performer with a special pass, and since it was so obvious he had been drinking and was already behaving less than appropriately, I knew I had no choice. As soon as he began walking away, I shrugged my shoulders as I looked at Carrie, and she indicated that she knew I had work to do. I ran over to the closest beer booth, and even though I was in "civvies," asked the bartender if anyone there had a radio. I explained as quickly as possible who I was, and fortunately, she knew I had been a performer, so she grabbed someone from the back who had a radio. As I quickly explained the situation, the gentleman with the radio called security and put them on the alert to look out for the knife-carrying pirate. I have no idea if they ever found him, but I know that I spent the rest of the day looking for him with no luck. I can only hope that means he was escorted from the premises [field notes].

This playtron was costumed inappropriately, wearing only a pirate coat and tights, had been drinking, was approaching people he assumed to be patrons and interacting with them in completely inappropriate ways, and was carrying a concealed weapon. This is the danger of people who think that the festival is their personal playground at which their admission fees pay for them to do whatever they wish. This man's actions, if indeed he was approaching patrons (and considering that is exactly what I looked like, I can only assume I was not his first victim), were crude and rude and could very negatively affect a visitor's perception of the festival, even though the person causing the problem is not an employee.

Other audience members have commented on the clothing as offensive, including one female returning patron between the ages of 31 and 40 who filled out a Royal Registry card with this simple and direct comment: "Dress Code! Some costumes are OBSCENE! Especially w/children." This interface between patrons who do not know each other illustrates some of the problems of a theatrical event that privileges carnivalesque conventions in which audience participation continuously transpires. While outside of the festival/carnival atmosphere some patrons might have high-powered jobs and tight-knit family relations, within the gates of Revel Grove they act with shameless sovereignty and a complete lack of decorum. Most visitors do not fall into this category, but it is important to realize that within a carnivalesque setting, where certain laws are temporarily suspended, some will venture across the threshold into indecency and offensiveness, and even into criminal activity against those laws which remain in effect.

Patron Interaction with Performers: The States of Intrasticiancy in Action

Many patrons have a genuine desire to play with the actors, not perform for the audience. This patron/performer interaction is part of what makes the festival a unique theatrical event. As performers and patrons mingle together, the intrastice is co-created. A fifty-three-year-old male playtron comments,

> While MDRF created the site, built the stages, and scripted the productions, the patron puts his money down and purchases the ticket; once through the gate, an interaction begins between player and audience hopefully permitting the audience to play for the player. To me, this is part of the magic of MDRF, allowing the audience to influence the performance of the players [field notes].

A magical aura draws this patron to the festival. That magic, I would argue, is the creation of the intrastice. Examining the patron/performer interaction offers an insight into the way people play. Considering what occurs during the interface between performer and patron provides an opportunity to analyze what is significant about this type of theatrical event to the patrons who attend the MDRF. As Victor Turner writes, "The way people play is perhaps more profoundly revealing of a culture than how they work, giving access to their 'heart values.'"[8] By considering how patrons engage in the different levels of intrasticiancy, it is possible to gain a greater understanding of what is important to them. A story from Melanie Butler, a member of the Royal Court in 2004, helps to explain how patrons find their ways to participate in the intrastice and frame the event. She recounts:

> Sarah [Middleton] (the Countess of Rutland) and I were working with Diane [Wilshere] and Stephen [Kirkpatrick] ([the] Marchioness of Exeter and [Baron] Cromwell) and were going around at the beginning of the day inquiring of patrons if they were for the Queen (Anne Boleyn) or the King. If they said the Queen, we would give them red stickers (like the scarlet letter) and indicate that they should accept our condolences to their families on their imminent demise.
>   There was a group of teenagers who really seemed to enjoy this bit and proceeded to follow us around for the rest of the hour trying to "warn" people who we approached that they should throw their support to the King (quite a few of

the group were "branded" as Queen supporters). Even through the rest of the day, whenever they would see me, they would indicate that they had had a change of heart and were now loyalists [field notes].

Based on the performer's words and the actions of the visitors, the impact of the MDRF lies in the very ability of the patrons to engage in public play. This opportunity to "perform" without facing the risks an actor confronts when taking the stage allows visitors to vicariously experience the exhilaration that actors feel when they bring a role to life.

For some patrons, the journey to Revel Grove each year is like a pilgrimage. Because of the limited run of the festival, there is a set beginning and ending time for this ceremonial attendance, which allows the patron to have pre-set boundaries. As these patrons mix and mingle with the performers, there is a sense of ritual: relationships renewed, conventions followed, states of being altered within the nineteen days of the MDRF run. Turner distinguished ritual and theatre in one way based upon the separation of performer and audience. He writes,

> Ritual, unlike theatre, does not distinguish between audience and performers. Instead, there is a congregation whose leaders may be priests, party officials, or other religious or secular ritual specialists, but all share formally and substantially the same set of beliefs and accept the same system of practices, the same sets of rituals or liturgical actions.[9]

At the MDRF, performers and patrons alike have established hierarchies of leadership among groups of people with a common set of beliefs and practices. Unlike conventional theatre, these belief systems become part of the performance on the streets of Revel Grove as the performers and the patrons together create the intrastice. As playtron Steve Jamison, who has attended the MDRF for seventeen seasons, comments, "Lots of hugs from faire friends you only see that time of year, it almost feels like a church fellowship at times to me" (field notes). This interface between performers and patrons allows for the MDRF theatrical event to sometimes provide ritualistic purpose through theatrical means. Ritual and theatre, as distinguished by Turner (see above), become less divided when the performers and the audience share the same space. A sharing of space that provides for a greater sense of *communitas* is one of the significant attributes that separates these contemporary festivals from conventional theatre and influences their ever-growing popularity as the twenty-first century begins.

A sixty-four-year-old retired electronics engineer with a Master's degree helps to illustrate the way the festival facilitates *communitas* by creating the intrastice. He states: "The faire is home for nine weekends. I would sleep there if I could. It is an alternate universe for me. I am no longer a government bureaucrat with a security clearance, but rather in my persona, a Scottish miller who grinds the best grain in the shire" (field notes). This "alternate universe" is in complete alignment with the intrasticious state. When this playtron comments that he would "sleep there," he is echoing others who have experienced intrasticiancy both at festivals and other venues. In her dissertation, Jennifer Gunnels relates the story of a woman she heard sobbing following the closing ceremony at the Michigan Renaissance Festival. Gunnels writes, "Through ragged breaths, I came to realize that she did not want to go home, but wanted to stay here, live here; she did not want it to end."[10] Like the electronics engineer, for this woman life within the intrastice was preferable to life outside of it. Some people who have experienced historic heritage sites have had similar reactions, even though they do not fulfill the fantasy of being a part of the village. Snow writes, "But no matter how much the experiential tourists say they want to play the Pilgrim role, in the end, they do not."[11] The visitors — both to Plimoth and the MDRF — in most cases eventually go back to their comfortable air conditioned houses, their wide screen TVs, and their fully functioning bathrooms. However, when visitors say they want to stay forever, they may truly intend to never leave because they are in an intrasticious state which allows them to be, for a moment, closer to the exciting and fantastical pretext of sixteenth-century England than they are to the actuality and comforts of twenty-first-century America. The movement from the pretext to the reality may involve more than crossing the threshold the gates of Revel Grove provide. At the end of this chapter, I delve more fully into this "re-entry" phenomenon.

There are exceptions; I do not mean that people actually live in the sixteenth century, though some performers and vendors do live in the villages in which they work, at least during the season. Sometimes, patrons who attend the faire as paying customers eventually become paid booth workers, performers, or vendors. David Thompson is one such patron, who began visiting the festival as a form of casual entertainment. Then he began purchasing garb, a muffin cap here, a pair of breeches there, and eventually his participation in the intrasticious state led to a life-altering moment. A retired professor with a Ph.D. in history (Tudor/Stuart minor emphasis), Thompson traded in academia for life as a Renaissance man when his work situation became unpleasant. He states:

> The whole tone of academe had been changing into a more "businesslike" environment, and thus a mere location change wasn't that attractive ... at least my university seemed to be treating "teaching/learning" as a mere product, an excuse to charge tuition. In a sense, faires are a form of learning-as-play, and thus attractive to me [field notes].

He now works several festivals each year selling books and maps and thereby participates in accordance with his interest in contemporary American Renaissance festivals as sites of "learning-as-play." This concept clearly equates to the living history focus of the MDRF, but it can also be linked to the actors' methods of guiding patrons while they are in the intrastice.

Performers facilitate these intrasticive and intrasticious states by working in the interactive improvisational environment. This acting form produces a different type of energy that promotes an audience member's ability to participate within the intrastice. According to Freddie Rokem, who writes on dramatic representations of the past, "The central point in any theatrical event is thus to fine tune the different energy sources of the actors as well as the spectators in order to make them flow within the new collective which has been created."[12] These energy sources flow freely in the streets of Revel Grove, noticeably because the collective is not restricted by the normal audience/actor barrier of conventional theatre. Rokem's concept of the energy sources combines well with Marie-Laure Ryan's writings on narrative. Ryan comments: "Whereas the designs that promote immersion keep the audience hidden from itself, the quintessential interactive architecture is a circular arena, such as a sports stadium, that allows spectators to see each other as well as the action on the field."[13] Ryan's assessment has merit except for the issue of choice. She contends that the stadium seating "allows" the audience members to see themselves and the performers. However, the interactive immersion on the streets of Revel Grove offers a combination of the two styles which provides the audience the choice of whether to recognize itself, the performers, both, or neither. The way the visitor frames the theatrical event is itself then an interface between an individual patron and the festival system. This interface then facilitates the patron's immersion into the intrastice. Just as performers must be able to assess what degree of intrasticiancy a visitor desires, patrons make choices regarding how deeply they will travel into the intrastice.

The cast members at Revel Grove have different ways of describing their roles in the process, but they acknowledge the need to guide the patrons and to assess their desires. Cast members may engage patrons directly or indirectly. Direct interfaces between performers and audience occur in a variety of ways. Diane Wilshere, cast as the Marchioness of Exeter, recounts how an audience member consistently approached her during the 2004 season to create the interface and enter the intrastice. She states, "I had one Fairever Pass patron who just about every day talked about what an evil person I was. He regularly followed the storyline and knew enough history to know what the Marchioness's point of view was" (field notes). This patron came to the festival daily, which Wilshere indicates by mentioning the Fairever Pass which allows entry every day for a price less than six individual day's tickets would cost. He sought out the interaction and actively participated in the storyline, indicating immersion into the intrasticious state. Wilshere's acknowledgement of the patron's desire to actively create his belief in the storyline led her to continue day after day to listen to his rants regarding her character. The repetition of the encounter indicates his deep immersion into the intrastice. This was not an isolated occurrence. The patron sought out the actor in order to participate, to experience the intrastice more deeply by actively creating belief in the pretext. If the patron simply wanted to illustrate his superior knowledge of history, one or two conversations would have been sufficient. If he merely wanted to experience the theatrical event intrasticially, he would have had no need to repeatedly comment upon the sixteenth-century events MDRF was portraying. Instead, it was important that he be an active part of the pretext created in Revel Grove, and he underwent a daily transformation from a twenty-first-century American to belief in himself as a sixteenth-century commentator in support of Anne Boleyn. He framed the theatrical event of MDRF as a means of experiencing sixteenth-century England with as much vigor as both the performers and he can create. This communication between the patron and the event as well as the cast member is indicative of the interface at both the systematic and individual levels.

Another way of engaging patrons directly occurs when cast members approach the visitors with a set idea in mind. Though he has never read David Lowenthal's *The Past is a Foreign Country*, actor Michael Winchester's method for guiding patrons through their Revel Grove experience could share the same title. According to Winchester,

> Our [actors] are trained to stay in character and an environment has been created to make everyone feel like they're in the sixteenth century from the moment they walk through the gates. Revel Grove is our town, our time, and what we make of it. The Americans from the twenty-first century are our guests. We encourage them to find out more about us and our customs and as a bit of entertainment we, as sixteenth-century characters, try to find out about them and the strange new ways they do things in their time and country [field notes].

This is truly an intrastice between the pretext of sixteenth-century England and the reality of twenty-first-century America. The majority of patrons about whom Winchester speaks participate in the intrasticive state. They play at belief even as the actors turn that action back upon them. In the words of Jean Baudrillard, the actor dissimulates, which "is to feign not to have what one has."[14] In this case, the actor is pretending to have no knowledge of the twenty-first-century America part of the intrastice. As patron and performer create the interface which allows for the mutual dissemination of information, the intrastice opens for both.

These two cases illustrate a direct manner of encouraging patrons to partake in the intrastice. However, the manner of engagement is often implicit, as two or more actors will perform a "bit" designed to entertain the audience, but in which neither persuades nor discourages the audience from becoming active participants. This technique is also used at venues such as Plimoth Plantation. Snow writes: "Although the interpreters do not usually collude about the premise of these improvised scenes, neither are the scenes always entirely spontaneous. Sometimes two or more interpreters will get together and prearrange actions that will take place in the village at a specific time."[15] Sometimes it is just the idea of what might happen that leads to an ongoing bit. These begin as improvisations, but if you do them for nineteen days, they eventually come to have a type of "script."

For example, my 2:45 P.M. daily robbing was never rehearsed. It was never even discussed between the three actors who created the playlet. As courtiers, and therefore the wealthiest characters in the village, we had been warned that the Merry Men characters might attempt to rob us. Therefore, we discussed amongst ourselves how we would handle the situation, but on the first day of the festival neither of the male performers in the bit had any idea what my retort to their attempted robbery was going to be or how the audience would react to it. Snow writes, that "such extemporaneous scenes resemble short one-act plays, except that the audience can ask questions and make comments, and the actors improvise all of their dialogue."[16] The audience made several comments, both encouraging and discouraging the robbery attempt, participating intrasticively. However, sometimes the audience did more than simply make comments. Occasionally, patrons chose to actively create belief, to participate intrasticiously, so that things became real. The occasion upon which the children attempted physically to prevent the robbery, which I detailed in the Introduction, is a prime example of intrasticious participation. Following its initial performance on the first day of the festival, we tried to meet at approximately the same time every day to perform the bit since the original audience response had been so overwhelmingly positive. Spectators reacted in different ways, depending upon how they framed the interaction. Some saw it as a piece of theatre, and contributed intrastically, willingly suspending their disbelief and showing their understanding of the theatrical convention by applauding at the end of the bit. Others would call out warnings to me or suggest that I should just pay the robbers since they were obviously "really good men," thereby partaking in the intrasticive state. And then there were the girls who wholeheartedly involved themselves intrasticiously as they actively created belief by physically and verbally participating in the action.

Only because of the carnivalesque atmosphere was it also possible for these young girls to "attack" a fully grown man. Obviously their parents were not afraid for their safety, for they did nothing to discourage the children from using Little John as a climbing wall. While the carnivalesque often provides a suspension of laws and mores which visitors could construe as an opportunity for a free-for-all, in this case, the lack of rules allowed these children to play openly and freely upon their instinct, which was to try to save "the lady" whose dress was being stolen. Though the young girls may have been playing intrasticiously, their parents were obviously aware of the theatrical nature of the scenario being played out in front of them, otherwise they would never have taken the chance that the girls could possibly be hurt by the large man upon whom they were climbing, jumping, and hanging. The parents were likely participating in an intrasticive state, encouraging the children while maintaining the understanding that for them it was only playing at belief.

The same performance can evoke different reactions depending upon the audience member's state of intrasticiancy. Rokem has written: "Why an individual spectator reacts in a specific way to a performance is no doubt very difficult to understand or to examine in detail."[17] How the individuals become involved, however, is easier to observe and may provide a guide for analyzing reactions to performances through exploring the state of intrasticiancy in which the patron was immersed. If we can evaluate how deeply immersed in the intrastice a spectator is at the end of a performance, we may then gain a greater understanding of why he or she reacted in a particular manner. Veteran cast member Lisa Ricciardi-Thompson explains how assessing a patron's level of intrasticiancy leads to a greater understanding of their needs and desires:

> Of course we want to make the experience complete for those patrons who wish to be taken out of themselves. These are people who have gone to plays and other live performances so they know how to be "patrons." And then there are those who not only want to be taken out of themselves, they want to disappear and be born from the ashes into something so far from their reality that they may escape whatever stresses or shortcomings they have in their regular day to day life [field notes].

The first type of patrons Ricciardi-Thompson describes participate in either the intrasticial or intrasticious states. They have framed the MDRF as a theatrical event, and their interfaces with the system lead them to certain reactions. However, the second group of patrons to whom Ricciardi-Thompson refers are those who participate decisively within the intrasticious state. These are the visitors to the village for whom the festival is ritual; it is compulsory. They do not merely want this in their lives; they yearn for it in order to be able to function when they return to the world outside the gates of Revel Grove. Why they react in a given way to a performance is a function of the intrasticious nature of their participation within that theatrical event. Turner posits that examining a person's way of playing could lead to a deeper understanding of a culture than analyzing his or her method of working. By analyzing the manner in which patrons participate in the MDRF, their needs and desires as well as their core values do become clearer. During intrasticial and intrasticive participation, patrons indicate a desire to play and reap the benefits of performance without experiencing anxiety over the normally attendant risks, illustrating both their desires and their fears. At the deepest level visitors yearn for a time which provides an escape from the modern world, but again because of the pre-set boundaries of the carnivalesque realm, the risk of completely losing themselves is minimized. In the first case, the patrons attain their goals with little to no personal threat. In the latter, the temporal and spatial boundaries serve to at least curtail the visitors' risks.

Patrons' Interaction Amongst Themselves

Despite the luxuries that exist in the modern society, some patrons still may view the MDRF as a perfect place free from the harsh realities of the world outside the gates, projecting for themselves in Revel Grove a form of utopia. According to Bakhtinian scholar Caryl Emerson, "No one doubted that Bakhtin's image of carnival was utopian fantasy."[18] Emerson seeks to illustrate that in Bakhtin's construction of carnival, he failed to acknowledge many of the major problems with it, including the abuse of alcohol, and thereby portrayed a dream world that never really existed. He looked back upon the carnival from a temporally-distanced perspective and romanticized it in many ways, neglecting and glossing over its seedier aspects, all of which are part and parcel of the carnival experience. Nonetheless, some people, such as the electronics engineer who wants to live in Revel Grove, hold on to that fantasy of the Renaissance festival as a utopian site, perhaps also neglecting to see any negative side. It may be easier to ignore the negatives within the village walls when the destructive realities of the outside world seem far greater. According to Emerson,

> The suspension of everyday anxieties during "holiday time" and "carnival space"—the specific locus being the vulnerable, yet superbly shame-free, grotesque body—rids both me and my most proximate neighbor of the excessive self-consciousness that keeps both of us lonely, our words insipid, and our outreaching gestures timid.[19]

Carnival, as expressed through the MDRF, therefore provides a way to escape the reality of twenty-first-century America. Though the nation has created connections on a global scale, in many ways, America has become more and more isolationist on the local level.

Neighborhoods once meant knowing everyone on the block, dropping in for coffee without making an appointment, and formally or informally supervising everyone's children. At the beginning of the twenty-first century it is not uncommon for people to live in the same place for years and never know their neighbors' names. When neighbors do greet each other, it is often without any air of familiarity, in ambivalent tones, and from a distance. Festival affords patrons the opportunity to interact without risk, to speak loudly and boldly, and gesture with brazenness and familiarity. Turner adds to the Bakhtinian concept upon which Emerson comments. He writes: "In tribal ritual, even the normally orderly, meek, and 'law-abiding' people would be *obliged* to be disorderly in key rituals, regardless of their temperament and character."[20] Many patrons at the festival act completely differently than they would in other circumstances, even those primarily social in nature. Not only is the opportunity presented to experience the wanton side of carnival, sometimes they feel compelled to play along. Often the experience begins with feeling obligated to follow a simple and safe ritual. It may begin with echoing the court as the audience bellows a hearty "God Save the King; God Bless the Queen." Later, if everyone else is bowing to their majesties as they enter a tavern, a patron may show reverence simply to not stand out by being the only one standing. The drinking of mead, cider, and ale can also be contagious as a patron sees everyone in a pub raising a tankard in toast. All of this may culminate for a patron in the carnivalesque experience known as "bodice diving," in which a male patron uses only his mouth in an attempt to remove an object — often a grape — from a female visitor's cleavage. Thompson comments,

> I personally know some women (and a couple of men) who are quite conservative sexually, but who have faire costumes showing a lot of cleavage, wear regimental kilts, and the like. And, consider the games like "grape diving" and "kilt checks." Faire provides a way to take on another persona, but still in a safe way [field notes].

Monday through Friday these patrons may wear suits to their places of employment, shuttle children back and forth to soccer games and dental appointments in jeans and polo shirts, and play tennis in shorts and t-shirts. On Saturday and Sunday, when carnival exists at the MDRF, they can become wenches and rogues, or members of the nobility, raising their social status, and their behavior for a time accords with their garb. Nonetheless, they are always surrounded by many people — friends who will ensure that events never go too far or get out of hand — so they are again able to play with minimal risk.

The reasons that playtrons continue to visit Revel Grove year after year are far more complex than the mere ability to commit lascivious acts in a situation which offers an absence of typical decorum. Visitors who make the pilgrimage to the MDRF an annual event have special relationships with their fellow playtrons. The retired electronics engineer quoted earlier said he began as a casual visitor to the village but discovered as time progressed that within Revel Grove he had found something far more fulfilling than an informal amusement, something that might, as Snow has written, "remove the pain of a centreless existence." He states,

> For many years I attended once or twice per season. I enjoyed the food, enter-
> tainment, and the general ambience. Then, one year I wore period attire (garb)
> and the whole involvement changed. I was no longer a visitor, but rather a citi-
> zen of Revel Grove. Patrons would stop me and ask questions. I began to feel
> that this was indeed my village. I fell in with a group of about a dozen people
> who felt the same. Now we go every day of the season, rain or shine. We sit
> together (usually at the White Hart) and have a great time. There have been
> three marriages in the group in the last four years [field notes].

This playtron links his deeper involvement to his decision to begin wearing garb. Once he began to look more like a "resident" of the village, people began to treat him as such, and he began to participate more in the intrasticious state. Those who treat him as a resident of the village include the typical twenty-first-century attired patron seeking directions to the closest privy, as well as other playtrons clad in garb. As he found others who dressed and acted similarly, and with whom he could share his intrasticious participation, he became part of a special group.

This collection of playtrons bonds as the members share their common interests within the intrastice. The process by which individuals form fac-tions at the theatrical event provides another example of interface in action, as the MDRF generates the opportunity for a subculture to exist within the larger structure of the MDRF. These groups may occur in other situations, such as cliques that form at corner taverns, in softball leagues, or PTA meet-ings. However, the members of those groups are acting as themselves. In the case of the MDRF groups, the playtrons are often portraying different peo-ple because of the liberties afforded by the carnivalesque nature of the faire. Furthermore, in the cases outside of theatrical events, the intrastice does not necessarily exist, since there is no counter to the current reality which would allow for the state betwixt and between to occur. In addition, while eventu-ally some of the relationships may continue outside the festival and the per-sonas contained therein, i.e. the above-referenced marriages, this is not a requisite for the formation of these groups. These factions are akin to what Turner calls "star groups." Turner writes of these units, "Most of us have what I like to call our 'star' groups or groups to which we owe our deepest loyalty and whose fate is for us of the greatest personal concern."[21] He further notes that the groups may be formal or informal and may be as intimate as family units or as public as national identification. Furthermore, Turner writes, that "a star group is the one with which a person identifies most deeply and in which he finds fulfillment of his major social and personal strivings and desires."[22] The group the miller-playing playtron describes has provided not only strong friendships that last from year to year, but also has produced several marriages, creating new family units, one of the more intimate forms of star groups. The festival star groups function to sanction the behavior of their members in attending the festival each day, in participating through use of costume, accent, and character unapproved in conventional theatre, and in perpetrating carnivalesque acts.

Other long-time faire attendees echo the engineer's sentiments. Thompson, who lives in Wisconsin but has traveled to the MDRF for many seasons, states:

> MD[RF] is one of those places where I have some very good friends, and the hugs are not pro forma at all. MD[RF] is one of several faires where I have people that I account "friends," and I believe reciprocate the feeling — but I usually see them only once a year, and usually only one weekend [field notes].

Despite only attending the festival in Maryland once each season, Thompson acknowledges the depth of the relationships he has with several local playtrons and performers. The ability to forge lasting relationships in a short time is another product of the interface. Because the MDRF provides an intrastician environment, meaningful communication occurs at the point that two individuals meet within a particular state of intrasticiancy. This interface allows for significant information to be exchanged in less time than usual because certain assumptions about the other person already exist for each participant in the dialogue based upon their mutual level of immersion in the intrastice.

This quick communication also permits a hastier movement from verbal communication to physical contact. A female playtron who met her now-husband in person for the first time at the MDRF comments,

> I love touching people. It never fails to amuse me, all the hugging and greeting people you've known for six years but if your life depended on it, you couldn't recall their names, but these are the same people you would trust to help you out when the chips are down, and you'd know they've got your back [field notes].

This playtron demonstrates the illusory nature of the festival realm in the intrastice by commenting that often she does not remember (if indeed she ever knew in the first place) fellow playtrons' names. Carnival allows her to freely bestow hugs and kisses upon these individuals. Such physical demonstrations of affection to acquaintances so unfamiliar that their names are unknown could easily be construed as a violation of personal space. Societal norms and rules of decorum dictate that intimacy of this nature is inappropriate in the public sphere and may even be illegal within the workplace. The carnivalesque nature of the festival removes those barriers, freeing playtrons to express themselves in ways they never would outside Revel Grove.

Furthermore, this playtron comments that these unnamed faire friends are the people upon whom she feels most likely to rely. Turner explains the significance of the star groups to fulfilling this role of trusted supporter when he writes,

> In every culture one is *obliged* to belong to certain groups, usually institutionalized ones — family, age-set, school, firm, professional association, and the like. But such groups are not necessarily one's beloved chosen star groups. It is in one's star group that one looks most for love, recognition, prestige, office, and other tangible and intangible benefits and rewards. In it one achieves self-respect and a sense of belonging with others for whom one has respect.[23]

Star groups, which are often referred to at festivals as "chosen family," serve as trusted bands of allies who provide love and a sense of belonging. An event which occurred at the final *Pub Sing* of the 2004 MDRF serves to illustrate Turner's point of the role of "trusted supporter." After the *Pub Sing* had "officially" ended — that end signified by the farewells from the cast on the stage, the ringing of the eight bells, and the firing of the closing cannon — amidst "hugs, and tears, and glasses raised," something unplanned by the performers happened. I quote in length here from the weblog of Dr. Jeffrey Huo because I feel it is necessary in order to fully convey the ramifications of the star group. I have made editorial changes only with regard to consistency of citations:

> And then, just as the gathered company was about to dissolve for the last time, from somewhere in a corner, the last song began. The song that wasn't on the set list.
>
> > Oh, the summertime is comin'
> > And the trees are sweetly blooming,
> > Where the wild mountain thyme
> > Grows around the blooming heather;
> > Will ye go, lassie, will ye go?
>
> I knew this song wasn't on the set list — one of the cast members in the table in front of us had a performer's copy of what was on the set list, and "Wild Mountain Thyme" wasn't. But from the far corner where it began the song rapidly spread, arresting everyone in their tracks to raise voices one last time. From a few people, the song swiftly swept over every corner of the pub, the performers and central cast and the King and Queen on stage to all of us there, from a few voices to hundreds inside of a few lines. By the end of the first verse the traditional ballad thundered from the pub, amidst the warm glow of the lamps and the warmer feeling of close-packed friends, one last, last song, spontaneous and heartfelt.[24]

Huo's statement as it stands is enough to clearly define the people gathered in various areas of the White Hart Tavern at the MDRF as part of star groups, but the tale speaks even further to the nature of the relationships festivals generate. Again, quoting from Huo:

> By itself, it would have been a special end to a special evening ... but what I later learned about why that last, unplanned song had happened pushes the moment from special to the stuff of legends....The performers on stage hadn't planned on singing it. But one man in the audience had planned to sing it even if no one else would. Sing it for the Lady he dearly loved.
>   They were husband and wife, and loved the Faire very much. And like many who share that love, and make plans even from across the country just to be there with old friends the last special pub Sing, so had they, together — and she had scheduled her cancer surgery so that she would not miss it.
>   ... "Wild Mountain Thyme" was her favorite Pub Sing song. For some reason, this Pub Season, it was not sung [often] at Pub Sing, and she missed it greatly. So he resolved, *together with the small circle of their friends* [emphasis added], that if it was not sung again that night at the Last Pub Sing, that they would sing it for her. What he wasn't expecting was for the entire White Hart Tavern to join in.[25]

Huo's recollections from the final day of the 2004 MDRF illustrate how deep-seated relationships emanate from the collectives Turner called star groups. Despite the somewhat ephemeral nature of these relationships, there exists a feeling among playtrons that these bonds created during carnival are legitimate. Though members of a star group may not see each other at all during the other forty-three weeks of the year, the belief that, if necessary, each one would readily support the others at any time during the non-carnival season is partially promulgated by the link to the more communal past of sixteenth-century England. Understanding that others share your desire for a romanticized past that is not quite attainable, but which can be visited in the intrastice, aids playtrons in continuing their overwhelming support for the MDRF and other faires throughout the country.

Carnivalizing the Carnivalesque

There is a particular and peculiar activity among playtrons at the MDRF that illustrates just how deeply immersed some patrons have become within the intrastice. Some playtrons consider the final day of the festival year to be the "Day of Wrong." According to the Faire Source website, the Day of Wrong is defined as "the closing day of faire, when many playtrons dress in outrageous clothing."[26] Outrageous does not begin to cover some of these clothing choices. A few of these outlandish costumes to which I have been a personal witness include: a Klingon, complete with forehead makeup;

Tigger, in a kilt, accompanied by Winnie the Pooh, in a pirate coat and hat; a man who is normally extremely well-dressed in doublet and tights instead clad in a full female court gown and French hood, complete with the attendant cleavage; and several can-can girls, some of whom were not anatomically women. These playtrons normally dress in their Renaissance costumes, assimilating into the village of Revel Grove as if it was their home. However, on the Day of Wrong, they take to the streets in these bizarre costumes.

When I first witnessed the Day of Wrong, I could not fathom why these visitors to the village would spend the time and money to create costumes they wear only once to festival. Furthermore, I could not understand why when they spent so much time trying to adhere to an illusion, they would suddenly so willingly break it. This phenomenon is not unique to the MDRF either. Many festivals across the country experience this peculiar invasion. During the week before the final weekend of the 2007 MDRF, the MDRF Friends of Faire Message Board was busy with people planning their costumes. These Day of Wrong invasions are neither casual nor improvisational; they are planned down to the last detail. Comments on the board included the following about costuming:[27]

> This is going to be a good day: Us 501st guys are going to be in Force, like last year, but with a twist. We'll spend some of the day in full armor and later we'll all have the upper half of our armor on and the bottom half will be Utilikilts. I'll also be doing my Raiders of the Lost Ark/Indy gear. (from Bakuhatsu)

And this:

> Go Wookiee. I'll have my lego Wookiee on my keychain; my first mug from Ulfric that has a Wookiee with a turkey leg and mug on it; my brown/tan Wookiee tye-dyed t-shirt; my brown winter "Chewie" Wookiee jacket (Wookiee fur around the hood and a pic of Chewie on the left side) ... and I think that's it. (from Spyke)

And this:

> I'm trying to go in Lolita, that should be fun. I dunno if I should wear the black lolie wig or not though ... I have a dress, minihat, boots or shoes, and socks/stockings. (from Kitten)

Several members chimed in with their opinions on Kitten's potential outfit, encouraging her to "Go with the wig" and "I'm so looking forward to seeing this in person, Kitten. The pics I saw were outstanding. Very well put together." In addition to questions regarding costumes, this commentary exchange about alcohol use occurred:

> This past weekend while discussing possible DoW outfits, Fahrv and I were discussing the possibility of having a sober day. What could be more wrong than the DotRT taking a day off from drinking? Would anyone actually be up for it? (from Violet)

Uh ... Have you lost your minds? (from Evil Katrina)

We've discussed this before: if the DoTRT quit drinking then our Faire will lose so much money that it will be forced to close. Do we want that?? I mean, what are the alternatives: asphalt at PARF and an open field at VARF?

While I do love seeing you peeps on my native soil, I'll deal with the mulch yellowjackets. Keep boozin'! (and leave the blaspheme for me!) (from The Deuce)

there is NO WAY im stayin sober on a pub sing weekend, my lord woman.... HAVE YOU LOST YOUR MIND??? (from Rifraf)

The discussions, both about costumes and about alcohol, clearly illustrate the pre-planning that the Day of Wrong takes. The playtrons discuss in detail their clothing, exchange pictures, ask each other advice, and insist on continuing on with their ability to imbibe alcohol during the festival day.

While initially the Day of Wrong appeared to be a strange anomaly that did not fit into my theory of the intrastice, upon further reflection, it began to make perfect sense. For some of these patrons, their normal immersion into the intrastice probably takes place at the deepest level, the intrasticious. They have found a place where a ritual transformation has taken place, and the village of Revel Grove (in this particular case), has become a home. There is such a sense of normalcy about the MDRF that dressing up in their Renaissance garb, putting on layers and layers of clothing, hats, shoes, and various accoutrements no longer suffices as carnival for them. Instead, they are forced to carnivalize the carnivalesque. They are so comfortable in the intrastice of Revel Grove, that pretext of sixteenth-century England, that they feel the need to create their own Rabelaisian marketplace. Because the Renaissance costuming has become normal, they need to add a new mask, so they dress up as Tigger or a Wookiee or Lolita. They refuse to give up the ability to use alcohol, as the drinking and feasting are common ground of carnival, and letting them go would take away from their experience of the freedom the Rabelaisian marketplace provides.

Recrossing the Threshold

Eventually, patrons and playtrons alike — no matter how deep their level of immersion — must leave the intrastice, ending their brief visit to the pretext of sixteenth-century Tudor Oxfordshire. As the performers get to the front gates, many peel off to go change into their "street clothes." Some members of the court will stay as long as they can to wave goodbye to patrons. Outside the gates, the performers still maintain their characters. Bakhtinian scholar Alexandar Mihailovic writes, "As delineated by Bakhtin, however, carnival ignores the hard-and-fast distinctions of spatial boundaries."[28] Surrounded by torchlight, performers in costume, and a darkened sky, some patrons forget that they must leave the festive freedom inside, which includes leaving all alcoholic beverages within the gates. When a patron tries to leave with alcohol, security will politely ask him or her either to finish the drink or dump it. If a patron pushes past security, the performers are often the only ones in their paths.

Several years ago one particular patron, who was unwilling to heed security and unable to easily pass by female performers in full court regalia, instead chose to swing his pewter mug at the actor closest to him. On account of height difference, the tankard headed directly for my face. It is a feeling I will never forget. I had less than a second to decide what to do, and I fortunately managed to get my hand between his mug and my cheekbone. While I blocked him from hitting my face, the impact of the mug on my hand was violent enough to leave it bruised and swollen. In an attempt not to ruin other people's enjoyment of the last vestiges of the intrastice, I tried to react in the best way possible. Paula and Larry Peterka, who were also involved in the incident, explain what happened in detail:

> LARRY: I was playing one of the King's guards that year. I was dressed as a Landsknecht captain. I was wearing a chain mail bishop's mantle and carrying a short sword. I was also carrying a lit torch (fire). This was after *Pub Sing;* I had escorted the Royals and several Nobles to the front gate for goodbye duty. The Royals had retired and several other characters were still doing good bye duty, including the Duchess of Norfolk (Tony Korol), Lady Kytson (Paula Peterka), and a couple of others.
>
> I was trying to keep an eye on everyone (actors) and still saying good night to patrons. I had moved farther to one side to keep the smoke from the torch away from people. I was keeping an eye out for patrons trying to leave with alcohol still in their cups. The security people had been having a lot of trouble with this and had asked us to keep an eye out for this in previous days/weekends while we were out front doing good bye duty. They were concerned about liquor law violations.
>
> I was startled to hear Tony call my real name. We were separated by about 10 to 15 feet, with patrons between us. When I turned slightly to look at her, I saw that there was an altercation going on. She looked to have an injury to her hand and was trying to hold onto a patron.
>
> PAULA: It was late in the season, and we marched to the front gate after pub sing escorted by torch-wielding Landsknechts, one of whom was my husband, Larry. I stood outside the gates wishing the departing guests safe journeys home, and bidding them to return to visit us again. Without warning or explanation, I heard Tony's voice cut over the general din with a very stark "Help! Larry!" I turned in the direction of the cry, my brain already registering that the use of my husband's given name and not his character's was an indication that something was very, very wrong. I didn't know whether it signified that Larry needed help or that she needed Larry's help, but I headed that way as fast as I could in a court dress in the dark. I cut through the crowd to find my friend

pointing at a man walking away from her "Stop him; don't let him get away!" she cried, and I saw that she was cradling her other hand. I turned, now with a very simple purpose in my brain, and proceeded after the man. I walked up behind him, and without saying a word, I grabbed him from behind with a bear hug around his waist, turned him around and started walking him back towards Tony. He didn't resist at all, or really even seem to notice, until she was right in front of him again [field notes].

Key in this part of the account is the surprise both Peterkas indicate at hearing me call Larry's given name. I purposefully yelled "Larry" because I knew that while no one else would realize the significance, other cast members nearby (and especially Larry himself) would realize that for me to break character meant there was a serious problem.

The altercation continued and escalated at this point:

LARRY: I had a burning torch in my hands and no where to put it safely. I stopped a patron and ordered him to hold it. I had to tell him twice. As I covered the last distance I yelled for Security and I dumped my sword on the ground (did not want to have it at my belt just in case).

PAULA: I had a firm hold on him, so he wasn't going anywhere, but he reached out to grab Tony, and threw himself sideways in the process. All three of us went to the right, to the left, back to the right, and then down to the ground. I struggled to try to regain my feet, but found I couldn't. I chalked it up to bad balance due to the corset and hoopskirt I was wearing, and decided to work with what I had, which were his legs. I wrapped myself around his calves, and ensured that, once again, he wasn't going anywhere.

LARRY: As I grabbed him by the doublet, buttons were popping off of it. This made me keep shifting my grip. I was also noticing the cuts on Tony's hand, and that she seemed to be in pain. At first I was just trying to restrain him as I tried to figure out/find out what happened. Tony said that he had hit her with the mug when she asked him to stop as security was trying to get him to stop since he had beer in the mug. At about this point he started trying harder to get away from me. I was still holding onto his doublet. We were all very close. At this point he started struggling more, demanding to be let go etc. He really could not take a step because Paula still had him by the ankles. He grabbed me to keep his balance and pulled me closer. When he realized that I would not let go he tried to head butt me in the face. I moved my head out of the way and he slammed his forehead and face into my chest that was covered with chain mail. When he looked back up he had cuts on his face and some blood.

PAULA: About this time, I heard Larry's voice from above. I couldn't quite make out what he was saying, but I could feel the guy I had hold of tense up and try to move. My adrenaline-fueled brain found it necessary to add to the argument, and I heard myself shouting "That's my husband! And if you hurt him, I'll kill you!" I'm still not sure quite where that came from, but I meant it. I then heard Larry shout to me: "Paula! Let him go!" "Is security here?" "No." "Then, no!" "Let him go!" "Do you have him?" "Yes!" I then threw my arms out to the sides and shouted "Clear." He called to me to get up, and as I tried to push myself up to my knees, I realized that the man was standing on my one of my Tudor bell sleeves, and preventing me from moving. "I can't!" "Why not?" "He's standing on my sleeve!" "No, I'm not!" the guy objected. I then poked him, hard, in the calf, and as he moved his leg in response, I scrambled to my feet. A hand came down to help me up, and I took it. "Yes. You were," I told the man.

I noticed that the guy had blood on his forehead and a distinctive woven-ring pattern embossed on his skin. Larry looked fine. I then turned to the helping hand. It belonged to someone that I recognized as a Festival booth-owner, and since Security had arrived, and Larry looked as though he had the situation in hand, I let him pull me into a hug, while I tried to get my breath back and my heart-rate down [field notes].

The very real effects of carnivalesque behavior are clearly indicated by the memories the Peterkas recall above. Both the intoxicated patron and I were wounded during this altercation.

Bakhtin neglected to accurately provide a detailed account of the inherent problems the mixture of alcohol and carnival setting generate, especially when the effects of imbibing outlast the duration of the festival. According to Emerson,

> These critics hold that Bakhtin was overall so enamored of his utopian carnival idea, so in need of its spiritual balm and convinced of its salvific qualities, so (perhaps) even conditioned by the lies that fueled the rhetoric of his era that he was taken in by the deceptions of carnival and remained blind to its potential for abuse.[29]

Exploitation of carnival at the MDRF has very real implications. I am attempting to illuminate these issues with which Bakhtin did not grapple in order to illustrate the true nature of intrasticiancy. It is not time travel. What happens within the pretext of sixteenth-century England that the festival attempts to provide has actual physical effect in twenty-first-century America. The space between is an amalgamation of the two, a both/and situation not a neither/nor circumstance. The drunken patron, who attempted to continue his carnivalesque exploits outside the gates which mark the threshold of Revel Grove and the pretext of sixteenth-century England, caused tangible consequences in twenty-first-century America. The altercation escalated with three performers eventually involved, an unsuspecting and very frightened patron holding a torch, and a somber reminder that for some alcohol becomes a far too easy path to an intrasticiancy most patrons and performers would rather not seek. The transformations and communication at festival are supposed to be part of an idealistic view of the sixteenth century. The festival provides port-o-potties and soap; performers are anxious to bathe when they remove the layers of sticky and dusty clothing; and vendors practice food safety and sanitation techniques unknown to the Tudors. While these actions and activities are anathema to the reality of sixteenth-century England, they are necessary to the idealistic pretext of it that the festival seeks to provide.

People caught up in carnival may forget that twenty-first-century rules and laws still apply, even if they are dressed as a sixteenth-century upwardly mobile merchant. Turner explains the rules of carnival that Bakhtin ignores:

> Public liminality is governed by public subjunctivity. For a while almost anything goes: taboos are lifted, fantasies are enacted, indicative mood behavior is reversed; the low are exalted and the mighty abased. Yet there are some controls: crime is still illicit; drunken bodies may be moved off the sidewalks.[30]

Sometimes entering too deeply into the intrastice may cause a patron to be unable to process the existence of the line between carnivalesque and criminal behavior. The patron who ignored the security guard, assaulted one performer, and attempted to attack another crossed that line. I cannot say for certain that alcohol was the only factor in his inability to understand the tangible effects of his actions, but I would argue that it was at least partly responsible. And as Turner writes, the crime was still a crime, and his body was removed from the area, but, in accordance with the long-standing history of the suspension of mores and laws during carnival. While the patron who attacked the actors did suffer the consequences from his actions with regard to his self-inflicted wounds, he did not have to submit to the laws of the twenty-first century. The Peterkas explain:

> LARRY: His companions had not interfered but I had tried to keep an eye on them. They now stepped up and just wanted us to let him go. I was trying to get Paula to let him go and get free. I told him that the police would be there shortly [and] to stop fighting me. Shortly after this a deputy did finally get there. None of the security had attempted to assist us nor did any patrons. Most of this happened very quickly. Even once the deputy got there he kept just trying to walk away.
>
> In the end the deputy decided to just let him go. They did not take any of his information or take any kind of report. The attitude was there was not property damage and his friends were going to take him home so everything was okay. I pointed out that one of the performers had been assaulted and was injured. At this point the deputy just shrugged his shoulders and walked away.
>
> PAULA: I ended up down at the costume house with Tony and the booth owner, decompressing and deconstructing what had just happened. Tony and I got each other undressed and changed back into street clothes, and waited for Larry. We tried to get Tony to agree to go to the hospital, but she wouldn't. Larry finally came back, and announced, much to our dismay, that security had not only not arrested him, but had not even detained him, nor prevented him from driving home, and didn't want to talk to either of us about the incident! [field notes].

The patron in question left the site with his friends. Though I am certain he was sore the following day, he did not have to face criminal charges for his actions, largely because they took place in the carnivalesque atmosphere that MDRF provides.

This example above, of course, is one in a million. For the overwhelming majority, the beautiful and Bakhtinian-exalted nature of carnival is the reality. However, for a miniscule minority, exiting the intrastice and leaving the pretext of sixteenth-century England behind can sometimes be dangerous if the patron has entered the intrasticious state too deeply, whether or not through the use of alcohol. Patrons may have tried to find something they wished not to leave and so used alcohol to aid them in carrying the carnival home. Sometimes the patron may experience the immersion merely through a desperate desire to disappear, and, as Ricciardi-Thompson so eloquently states, "be born from the ashes" into something completely new. Others simply take a bit of the intrastice with them, and they use it accordingly throughout the year once they have re-crossed the threshold. Performers are constantly mindful that all types of patron exist, and they will often attempt to ease the visitor out of the intrastice and back to the reality of twenty-first-century America, if it is at all possible.

Afterword: "The Beer Is in the Pick-Up Truck"; or, "Put Down the Accent, Step Away from the Character, and Nobody Gets Hurt!"

Following an entire day of participation at the MDRF, it is sometimes difficult for both performers and patrons to reintegrate into the twenty-first-century American reality. Though no time travel has occurred, eight or more hours in character often does not come to a screeching halt just because the cannon sounds. Victor Turner chronicled a similar situation when he wrote about a mock wedding in which he had participated:

> It was interesting, too, to observe which persons "stayed in role" longest and who could or could not suspend disbelief in order to play their roles properly. The "bride" caught herself on numerous occasions following the performance talking about her "wedding" as though it was real.[1]

As the patrons stream out of the village and performers return to the costume house to remove layers of clothing, it is not unusual to hear someone accidentally continue to speak in accent or act as his or her character. When performers commit the *faux pas* of persisting to speak in an English accent, they are often greeted with either a hearty, "The beer is in the pick-up truck!" said in an overly exaggerated southern accent or a somewhat more sarcastic "Put down the accent, step away from the character, and nobody gets hurt!" (field notes). If actors continue to portray characters — and they are usually of high station — it is likely that they will be quickly removed from their self-proclaimed pedestals with such comments similar to, "You're not really the duke; you're a government worker in Washington!" (field notes). These admonitions against accent and character continuation are friendly, but important, reminders that the intrastice is closed for the day.

Nonetheless, memories of the time at faire and within the intrastice travel with performer and patron alike. For some patrons, the effects of festival linger far longer than the drive home. The memory of the man who sang "Wild Mountain Thyme" to his wife at the final *Pub Sing* of 2004 certainly lives on for many who were there, made perhaps even more poignant because the valiant woman eventually lost her battle with cancer. Likewise, others bring their memories of festival home, perhaps thinking about them rarely until something jars them and reminds them of the intrastice. Following the death of Bill Huttel, the man who portrayed King Henry VIII until 2001, an article appeared in *The Capital*, an Annapolis, Maryland, newspaper. Asked about her favorite memory of Huttel, MDRF entertainment director Carolyn Spedden responded with a story told by Mary Ann Jung, 2004's Anne Boleyn. According to the article by Jennifer Donatelli:

> Mr. Huttel was visiting Mrs. Jung and her husband at a party that ended late. When the party ended, Mr. Huttel learned he parked in a neighbor's space and the neighbor parked him in, Ms. Spedden said. "He had to knock on my neighbor's door at 2 in the morning to wake him up," Mrs. Jung told Ms. Spedden. "So there he is, and there's my neighbor whom he's never met before and Bill says, 'I'm sorry. I seem to have parked in your reserved space.' And my neighbor looks at him and doesn't blink. 'That's no problem, Your Majesty,' he says. 'I'll move my car at once.'"[2]

No costume. No accent. No site. Just the memory of the intrastice on which to rely, and the neighbor found himself responding as if King Henry himself had roused him from bed to move a carriage.

Memories of the faire and its culture linger on for both patrons and performers. My ethnography of the MDRF concerns only one of many festival sites throughout the country, but this work provides a backdrop against which scholars can analyze other faires. Furthermore, research into the intrastice allows scholars to examine diverse performances with regard to immersive level of interaction. From living history sites to murder mystery dinners, events along the theatrical continuum contribute to differing levels of immersion within the intrastice. Beyond the theatrical pale, examining the roles people play in everyday life offers an opportunity to explore the intrastice in further depth.

This work focuses heavily on cast members and patrons, paying small homage to stage acts and musicians at the contemporary American Renaissance festival. With the exception of the section of the chapter on the history of faires, which treats the difference between small and large festivals, and the third chapter (on the sensescape), another significant contributor to the atmosphere of the MDRF and other faires is decidedly missing from these pages and deserves further attention: the role of the vendor. The thousands of crafts-people who create the wares that serve as artifacts of the intrastice lead a very different life than the actors. Their own performances within the intrastice could well fill the pages of another book entirely.

In addition, there is a significant gap in the literature regarding the audi-ence for the contemporary American Renaissance festival. Who are the peo-ple who attend? Is the information garnered about the MDRF patrons applicable to festivals across the country? Do the same types of patrons attend both the small and large faires? Do different eras (Elizabethan versus Henri-cian) or locales (England versus France) draw differing visitors? Is there a cross-over between festival attendees and patrons at other entertainment gath-erings such as science fiction conventions? And, how do any of these factors effect the patron's immersion in the intrastice?

From a historical standpoint, there is much research to be completed on the selection of "historical fact" presented not just at the contemporary Amer-ican Renaissance festival, but at living history sites both in the United States and abroad. For example, at Kentwell Manor in Long Melford, England, Tudor recreations are an on-going enterprise through various times of the year. How do the entertainers at Kentwell choose which eras to portray? From what sources do they receive their historical research information? How do the managers of the site train their staff on both history and interactive improvisation? Do their patrons ever appear in costume? If not, how does the lack of patron participation affect the overall immersive experience?

Finally, there is also a large festival community which exists on-line, on the Internet. The seeming dichotomy, which is espoused by a group of peo-ple who purport to live in the past and experience the intrastice in varying depths yet keep connected throughout the year via the technology of the world wide web, is definitely worthy of study. Alt.Faires.Renaissance (and Alt.Fairs.Renaissance) was once the on-line community of choice for festi-val-goers. Now A.F.R. has been supplanted by Live Journal (LJ), although occasional posts on the former continue, usually accompanied by lamenta-tions for its demise. RenSpace.com (a Renaissance festival and faire version of the very popular MySpace.com) caters particularly to the patrons and per-formers of Renaissance festivals. Other popular sites include RenRadio.com, where songs often heard only at festivals stream on-line, and FaireNews.com, which provides information about performers, upcoming events, and general festival information. The maintenance of a community of people who cele-brate the sixteenth century, in reality a world lit only by fire, via the most modern means of technology possible is rife for examination.

I suggest these possibilities and questions as a means of extending the use of the study of the intrastice beyond the borders of the contemporary American Renaissance festival, both into other venues and into the cyber world. While I have filled the pages of this book with my own ethnographic experiences and those of the people with whom I have been fortunate enough to work, there are so many other venues that can benefit from this form of research. Yet, I come back to the issue of festivals and immersion time and again, questioning how embodied performance changes our perception of history over time. Memories from the 2004 season at MDRF linger in my mind even as I built new ones at the WHRF in 2008. Contrasts of Henrician versus Elizabethan dress and dance, large versus small venue, extended run versus short run, and established versus emerging continue to engage me. Both festivals provide a unique experience and a vastly different look into the Tudor life, as they should. Yet, both entice me back to perform, to visit with old friends and to make new ones, and to continuously re-evaluate what I have learned in my own time in the intrastice amidst the trees, the accents, the songs, the merchants, the smiles, the laughs, and the tears. This is a journey just begun, not one concluded.

So I say, "Go carefully upon thy journey and fare thee well."

Chapter Notes

Introduction

1. All of the quotations in this section and description of the event are from field notes I wrote of my personal experience, as well as from conversations with the others involved in the scenario. In other places in this work, I will indicate the use of field notes immediately following quotations.

2. Victor Turner, *From Ritual to Theatre: The Human Seriousness of Play* (New York: PAJ Publications 1982), 41.

3. Mikhail Bakhtin, *Rabelais and His World*, trans. Hélène Iswolsky (Bloomington, IN: Indiana University Press 1984), 410.

4. V. Turner, 43.

5. Richard Schechner, "Victor Turner's Last Adventure" in *The Anthropology of Performance*, by Victor Turner (New York: PAJ Publications 1988), 9.

6. V. Turner, 43.

7. All of the notations on meanings of suffixes are culled from the *Oxford English Dictionary Online*.

8. Erving Goffman, *Frame Analysis: An Essay on the Organization of Experience* (New York: Harper and Row, 1974; reprint, Boston: Northeastern University Press 1986), 10–11. (Page citations are in the reprint edition.)

9. Ibid., 21.

10. Temple Hauptfleisch, "Eventification: Using the Theatrical System to Frame the Event" in *Theatrical Events: Borders Dynamics Frames*, ed. Vicki Ann Cremona et al. (Amsterdam: Rodopi 2004), 281. (emphasis in original)

11. E. Goffman, 45.

12. Victor Turner, *The Anthropology of Performance* (New York: PAJ Publications 1988), 140.

13. Unless otherwise cited, the definitions from Conquergood that I offer here come from class notes I took during the final two classes he taught at Northwestern University: Critical/Performance Ethnography (Winter 2003) and Field Methods in Performance Studies (Spring 2003).

14. V. Turner, *Anthropology*, 89.

15. Dwight Conquergood, "Performance Studies: Interventions and Radical Research," *TDR: The Drama Review* 46, no. 2 (2002): 146.

16. Jenny Adams, "Marketing the Medieval: The Quest for Authentic History in Michael Crichton's *Timeline*," *Journal of Popular Culture: Comparative Studies in the World's Civilizations* 36, no. 4 (2003): 708.

17. In Chapter 3, I touch upon these ideas and ideals of authenticity, but only insofar as they relate to the immediate case study of living history.

18. Many scholars have told me that Renaissance festivals are unworthy of academic study because they are neither "living history sites" nor "cutting edge theatre"; some academics have referred to them as "fluff." For treatment of the highbrow/lowbrow issue, see Lawrence M. Levine, *Highbrow/Lowbrow: The Emergence of Cultural Hierarchy in America* (Cambridge, MA: Harvard University Press 1990).

19. Jennifer Sue Moore, "A Descriptive Study of the Michigan Renaissance Festival"

185

(M.A. Thesis Michigan State University, 1997); Jennifer Sue Gunnels, "Let the Car Burn, We're Going to the Faire: History, Performance, Community and Identity within the Renaissance Festival" (Ph.D. Dissertation, University of Texas — Austin, 2004). Gunnels's dissertation was the only Ph.D. work upon which I had to rely. The other graduate studies were all M.A. theses.

20. Raymond Williams, *Keywords: A Vocabulary of Culture and Society* (New York: Oxford University Press 1976).

21. Kimberly O'Brien, "The Effectiveness of Persuasion: A Promotional Videotape for the Michigan Renaissance Festival" (M.A. Thesis, Michigan State University, 1987); Brenda Reneé Pontiff, "The American Renaissance Festival" (M.A. Thesis, Kansas State University, 1986); Delanna Kay Reed, "A Readers Theatre in Performance: The Analysis and Compilation of Period Literature for a Modern Renaissance Faire" (M.A. Thesis, University of North Texas, 1987).

22. See Richard Handler, *The New History in an Old Museum: Creating the Past at Colonial Williamsburg* (Durham, NC: Duke University Press 1997); and Anders Greenspan, *Creating Colonial Williamsburg,* (Washington, D.C.: Smithsonian Institution Press 2002).

23. See Rory Turner, "Bloodless Battles: The Civil War Reenacted," *TDR* 34, no. 4 (1998): 123–136.

24. See Stephen Eddy Snow, *Performing the Pilgrims: A Study of Ethno-Historical Role-Playing at Plimoth Plantation* (Jackson, MS: University of Mississippi Press 1993).

25. See Kurt Lancaster, *Warlocks and Warpdrive: Contemporary Fantasy Entertainments with Interactive and Virtual Environments* (Jefferson, NC: McFarland and Company, Inc., 1999).

Chapter 1

1. M. Bakhtin, 7–8.

2. In her dissertation on the Texas, Scarborough, and Michigan Renaissance festivals, Jennifer Gunnels ascribes particular reliability to the SCRIBE network, <http://scribe.faire.net/>

3. Ben Simons, "A Brief History of the Renaissance Faire," *Renaissance Magazine* 6, no. 23 (2001): 34.

4. K. Lancaster, 45.

5. B. Simons, 36.

6. Phyllis Patterson, "Letter to AFR," (14 October 1999), alt.faires.renaissance (accessed 31 October 2005).

7. B. Simons, 35.

8. See Laura Shapiro, *Something from the Oven: Reinventing Dinner in 1950<ft>s America* (New York: Viking 2004); and William H. Young, *The 1950s* (Westport, CT: Greenwood Press 2004).

9. M. Bakhtin, 33.

10. See Alexander Bloom, ed., *Long Time Gone: Sixties America Then and Now* (Oxford and New York: Oxford University Press 2001); Stephen J. Bottoms, *Playing Underground: A Critical History of the 1960s Off-off–Broadway Movement* (Ann Arbor, MI: University of Michigan Press 2004); Alice Echols, *Shaky Ground: The '60s and its Aftershocks* (New York: Columbia University Press 2002); Michael W. Flamm, *Law and Order: Street Crime, Civil Unrest, and the Crisis of Liberalism in the 1960s* (New York: Columbia University Press 2005); and Simon Hall, *Peace and Freedom: The Civil Rights and Antiwar Movements in the 1960s* (Philadelphia: The University of Pennsylvania Press 2005).

11. M. Bakhtin, 34.

12. Ibid., 9.

13. For examples, see the artwork of Francois Clouet (*Agnes Sorel* after Jean Fouquet), Jean Clouet (*Marguerite d'Angouleme*), and Hans Holbein (*Artist's Wife and Children, Katherine of Aragon, Lais Corinthiaca,* and *Lady Guildford*).

14. B. Simons, 35.

15. S. Blazer, 36.

16. P. Patterson.

17. Janet Novack and Fleming Meeks, "Ye Olde Money Pit," *Forbes* 152, no. 14 (20 December 1993): 206.

18. Ibid.

19. The information chronicling the portrayal of Henry VIII and his wives at the MDRF is taken from personal conversations with Carolyn Spedden, Mary Ann Jung, and Paula Peterka, as well as from festival playbills from several seasons.

20. M. Bakhtin, 9.

21. Nicole Fuller, "Officials hoping to keep festival: As Renaissance event seeks new home, officials call it economic boon to county" *Baltimore Sun,* 6 November 2008

<http://www.baltimoresun.com/news/local/a nnearundel/bal-ar.festival06nov06,0,6090. story> (accessed 11 November 2008).

22. "Festivals International," www.festint.com/about.shtml (accessed 10 September 2008).

23. U.S. Census Bureau, <http://factfinder. census.gov/servlet/GCTTable?_bm=n&_lang =en&mt_name=DEC_2000_PL_U_GCTPL_ ST7&format=ST7&_box_head_nbr=GCTPL &ds_name=DEC_2000_PL_U&geo_id= 04000US29>

24. Charles Taylor passed between the first and second seasons of the White Hart Renaissance Faire. The information about his involvement is taken from conversations with Di Johnson-Taylor, his wife, and his resume, which she provided. All further information about the WHRF is from personal field notes or interviews and will be cited in the same way as the MDRF field notes.

25. This particular conversation with Brother William was conducted via e-mail, and the emphasis is his.

26. "Faire a la Carte," <http://fairealacarte. com> (accessed 28 September 2008).

27. S. Blazer, 32.

28. M. Bakhtin, 149.

29. Ibid, 7.

30. Ibid.

31. Ibid., 410.

32. V. Turner, *Anthropology*, 22.

33. M. Bakhtin, 89.

Chapter 2

1. Thomas Doherty, *Projections of War: Hollywood, American Culture, and World War II* (New York: Columbia University Press 1993), 182.

2. Parris N. Glendening, "Governing after September 11th: A New Normalcy," *Public Administration Review* 62, Special Issue: Democratic Governance in the Aftermath of September 11, 2001, (Sept. 2002), 21–22.

3. John Bush Jones, *The Songs that Fought the War: Popular Music and the Homefront, 1930–1945* (Waltham, MA: Brandeis University Press; Hanover and London: University Press of New England 2006), 31.

4. Brenda Ralph Lewis, *Women at War: The Women of World War II — At Home, at Work, on the Front Line* (Pleasantville, NY:

The Reader's Digest Association, Inc. 2002), 221.

5. The USO performs for the nation's troops across the world, providing entertainment for men and women of the armed forces who are deployed in far-flung destinations as part of the United States's military efforts.

6. Bill Adler with Tracy Quinn McLennan, eds., *World War II Letters: A Glimpse into the Heart of the Second World War Through the Words of Those Who Were Fighting It* (New York: St. Martin's Press 2002), 174–175.

7. Maxine Andrews and Bill Gilbert, *Over Here, Over There: The Andrews Sisters and the USO Stars in World War II* (New York: Zebra Books 1993), 6.

8. *The Rosie O'Donnell Show*, New York, NY: 18 September 2001.

9. Randall Collins, "Rituals of Solidarity and Security in the Wake of Terrorist Attack," *Sociological Theory* 22, no. 1 (2004): 74–75.

10. Snow, 171.

11. www.mapquest.com

12. M. Bakhtin, 178.

13. "Life Lines," *The Washington Post*, 9 October 2001.

14. Carolyn Spedden, *The Grand Event* (Crownsville, MD: Maryland Renaissance Festival 2001), 15.

15. R. Collins, 67.

Chapter 3

1. V. Turner, *Ritual to Theatre*, 9.

2. Wendy Griswold, *Cultures and Societies in a Changing World* (Thousand Oaks, CA: Pine Forge Press 1994), 11.

3. Paul Groth, "Frameworks for Cultural Landscape Study," in Paul Groth and Todd W. Bressi, eds. *Understanding Ordinary Landscapes* (New Haven, CT: Yale University Press 1997)1–21: 1.

4. Otto E. Laske, "Verification and Sociological Interpretation in Musicology," *International Review of the Aesthetics and Sociology of Music* 8, no. 2 (Dec. 1977), 211–236: 230.

5. Ibid.

6. Elinor Fuchs, "Reading for Landscape: The Case of American Drama," in *Land/ Scape/Theater*, eds. Elinor Fuchs and Una Chaudhuri (Ann Arbor, MI: The University of Michigan Press 2002), 30.

7. Lewis Thomas, *Late Night Thoughts on*

Listening to Mahler's Ninth Symphony (New York: Viking Press 1980), 42.

8. Marie-Laure Ryan, *Narrative as Virtual Reality: Immersion and Interactivity in Literature and Electronic Media* (Baltimore: Johns Hopkins University Press 2001), 288–289.

9. Michel de Certeau, *The Practice of Everyday Life* (Berkeley and Los Angeles: University of California Press 1984), 99.

10. V. Turner, 25.

11. David Howes, "Introduction: 'To Summon All the Senses,'" in *The Varieties of Sensory Experience: A Sourcebook in the Anthropology of the Senses*, ed. David Howes (Toronto: University of Toronto Press 1991), 4. (emphasis in original)

12. S.E. Snow, 180.

13. Alice Rayner, "Rude Mechanicals and the *Specters of Marx*," *Theatre Journal* 54 (2002), 535–554: 535.

14. Thomas Luckmann, "Constitution of Human Life in Time," in *Chronotypes: The Construction of Time*, ed. John Bender and David E. Wellbery (Stanford, CA: Stanford University Press 1991), 156.

15. Ibid.

16. Margaret Thompson Drewal, "Dancing for Ogun in Yoruba land and in Brazil" in *Africa's Ogun: Old World and New*, ed. Sandra T. Barnes (Bloomington & Indianapolis: Indiana University Press 1989), 199.

17. M. Bakhtin, 231.

18. Caryl Emerson, *The First Hundred Years of Mikhail Bakhtin* (Princeton, NJ: Princeton University Press 1997), 163.

19. Brooks McNamara, Jerry Rojo, and Richard Schechner, *Theatres, Spaces, Environments: Eighteen Projects* (New York: Drama Book Specialists 1975), 3. Note that at the Maryland Renaissance Festival, hat passing is not allowed. All performers are paid from "the King's purse."

20. Paolo Prato, "Music in the Streets: The Example of Washington Square Park in New York City," *Popular Music* 4 (1984), 151–163: 151.

21. Ibid., 157.

22. Ibid.

23. David Howes, "Olfaction and Transition," in *The Varieties of Sensory Experience: A Sourcebook in the Anthropology of the Senses*, ed. David Howes (Toronto: University of Toronto Press 1991), 142. (emphasis in original)

24. Though elephants were not often seen in England in the sixteenth century, pastures of sheep and cows filled the rural areas, and the smell of dung is one modern audiences associate with the time period. Contemporary films about medieval and early modern England often feature specific references to the smell of feces, and today's festival attendee is often a viewer of films of the period (field notes). See such films as *Braveheart, Robin Hood: Prince of Thieves, A Knight's Tale,* and *Shakespeare in Love* for examples of animal and human proximity and commentary on feces.

25. M. Bakhtin, 235–236.

26. Ibid., 182.

27. C. Emerson, 163.

28. M. Bakhtin, 39–40.

29. Maurice Merleau-Ponty, *Nature: Course Notes from the Collège de France*, trans. Robert Vallier (Evanston, IL: Northwestern University Press 2003), 221.

30. Shai Burstyn, "In Quest of the Period Ear," *Early Music* 25, no. 4 (1997): 696.

31. M. Bakhtin, 80.

32. Anthony Synnott, "Puzzling over the Senses: From Plato to Marx," in *The Varieties of Sensory Experience: A Sourcebook in the Anthropology of the Senses*, ed. David Howes (Toronto: University of Toronto Press 1991), 64–65.

33. Matthew Wilson Smith, "Bayreuth, Disneyland, and the Return to Nature," ed. Elinor Fuchs and Una Chaudhuri (Ann Arbor, MI: The University of Michigan Press 2002), 265.

34. Dwight Conquergood, "Of Caravans and Carnivals: Performance Studies in Motion," *TDR: The Drama Review* 39, no. 4 (1995), 138.

35. M. Bakhtin, 259.

36. Barbara Kirshenblatt-Gimblett, *Destination Culture: Tourism, Museums, and Heritage* (Berkeley, CA: The University of California Press 1998), 192.

37. Ibid., 194.

Chapter 4

1. Jay Anderson, *Time Machines* (Nashville: American Association for State and Local History 1984), 42.

2. Jean Baudrillard, *Simulacra and Simulation*, trans. Sheila Faria Glaser (Ann Arbor,

MI: The University of Michigan Press 1994), 6.

3. R. Turner, 124.

4. Scott Magelssen. "Living History Museums and the Construction of the Real Through Performance," *Theatre Survey* 45, no. 1 (May 2004): 65.

5. Ibid., 61.

6. I was a member of the Guild of St. Genesius in 1998, assistant guild mistress of the Household of Hengrave Hall in its first year of existence in 1999, and subsequently served as a *de facto* dramaturg.

7. Carolyn Spedden, Artistic Director, International Renaissance Festivals, Inc., interview by author, 7 December 2001, Crownsville, MD in Kimberly Tony Korol, "God is in the Details: The Development of the Guild of St. George, the Living History Component of the Maryland Renaissance Festival," written for University of Maryland Theatre Historiography (THET 712), 17 December 2001, 9–10.

8. Carolyn Spedden, Crownsville, MD, to actors in the companies of St. Genesius and St. George, April 2000, International Renaissance Festivals, Inc.

9. Paula Peterka, Crownsville, MD, to the Hengrave Hall Yahoo Groups listserve, via e-mail, 15 May 2002.

10. Ibid.

11. R. Turner, 125.

12. S.E. Snow, 168.

13. For more information on Menzer's work, see <www.furman.edu/~mmenzer/gvs>

14. See Diana Taylor, *The Archive and the Repertoire.*

15. R. Turner, 127.

16. For further insight into patrons' immersion into the intrastice and creation of personal storylines amongst themselves, see Chapter 6.

17. *The Free Lancers* <http://freelancers. faire.net/freelancers.html> (accessed 1 October 2005).

18. Ibid.

19. Freddie Rokem, *Theatrical Representations of the Past in Contemporary Theatre* (Iowa City: University of Iowa Press 2000), 201.

Chapter 5

1. Marvin Carlson, *The Haunted Stage: The Theatre as Memory Machine* (Ann Arbor,

MI: The University of Michigan Press 2001), 17.

2. S.E. Snow, 170.

3. Ibid., 175.

4. V. Turner, *Ritual to Theatre*, 25.

5. S.E. Snow, 173.

6. Ibid., 180.

7. E. Goffman, 45.

8. Ibid.

9. S.E. Snow, 178.

10. Carolyn Spedden, *The Royal Arrival*, Maryland Renaissance Festival, Crownsville, MD, September 2004.

11. Ibid.

12. Michael Worton and Judith Still, eds. *Intertextuality: "Theories and Practices,"* (Manchester and New York: Manchester University Press 1990), 6.

13. Carolyn Spedden, *Katherine's Story*, Maryland Renaissance Festival, Crownsville, MD, 15 October 2004.

14. E. Goffman, 45.

15. Tracy C. Davis, "Do You Believe in Fairies?: The Hiss of Dramatic License," *Theatre Journal* 57, no. 1 (2005), 78.

16. E. Goffman, 38.

17. S.E. Snow, 175.

18. Freddie Rokem, 202.

19. S.E. Snow, 179.

20. V. Turner, *Anthropology*, 22.

21. M. Bakhtin, 248.

Chapter 6

1. Gary Alan Fine, *Shared Fantasy: Role-Playing Games as Social Worlds* (Chicago: University of Chicago Press 1983), 196.

2. T. Davis, 81.

3. S.E. Snow, 164.

4. E. Goffman, 124.

5. Ibid., 22.

6. Bladed weapons sold at the festival are wrapped in paper or boxes. Vendors inform patrons of the rules against carrying unwrapped bladed weapons. If a patron removes the wrapping and attempts to openly carry the weapon, it is likely that security will stop him or her and ask the patron to take the weapon to his or her vehicle.

7. M. Bakhtin, 247.

8. V. Turner, *Anthropology*, 124.

9. V. Turner, *Ritual to Theatre*, 112.

10. J.S. Gunnels, 238.

11. S.E. Snow, 167.

12. F. Rokem, 200.

13. M. Ryan, 298.

14. J. Baudrillard, 3.

15. S.E. Snow, 177.

16. Ibid., 178.

17. F. Rokem, 202.

18. C. Emerson, 164.

19. Ibid., 163.

20. V. Turner, *From Ritual to Theatre*, 43.

21. Ibid., 69.

22. Ibid.

23. Ibid.

24. "The Tales of Peter Geoffrey of Turnberry,"<http://www.personal.umich.edu/~jeffshuo/2ktwmt.html> (accessed 20 May 2008).

25. Ibid. Huo notes in a postscript to his story that he "later learned his name was Jeff. Her name was Bonnie.... She did survive her surgery, and fought on valiantly beyond that, for almost another two years. In the end, she finally lost her struggle in July of 2006." Huo garnered the information about Jeff and Bonnie from the alt.fairs.renaissance site, in two separate posts. In the first, Jeff recounts the same story as his "favorite faire memory," and in the second, Jeff announces Bonnie's death on 4 July 2006.

26. "RenSpeak," *The Faire Resource*, <http://thefairesource.com/renspeak.aspx> (accessed 30 September 2008).

27. All quoted comments in this section are taken from the following website: "Message Boards," *MDRF Friends of Faire*, <http://mdfof.proboards55.com/index.cgi?action=display&board=92007&thread=1277&page=1> (accessed 30 September 2008).

28. Alexandar Mihailovic, *Corporeal Words: Mikhail Bakhtin's Theology of Discourse* (Evanston, IL: Northwestern University Press 1997), 153.

29. C. Emerson, 170.

30. V. Turner, *Anthropology*, 120.

Afterword

1. V. Turner, *Anthropology*, 142–144.

2. Jennifer Donatelli, "Festival 'king' dies of heart attack," *The Capital*, 17 November 2001.

Bibliography

Adams, Jenny. "Marketing the Medieval: The Quest for Authentic History in Michael Crichton's *Timeline*." *Journal of Popular Culture: Comparative Studies in the World's Civilizations* 36, no. 4 (2003): 704–723.

Adams, Michael C. C. "Preface: Citizens Who Quest (For Knowledge)," "Knights on Horseback," and "Afterword: Historians with Axes (To Grind)." In *Echoes of War: A Thousand Years of Military History in Popular Culture*. Lexington, KY: The University Press of Kentucky, 2002.

Anderson, Jay. *Time Machines*. Nashville: American Association for State and Local History, 1984.

Anne of a Thousand Days (1969). Dir. Charles Jarrott. Universal Studios, 1988. Videocassette.

Bakhtin, Mikhail M. *Rabelais and His World*. Translated by Hélène Iswolsky. Bloomington: Indiana University Press, 1984.

Baudrillard, Jean. *Simulacra and Simulation*. Translated by Sheila Faria Glaser. Ann Arbor: The University of Michigan Press, 1994.

Becker, Howard S. *Art Worlds*. Berkeley, CA: University of California Press, 1982.

Benson, Susan Porter, Steven Brier, and Roy Rosenzweig, eds. *Presenting the Past: Essays on History and the Public*. Philadelphia: Temple University Press, 1986.

Blatti, Jo, ed. *Past Meets Present: Essays About Historic Interpretation and Public Audiences*. Washington, D.C.: Smithsonian Institution Press, 1987.

Blazer, Sam. "The Renaissance Pleasure Faire," *TDR: The Drama Review* 20, no. 2 (1976): 31–37.

Bloom, Alexander, ed. *Long Time Gone: Sixties America Then and Now*. Oxford and New York: Oxford University Press, 2001.

Bottoms, Stephen J. *Playing Underground: A Critical History of the 1960s Off-off-Broadway Movement*. Ann Arbor: University of Michigan Press, 2004.

Bordo, Susan. *Unbearable Weight: Feminism, Western Culture, and the Body*. Berkeley: University of California Press, 1993.

Boyd, Morrison Comegys. *Elizabethan Music and Musical Criticism*. 2nd ed. Philadelphia: University of Pennsylvania Press, 1962.

Braveheart (1995). Dir. Mel Gibson. Paramount Studios, 1995. Videocassette.

Buckley, Ann. *Hearing the Past: Essays in Historical Ethnomusicology and the Archaeology of Sound*. Liege: ERAUL, 1986.

Burstyn, Shai. "In Quest of the Period Ear." *Early Music* 25, no. 4 (1997):692–697, 699–701.

Caillois, Roger. *Man, Play, and Games.* Translated by Meyer Barash. New York: Free Press of Glencoe, 1961.

Camus, Renee. "Historical Re-Enactment: Fact or Fiction? Can We Achieve Historical Accuracy When Re-Enacting Period Social Dance?" Paper presented at the Congress on Research in Dance, New York University 2001.

Carlson, Marvin. *The Haunted Stage: The Theatre as Memory Machine.* Ann Arbor: University of Michigan Press, 2001.

Castle, Terry. *Masquerade and Civilization: The Carnivalesque in Eighteenth-Century English Culture and Fiction.* Stanford, CA: Stanford University Press, 1986.

Certeau, Michel de. *The Practice of Everyday Life.* Berkeley and Los Angeles: University of California Press, 1984.

Clifford, James. *Predicament of Culture: Twentieth Century Ethnography, Literature and Art.* Cambridge: Harvard University Press, 1988.

Clopper, Lawrence M. *Drama, Play, and Game: English Festive Culture in the Medieval and Early Modern Period.* Chicago: University of Chicago Press, 2001.

Comaroff, John & Jean. *Ethnography and the Historical Imagination.* Boulder, CO: Westview Press, 1992.

Conquergood, Dwight. Northwestern University: Critical/Performance Ethnography (Winter 2003) and Field Methods in Performance Studies (Spring 2003).

_____. "Of Caravans and Carnivals: Performance Studies in Motion," *TDR: The Drama Review* 39, no. 4 (1995): 137–141.

_____. "Performance Studies: Interventions and Radical Research." *TDR: The Drama Review* 46, no. 2 (2002): 145–156.

Crane, Susan, ed. *Museums and Memory.* Stanford, CA: Stanford University Press, 2000.

Dangerous Beauty (1998). Dir. Marshall Herskovitz. Warner Studios, 1998. Videocassette.

Davis, Tracy C. "Do You Believe in Fairies?: The Hiss of Dramatic License." *Theatre Journal* 57, no. 1 (2005): 57–81.

The Dietary of Ghostly Helthe. London: Henry Pepwell, 1523.

Donatelli, Jennifer. "Festival 'king' dies of heart attack." *The Capital.* 17 November 2001.

Drewal, Margaret Thompson. "Dancing for Ogun in Yoruba Land and in Brazil." In *Africa's Ogun: Old World and New,* edited by Sandra T. Barnes, 199–234. Bloomington & Indianapolis: Indiana University Press, 1989.

Echols, Alice. *Shaky Ground: The '60s and its Aftershocks.* New York: Columbia University Press, 2002.

Eco, Umberto. *Carnival.* New York: Mouton Publishers, 1984.

Elizabeth (1998). Dir. Shekar Kapur. Umvd, 2003. Videocassette.

Elton, G.R. *England Under the Tudors.* 3rd ed. London and New York: Routledge, 1991.

Emerson, Caryl. *The First Hundred Years of Mikhail Bakhtin.* Princeton: Princeton University Press, 1997.

Excalibur (1981). Dir. John Boorman. Warner Studios, 1981. Videocassette.

Fine, Gary Alan. *Shared Fantasy: Role-Playing Games as Social Worlds.* Chicago: University of Chicago Press, 1983.

First Knight (1995). Dir. Jerry Zucker. Columbia/TriStar Studios, 1995. Videocassette.

Flamm, Michael W. *Law and Order: Street Crime, Civil Unrest, and the Crisis of Liberalism in the 1960s.* New York: Columbia University Press, 2005.

Fraser, Antonia. *The Wives of Henry VIII.* New York: Vintage Books, 1994.

"The Free Lancers." <http://freelancers.faire.net/freelancers.html>

Fuchs, Elinor. "Reading for Landscape: The Case of American Drama." In *Land/Scape/Theater,* edited by Elinor Fuchs and Una Chaudhuri, 30–50. Ann Arbor: University of Michigan Press, 2002.

Galpin, Francis W. *Old English Instruments of Music: Their History and Character.* 4th ed. London: Methuen & Co., 1965.

Geertz, Clifford. *The Interpretation of Cultures: Selected Essays*. New York: Basic Books, 1973.

Gent, Lucy and Nigel Llewellyn, eds. *Renaissance Bodies: The Human Figure in English Culture, c. 1540–1660*. London: Reaktion Books, 1990.

Glendening, Parris. "Governing after September 11th: A New Normalcy," *Public Administration Review* 62, Special Issue: Democratic Governance in the Aftermath of September 11, 2001. (Sept., 2002), 21–23.

Goffman, Erving. *Frame Analysis: An Essay on the Organization of Experience*. New York: Harper and Row, 1974. Reprint, Boston: Northeastern University Press, 1986.

_____. *The Presentation of Self in Everyday Life*. New York: Doubleday, 1959.

Goodacre, Elizabeth Jane and Gavin Baldwin. *Living the Past: Reconstruction, Recreation, Re-enactment, and Education at Museums and Historical Sites*. London: Middlesex University Press, 2002.

Greenspan, Anders. *Creating Colonial Williamsburg*. Washington, D.C.: Smithsonian Institution Press, 2002.

Griswold, Wendy. *Cultures and Societies in a Changing World*. London: Pine Forge Press, 1994.

Groth, Paul. "Frameworks for Cultural Landscape Study." In *Understanding Ordinary Landscapes,* edited by Paul Groth and Todd W. Bressi, 1–21. New Haven, CT: Yale University Press, 1997.

Gunnels, Jennifer Sue. "Let the Car Burn, We're Going to the Faire: History, Performance, Community and Identity within the Renaissance Festival." Ph.D. dissertation, University of Texas — Austin, 2004.

Hagan, Joan and David Hagan. *Civil War Re-Enactment*. Atglen, PA: Schiffer Pub., 1996.

Hall, Simon. *Peace and Freedom: The Civil Rights and Antiwar Movements in the 1960s*. Philadelphia: The University of Pennsylvania Press, 2005.

Hamlet (1991). Dir. Franco Zeffirelli. Warner Home Video, 2004. DVD.

Handler, Richard. *The New History in an Old Museum: Creating the Past at Colonial Williamsburg*. Durham, NC: Duke University Press, 1997.

Harrison, William. *The Description of England: The Classic Contemporary Account of Tudor Social Life*. Edited by Georges Edelen. Washington, DC and New York: The Folger Shakespeare Library and Dover Publications, Inc., 1994.

Haskell, Harry. *The Early Music Revival: A History*. London: Thames and Hudson, 1988.

Hauptfleisch, Temple. "Eventification: Using the Theatrical System to Frame the Event" in *Theatrical Events: Borders Dynamics Frames*, edited by Vicki Ann Cremona, Peter Eversmann, Willmar Sauter, and John Tulloch. Amsterdam: Rodopi, 2004.

Henry V (1989). Dir. Kenneth Branagh. MGM/UA Video, 2000. DVD.

Henry VIII: A&E Biography. A&E Entertainment, 2000. Videocassette.

Here Beginneth a Treatise of a Galau[n]t. London: Wynkyn de Worde, 1510.

Here Foloweth a lytell treatyse of the beaute of women newly translated out of Frenshe in to Englishe. London: Rycharde Fawkes, 1525.

Horwitz, Tony. *Confederates in the Attic: Dispatches from the Unfinished Civil War*. New York: Pantheon, 1998.

Howes, David. "Introduction: 'To Summon All the Senses.'" In *The Varieties of Sensory Experience: A Sourcebook in the Anthropology of the Senses*, edited by David Howes, 3–24. Toronto: University of Toronto Press, 1991.

_____. "Olfaction and Transition." In *The Varieties of Sensory Experience: A Sourcebook in the Anthropology of the Senses*, edited by David Howes, 128–147. Toronto: University of Toronto Press, 1991.

Hudson, Kenneth. *Social History of Museums: What the Visitors Thought*. London: Macmillan, 1975.

Huizinga, Johan. *Homo Ludens: The Study of the Play-Element in Culture*. Boston: Beacon, 1995.

Izzo, Gary. *Acting Interactive Theatre: A Handbook*. Portsmouth, NH: Heinemann, 1998.

_____. *The Art of Play: The New Genre of Interactive Theatre*. Portsmouth, NH: Heinemann, 1997.

Joseph, Suad. "Relationality and Ethnographic Subjectivity: Key Informants and the Construction of Personhood in Fieldwork." In *Feminist Dilemmas in Fieldwork*, edited by Diane L. Wolf, 107–121. Boulder, CO: Westview Press, Inc., 1996.

Kirshenblatt-Gimblett, Barbara. *Destination Culture: Tourism, Museums, and Heritage*. Berkeley: University of California Press, 1998.

A Knight's Tale (2001). Dir. Brian Helgeland. Columbia/TriStar, 2003. Videocassette.

Kulick, Don and Margaret Willson. *Taboo: Sex, Identity and Erotic Subjectivity in Anthropological Fieldwork*. London: Routledge, 1995.

Lancaster, Kurt. *Warlocks and Warpdrive: Contemporary Fantasy Entertainments with Interactive and Virtual Environments*. With a forward by Brooks McNamara. Jefferson, NC: McFarland & Company, Inc., 1999.

Laske, Otto E. "Verification and Sociological Interpretation in Musicology," *International Review of the Aesthetics and Sociology of Music* 8, no. 2 (1977): 211–236.

Laurent, Dominican. *The Boke Named the Royall*. London: Wynkyn de Worde, 1507.

Levine, Joseph M. *Re-enacting the Past: Essays on the Evolution of Modern English Historiography*. Burlington, VT: Ashgate, 2004.

Lindsey, Karen. *Divorced, Beheaded, Survived: A Feminist Reinterpretation of the Wives of Henry VIII*. Cambridge, MA: Perseus Publishing, 1995.

Lofland, John and Lyn H. Lofland. *Analyzing Social Settings: A Guide to Qualitative Observation and Analysis*. Belmont, CA: Wadsworth, 1995.

Lowenthal, David. *The Past is a Foreign Country*. Cambridge, UK: Cambridge University Press, 1985.

Luckmann, Thomas. "Constitution of Human Life in Time." In *Chronotypes: The Construction of Time*, edited by John Bender and David E. Wellbery, 151–165. Stanford, CA: Stanford University Press, 1991.

Lumley, Robert, ed. *The Museum Time-Machine: Putting Cultures on Display*. London and New York: Routledge, 1988.

Magelssen, Scott. "Living History Museums and the Construction of the Real Through Performance." *Theatre Survey* 45, no. 1 (2004): 61–74.

_____. "Resuscitating the Extinct: The Backbreeding of Historic Farm Animals at U.S. Living History Museums." *TDR: The Drama Review* 47, no. 4 (2003): 98–109.

A Man for All Seasons (1966). Dir. Fred Zinneman. Columbia/TriStar, 1998. Videocassette.

McNamara, Brooks, ed. *American Popular Entertainments: Jokes, Monologues, Bits, and Sketches*. New York: PAJ Publications, 1983.

_____. *Day of Jubilee: The Great Age of Public Celebrations in New York, 1788–1909: Illustrated from the Collections of the Museum of the City of New York*. New Brunswick, NJ: Rutgers University Press, 1997.

_____. *The New York Concert Saloon: The Devil's Own Nights*. Cambridge: Cambridge University Press, 2002.

McNamara, Brooks, Jerry Rojo, Richard Schechner, eds. *Theatres, Spaces, Environments: Eighteen Projects*. New York: Drama Book Specialists, 1975.

Merleau-Ponty, Maurice. *Nature: Course Notes from the Collège de France*. Translated by Robert Vallier. Evanston, IL: Northwestern University Press, 2003.

Mihailovic, Alexandar. *Corporeal Words: Mikhail Bakhtin's Theology of Discourse*. Evanston, IL: Northwestern University Press, 1997.

Monty Python and the Holy Grail (1975). Dir. Terry Gilliam and Terry Jones. Columbia/TriStar 2001. Videocassette.

Moore, Jennifer Sue. *A Descriptive Study of the Michigan Renaissance Festival.* M.A. Thesis, Michigan State University, 1997.

Newton, Esther. *Margaret Mead Made Me Gay: Personal Essays, Public Ideas.* Durham, NC: Duke University Press, 2000.

Novack, Janet and Fleming Meeks, "Ye Olde Money Pit," *Forbes* 152, no. 14 (20 December 1993), 206–207.

O'Brien, Kimberly. "The Effectiveness of Persuasion: A Promotional Videotape for the Michigan Renaissance Festival." M.A. Thesis, Michigan State University, 1987.

Oreglia, Giacomo. *The Commedia dell'Arte.* Translated by Lovett F. Edwards. New York: Hill and Wang, 1964.

Patterson, Phyllis. "Letter to AFR," 14 October 1999. <alt.faires.renaissance> (accessed 31 October 2005).

Pearce, Susan M., ed. *Museums and the Appropriation of Culture.* London: Athlone Press, 1994.

Peterka, Paula. Crownsville, Maryland, to the Hengrave Hall Yahoo Groups listserve, via e-mail, 15 May 2002.

Peterson, Richard A. *Creating Country Music: Fabricating Authenticity.* Chicago: University of Chicago Press, 1997.

Pontiff, Brenda Reneé. "The American Renaissance Festival." M.A. Thesis, Kansas State University, 1986.

Prato, Paolo. "Music in the Streets: The Example of Washington Square Park in New York City," *Popular Music* 4 (1984): 151–163.

Price, David C. *Patrons and Musicians of the English Renaissance.* New York: Cambridge University Press, 1981.

Private Life of Henry VIII (1933). Dir. Alexander Korda. Timeless Video, Inc., 1994. Videocassette.

Ralph, James. *The Touch-stone: or, Historical, critical, political, philosophical, and theological essays on the reigning diversions of the town.... In which everything antique, or modern, relating to musick, poetry, dancing, pantomimes, choruses, cat-calls ... circus, bear-garden, gladiators, prize-fighters ... is occasionally handled. By a person of some taste and some quality.* London, 1728.

Rayner, Alice. "Rude Mechanicals and the *Specters of Marx,*" *Theatre Journal* 54 (2002): 535–554.

Reed, Delanna Kay. "A Readers Theatre in Performance: The Analysis and Compilation of Period Literature for a Modern Renaissance Faire." M.A. Thesis, University of North Texas, 1987.

Ridley, Jasper. *Henry VIII.* London: Constable, 1984.

Robin Hood: Prince of Thieves (1991). Dir. Kevin Reynolds. Warner Studios, 2004. Videocassette.

Rokem, Freddie. *Theatrical Representations of the Past in Contemporary Theatre.* Iowa City: University of Iowa Press, 2000.

Roth, Stacy F. *Past Into Present: Effective Techniques for First-Person Historical Interpretation.* Chapel Hill, NC and London: The University of North Carolina Press, 1998.

Rosenfeld, Sybil Marion. *The Theatre of the London Fairs in the 18th Century.* Cambridge: Cambridge University Press, 1960.

Ryan, Marie-Laure. *Narrative as Virtual Reality: Immersion and Interactivity in Literature and Electronic Media.* Baltimore: Johns Hopkins University Press, 2001.

Sands, Mollie. *The Eighteenth-Century Pleasure Gardens of Marylebone, 1737–1777.* London: Society for Theatre Research, 1987.

Sanjek, Roger, ed. *Fieldnotes: The Makings of Anthropology.* Ithaca, NY: Cornell University Press, 1990.

Schechner, Richard. "Victor Turner's Last Adventure." In *The Anthropology of Performance,* Victor Turner, 7–20. New York: PAJ Publications, 1988.

_____. *Between Theatre and Anthropology.* Philadelphia: University of Pennsylvania Press, 1985.

_____. *Environmental Theatre: An Expanded New Edition including "Six Axioms for Environmental Theatre."* New York: Applause, 1994.

Schechner, Richard and Mady Schuman, eds. *Ritual, Play, and Performance: Readings in the Social Sciences/Theatre.* New York: Seabury Press, 1976.

Schechter, Joel, ed. *Popular Theatre: A Sourcebook.* London and New York: Routledge, 2003.

"The Scribe Network," <*www.faire.net/SCRIBE/*>.

Shakespeare in Love (1998). Dir. John Madden. Miramax Home Entertainment, 2003. Videocassette.

Shapiro, Laura. *Something from the Oven: Reinventing Dinner in 1950's America.* New York: Viking, 2004.

Sherman, Bernard D. *Inside Early Music: Conversations with Performers.* New York: Oxford University Press, 1997.

Simons, Ben. "A Brief History of the Renaissance Faire," *Renaissance Magazine* 6, no. 23 (2001): 33–40.

The Six Wives of Henry VIII. Bfs Entertainment and Multimedia, 2000. Videocassette.

Smith, Bruce R. *The Acoustic World of Early Modern England: Attending to the O-factor.* Chicago: University of Chicago Press, 1999.

Smith, Lacey Baldwin. *Henry VIII: The Mask of Royalty.* Chicago: Academy, 1982.

Smith, Matthew Wilson. "Bayreuth, Disneyland, and the Return to Nature." In *Land/Scape/Theater*, edited by Elinor Fuchs and Una Chaudhuri, 252–279. Ann Arbor: University of Michigan Press, 2002.

Snow, Stephen Eddy. *Performing the Pilgrims: A Study of Ethnohistorical Role-Playing at Plimoth Plantation.* Foreword by Barbara Kirshenblatt-Gimblett. Jackson: University Press of Mississippi, 1993.

Spedden, Carolyn. Artistic Director, International Renaissance Festivals, Inc. Interview by author, 7 December 2001, Crownsville, Maryland, in Kimberly Tony Korol, "God is in the Details: The Development of the Guild of St. George, the Living History Component of the Maryland Renaissance Festival," written for University of Maryland Theatre Historiography (THET 712), 17 December 2001, 9–10.

_____. Crownsville, Maryland, to actors in the companies of St. Genesius and St. George, April 2000, International Renaissance Festivals, Inc.

_____. *The Grand Event.* Crownsville, Maryland: Maryland Renaissance Festival, 2001.

_____. *Katherine's Story.* Maryland Renaissance Festival, Crownsville, Maryland, 15 October 2004.

_____. *The Royal Arrival.* Maryland Renaissance Festival, Crownsville, Maryland, September 2004.

Stack, Carol B. "Writing Ethnography: Feminist Critical Practice." In *Feminist Dilemmas in Fieldwork*, edited by Diane L. Wolf, 96–106. Boulder, CO: Westview Press, Inc., 1996.

Stallybrass, Peter and Allon White. *The Politics and Poetics of Transgression.* Ithaca, NY: Cornell University Press, 1986.

Starkey, David. *Six Wives: The Queens of Henry VIII.* New York: HarperCollins Publishers, 2003.

Stevens, John E. *Music and Poetry in the Early Tudor Court.* London: Methuen, 1961.

_____. "Music at the Court of Henry VIII." *Musica Britannica xviii*, 1962.

Stover, Kate. "Is it Real History Yet?" *Journal of American Culture* 12, no. 4 (1991): 113–117.

Synnott, Anthony. "Puzzling over the Senses: From Plato to Marx." In *The Varieties of Sensory Experience: A Sourcebook in the Anthropology of the Senses*, edited by David Howes, 61–76. Toronto: University of Toronto Press, 1991.

"The Tales of Peter Geoffrey of Turnberry," <http://www.personal.umich.edu/~jeffshuo/2ktwmt.html> (accessed 20 May 2008).

The Three Musketeers (1993). Dir. Stephen Herek. Disney Studios, 2001. Videocassette.

Thomas, Lewis. *Late Night Thoughts on Listening to Mahler's Ninth Symphony.* New York: Viking Press, 1980.

Turner, Rory. "Bloodless Battles: The Civil War Reenacted." *TDR: The Drama Review* 34, no. 4 (1998): 123–136.

Turner, Victor. *The Anthropology of Performance.* New York: PAJ Publications, 1988.

_____, ed. *Celebration: Studies in Festivity and Ritual.* Washington, DC: Smithsonian Institution Press, 1982.

_____. *The Forest of Symbols: Aspects of Ndembu Ritual.* Ithaca, NY: Cornell University Press, 1967.

_____. *From Ritual to Theatre: The Human Seriousness of Play.* New York: PAJ Publications, 1982.

_____. *Image and Pilgrimage in Christian Culture: Anthropological Perspectives.* New York: Columbia University Press, 1978.

_____. *The Ritual Process: Structure and Anti-Structure.* New York: Aldine de Gruyter, 1995.

Vince, Ronald W. *Renaissance Theatre: A Historiographical Handbook.* Westport, CT: Greenwood Press, 1984.

Weir, Alison. *Henry VIII: The King and His Court.* New York: Ballantine Books, 2001.

Westfall, Suzanne R. *Patrons and Performance: Early Tudor Household Revels.* Oxford: Clarendon Press, 1990.

Wiles, David. *A Short History of Western Performance Space.* Cambridge, UK: Cambridge University Press, 2003.

William Shakespeare: Life of Drama, A&E Biography. A&E Entertainment, 1997.

Williams, Raymond. *The Country and the City.* New York: Oxford University Press, 1973.

_____. *Keywords: A Vocabulary of Culture and Society.* New York: Oxford University Press, 1976.

Wilshire, Bruce. "The Concept of the Paratheatrical." *The Drama Review* 34.4 (Winter 1990): 169–178.

Wolf, Diane L. "Situating Feminist Dilemmas in Fieldwork." In *Feminist Dilemmas in Fieldwork,* 1–55. Boulder, CO: Westview Press, Inc., 1996.

Workman, Mark E. "The Differential Perception of Popular Dramatic Events." *Keystone Folklore* 23, no.3 (1979): 1.

Worton, Michael and Judith Still, eds. *Intertextuality: "Theories and Practices."* Manchester and New York: Manchester University Press, 1990.

Young, William H. *The 1950s.* Westport, CT: Greenwood Press, 2004.

Index

Numbers in **bold italics** indicate pages with photographs.